BHAGAVAD GITA

Simplified

AN UNBIASED INTERPRETATION

BHAGAVAD GITA

Simplified

AN UNBIASED INTERPRETATION

Organized by Major Topics

Emphasis on Krishna's explanations
Simplified English Translation
Easy to understand
Extensive background Information
Knowledge of Philosophy not Necessary

VINO MODY

Author and Management Consultant

www.whitefalconpublishing.com

BHAGAVAD GITA
Vino Mody

www.whitefalconpublishing.com

ISBN - 978-1-63640-231-4

Dedicated to

My Sadguru Dev Sri Sri Saidas Baba,
whose inspiration and guidance were the sole reasons
for the completion of this work.

My wife Anita Mody for her encouragement and cooperation.

Thanks to

Prof. Dr. Charles Elerick, Professor of Languages and
Linguistics, University of Texas at El Paso, for his help with
the final editing of this book.

Book Index

Foreword...ix

Preface..xi

Notation of Verses...xv

Why Is the Book Formatted by Topics, Not by Chapters? xvii

Block Chart on Book Format xix

Index of Topics xxi

Table of Sub-Topics (Four Pages) xxiii

Quantitative Summary of Gita's Verses xxix

Introduction.. xxxi

Did Krishna Pronounce in Gita He Was Brahm?...................... 1

Topic Contents (1 to 44)... 13

Bibliography.. 205

Endorsement... 206

Other Publications of The Author 207

Foreword

This book, a treasure of its kind, is the product of the author's meticulous research and effort to collate the key concepts of one of the most valuable Hindu scriptures, bringing out unbiased explanations and meaning of the way of life as taught by Krishna to Arjun in the battlefield of the Great Mahabharat war. The author has gone to great lengths, putting together the key concepts, piece-by-piece, text-by-text, and the gist of all that was said in an easy-to-understand way, to benefit one and all, irrespective of religion.

The mode of translation through logical reasoning and interpretation of the text in an easy-to-read language is sure to bring light to the puzzles of life and present a way of living and looking at life through a much broader perspective than we generally tend to have, for our limited time. The author's work in chalking out and putting the related concepts together, from various parts of the Gita, requires great patience, in addition to an immense understanding and knowledge of the subject as well as the text, besides translating it from the original language to the one more common nowadays. This unique way of presenting the Gita, topic-wise, or rather concept-wise, is sure to benefit the reader in not only grasping the teachings quite easily but also being able to bring them to practice in daily life.

Reading such a work of dedication, put together with love and the sole reason of bringing out the true meaning of the otherwise, many times, misinterpreted text, adds even more faith in this blissful way of looking at, and leading one's life.

With this note, we would like to welcome you, the reader, into this work of unbound knowledge and reap the benefit of the author's fastidious resolve and immense dedication to bring this way of life to you, as taught by Krishna.

– Amit Sarren, Editor
White Falcon Publishing

Preface

Krishna discloses in Gita certain philosophical doctrines of Karma Yoga, Bhakti Yoga, Ashtang Yoga, and Jnana Yoga. It comprises Krishna's elaborate answers to questions raised by Arjuna, at a bizarre venue, in the middle of the Kurukshetra battlefield. The cousins Pandavas and Kauravas fought there 5,000 years ago to settle an old dispute about the legal ownership of the Hastinapur kingdom which the Kauravas had seized adamantly declining to give up the Pandava's share of the kingdom. The prominent ancient sage and author Ved Vyas wrote the dialogue between Arjuna and Krishna for the benefit of all people of faith, who aspire to learn the science of spirituality.

According to many spiritual leaders, no literature in the world can guide the seekers of truth from ignorance to enlightenment, as thoroughly as Gita does. It is a treasure of wisdom, a source of bliss, and the pride of Sanatana Dharma. It extracts the truths from the Vedas and Upanishads to chart the path for eternal peace for those afflicted by miseries of this mortal world. Gita in its essence means the same as wisdom, love, peace, God, truth, and liberation.

Gita reflects an open-minded attitude, not a rigid thought process. To the seekers of truth, it provides several possibilities to suit their aptitude and inclination. Gita's message maintains respect for all and contains no criticism for any faith, even those that disagree with its premise. Krishna eloquently presented the transcendental spiritual science from scriptures to Arjuna to eradicate his weakness, driven by ignorance, and thus, indirectly bestowing a great favor to the mankind by offering solutions for their problems and doubts in life. The depth and breadth of the teachings it contains can overwhelm beginners, raising doubt in their mind about the plausibility of practicing such an extensive discipline put forward by Krishna. Swami Vivekananda said that just following the spirit of a single verse of Gita sincerely has the power to transform anyone on a journey to the supreme.

While Gita is an authentic source of knowledge for the Sanatana Dharma, Krishna's guidance and teachings on Yoga are not limited to a country or a religion or a cult; these are for the whole world. Originally written in Sanskrit, it is translated into virtually all major languages of the world, many times in English. Several elevated personalities like Sankaracharya, Yogananda Paramhansa, Maharshi Aurobindo, Swami Chinmayananda, Swami Mukundananda, and many western philosophers have written dazzling commentaries on Gita. Some of these are published in enormous volumes, each reflecting an individual ideology of the writer, thus providing the readers a broader vista of Krishna's teaching.

Swami Shivananda characterizes the significance of Gita in simple terms, "The world is a battlefield. The real Kurukshetra is within you. The battle is still raging within us. Ignorance is Dhritarashtra; the individual soul is Arjuna; the super soul in your heart is Lord Krishna, the charioteer; the body is the chariot; the senses are the five horses; the terrible enemies you must confront and vanquish are the uncontrolled mind, ego, mental impressions, senses, cravings, likes and dislikes, lust, jealousy, greed, pride, and hypocrisy." Gita is not limited to this or that doctrine although, for example, some Vedantic thinkers may lead you to think it is only about Vedanta, or the followers of the path of devotion may say Gita is strictly about the path of devotion. Krishna's teaching is all-inclusive of many paths to the supreme.

Gita relates the war within us, the struggle we must wage to overcome the weakness in confronting the tasks staring at us and our vulnerability to vacillations and delusions. We must fight "the war" courageously but righteously and compassionately. A clear heart, free of attachment and selfish interests, sees God in all beings. Krishna says all life is his manifestation and part of him. So, we should feel the joy and sorrow of others. At this point, the most fitting slogan Satya Saibaba lived by comes to mind, "Love all, hurt none".

Gita enumerates three paths to the supreme; Jnana Yoga for the logical-minded devotees, Bhakti Yoga for sentimental devotees who love God's form, and Karma Yoga for action-oriented people. Furthermore, it comprises a variety of options within each path and their combinations. They are all in harmony, equally effective, and lead to the same goal; they are not in conflict with each other, although the myopic interpretations result in debates and doubts. The self-realized saints say that the convergence of all paths come in the view from the higher level of spirituality. Like the one at the peak of the mountain sees all routes pointing to the top, the one standing at the bottom can only see their route going to the top; no wonder some people would insist that theirs is the only way.

Gita contains dozens of verses that reveal the secret of how one can attain the Supreme. The wise suggest just pick one that suits your temperament and practice it diligently to open the door to the higher world. Krishna slowly and systematically coaches Arjuna to rescue him from the deplorable state of despondency and refusal to perform his duty as a Kshatriya (warrior). He imparts Arjuna the secret doctrine of the soul and goes on to cover many subjects, such as Karma Yoga. Krishna repeatedly tells Arjuna to conquer ego, desire, and lust, and rise above the likes and dislikes. He explains to Arjuna that the selfless and detached actions, done enthusiastically, as a prescribed duty in dedication and devotion to God, and without the ego of ownership and anticipation of a reward, will be free of any karmic reactions and will not bind you.

The Sanatana Dharma scriptures accept and sing merits of other names besides Krishna, by which people recognize Brahm. This book welcomes all names of Brahm as followed by other faiths, but does not discuss them to remain focused on the purpose of the book - to organize Gita by major topics discussed by Krishna and offer a simple interpretation that most people can understand and easily relate to. Unfortunately, some people are full of doubt and often question and ridicule the essence of Gita. The doubtful mind may not believe that God exists or whether reincarnation is possible, or if Krishna is real or mythical, or why Krishna engaged Arjuna in the violent war with the evil enemy (refer to 2.17 under topic 8 on the concept of Ahimsa). However, this book is not intended to address such reservations raised by those lacking the faith or offer arguments to them. The last few verses of Gita beacon the sincere spiritual aspirants to not argue with those who disagree with the teachings presented in it. We must be practical and accept the reality that "To the one without faith, no proof is enough, and the faithful requires no proof."

Writing a book on complex philosophy like Gita accompanies certain unique challenges. Translating Sanskrit into English is difficult, as often it requires several English words to interpret a single Sanskrit word. For instance, the Sanskrit word Avyaktam can mean unmanifested prakriti or formless God. Another example, the Sanskrit word dharma, is commonly translated as religion. However, it also means one of the many attributes such as responsibilities, duties, thoughts, and actions. Therefore, beyond the translation, the understanding of the intent and the force behind the prefixes, words, or phrases is crucial, and that is only possible with expert guidance based on an understanding of Gita as a whole, not just a verse here and a verse there. Only a realized Guru, free of any sectarian mindset, can accurately interpret what Krishna said and meant; only such a Guru can reveal the absolute truth and point you in the right direction.

A question may arise why another book on Gita while there are hundreds already written by prominent experts like Lokmanya Tilak, highly learned individuals like Dr. Radhakrishnan, and realized personalities like Satya Saibaba, Yogananda Paramhansa, Swami Mukundananda, and Swami Shivananda? Well, Gita is like a dark deep ocean that contains enormous valuable treasures and gems. People of all age groups and skills can dive deep into its depths with faith and a receptive mind to collect the "gems" and absorb its profound teachings. The divine subject of Gita is endless; no matter how many times it is transcribed, it is not possible to write enough about it.

The original Gita has 18 chapters on various methods of yoga that cover over forty major topics. A conventional book on Gita would follow suit and pursue the same sequential order while interpreting and translating it. However, one needs to understand that the discussion of a topic is not limited to a single chapter, rather it is scattered across all 18 chapters. So, the deep study of a particular topic would require the reading of all chapters. This is where the uniqueness of this book lies, in how it formats the contents compared to a typical book on Gita organized by chapters. This book compiles all verses relating to each topic from wherever the topic is discussed across Gita, thus making an in-depth study of a topic easier. The block chart at the beginning of this book attempts to clarify the formatting concept.

A conventional book on Gita contains many esoteric terms and complex contents hard to comprehend for the beginners and younger generation, lacking prior knowledge and access to expert guidance. Most of these books are very lengthy, hundreds of pages long, and use bewildering language, which a majority of readers may never completely read, and even if they do, they're unable to grasp the meaning of the text. As a result, such books end up being shelved away to decorate the bookcases.

However, this book explains the contents and terminology in compact and conversational language wherever possible. Also, it allows the readers to select and read only the topic(s) of interest without having to go through the entire content. Anyone who reads this book will gain knowledge of the subjects they choose to read, even if they do not read the complete book. The readers will also enjoy and learn from the sub-topics tabulated in this book that provide interesting information related to the verses from the scriptures. We hope the younger generation and beginners will also enjoy this translated version of Gita and apply its teaching to improve the quality of their life.

This book interprets the intent of the verses as written by relying on the author's knowledge of Sanskrit and by referring to a few books on Gita written by renowned spiritual personalities mentioned in the Bibliography. Interestingly, no two books contain identical translation and interpretation of the verses, all the more reason for reaching out to the books by experts. The author included the translation and interpretation as close to the intended message of the verses as possible. The readers are requested to forgive unintended errors in this sincere and humble presentation. The sole purpose of this book is to spread the marvelous teaching by Lord Krishna to people of all backgrounds.

समस्ता: लोका: सुखीनो भवन्तु
Samastah Lokaha Sukhino Bhavantu
May the Entire Universe Be Happy

Notation of Verses

Please note that this book designates verses to reflect the standard Gita chapter number followed by the verse number. For instance, verse 14.1 means verse number 1 in Chapter 14 of the original Gita. The verse numbers, chapter numbers, and Sanskrit lyrics are identical in all books on Gita; the English translation and interpretation of the verses vary from author to author. All verses compiled under a topic in this book cross-reference to all chapters and verse numbers in the classical format of Gita. The Sanskrit Verses are sourced from the original Gita. English translation is offered in regular fonts following the Sanskrit text. The author's interpretation of the verses is in the Italics.

Embodied or Bonded Soul

What does the term "embodied or bonded soul" mean, as frequently mentioned in books on Gita? The individual soul undergoes evolution by gradual detachment from its ancient association with the senses, mind, ego and intellect, on its way to freedom and merger with the Source; i.e., Brahm. The book chooses the word "embodied or bonded soul" as it is commonly known and described in discussions and literature on Bhagavad Gita.

Brahm (ब्रह्म), Brahma (ब्रह्मा), Brahman (ब्राह्मण)

The English spelling of the above words can be confusing as these words are spelled interchangeably. Brahm (ब्रह्म) is the supreme God frequently spelled as Brahman. However, the word Brahman (ब्राह्मण) also means a priest who conducts religious rituals. Brahma (ब्रह्मा) is one of the three divine entities – Vishnu, Brahma and Shiva.

Why Is the Book Formatted by Topics, Not by Chapters?

Most books while interpreting Gita follow the standard format, the original chronological order of the eighteen chapters. Each chapter carries a Sanskrit title, which contains the word 'Yoga' at the end because Gita introduces the original systems of yoga. 'Yoga' means to unite. In this context, it means for the soul to unite with God. Yoga in the Gita lingo is a spiritual science much broader than a set of physical postures and breathing exercises we generally associate it with. The classical Gita has 18 chapters; Chapter 1, for instance, is titled Arjuna Viṣada Yoga (The Yoga of Arjuna's Dejection), and Chapter 2 is called Sankhya Yoga (The Yoga of Analysis of the Soul), and so on.

Implanted in the eighteen chapters of Gita are several valuable topics, reiterated in various verses in multiple chapters throughout Gita. Combining the verses related to a topic from across Gita would allow a deeper appreciation of the emphasis Krishna placed on each topic. This book takes an unconventional approach for organizing the contents with the help of a computer. Instead of grouping the book by classical chapters, it identifies various topics as discussed by Krishna and presents them in the Index of Topics. For instance, Bhakti Yoga (The Path of Devotion) is discussed in chapter 12 of Gita, entitled Bhakti Yoga, however, several other chapters also contain verses on Bhakti Yoga. In other words, Krishna emphasizes Bhakti Yoga heavily in many other chapters too, and not just in Chapter 12. This book extracts all verses on Bhakti Yoga from different chapters by a comprehensive cross-referencing exercise and combines them under the topic entitled Bhakti Yoga (Topic 1) to accentuate its collective impact in spiritual pursuit.

Similarly, Krishna's discourses on Karma Yoga prevail throughout Gita, besides the third chapter on Karma Yoga. So, this book extracts all verses relating to Karma Yoga and places them under the topic of Karma Yoga (Topic 3). Similarly, the book compiles the other topics of Gita; altogether it organizes 44 significant topics as included in the Index of Topics. Again, formatting the Index by key topics reveals the collective impact of a subject and simplifies an enhanced study of a topic of interest to the reader, without having to read the whole Gita.

For the general information of those who have little or no previous exposure to Gita, note that a standard book on Gita contains 18 chapters on different yoga matters, which look like as below:

Chapter 1: Arjuna Visada Yoga - Arjuna's Dejection
Chapter 2: Sāṅkhya Yoga – Analysis
Chapter 3: Karma Yoga – Science of Action
Chapter 4: Jnana Yoga – Divine Knowledge
Chapter 5: Sannyasa Yoga – Renunciation
Chapter 6: Dhyana Yoga – Meditation
Chapter 7: Vijnana Yoga – Wisdom
Chapter 8: Taraka Brahm Yoga - Attaining Brahm
Chapter 9: Raja Vidya Raja Guhya Yoga – Secret Royal Knowledge
Chapter 10: Vibhuti Yoga – Opulations
Chapter 11: Viśva Rupa Darshana Yoga – The Cosmic Form
Chapter 12: Bhakti Yoga – Devotion and Surrender
Chapter 13: Prakṛti Puruṣa Viveka Yoga – Matter and Spirit
Chapter 14: Guṇa Traya Vibhaga Yoga - The Three Modes (Triguna)
Chapter 15: Puruṣottama Yoga – The Ultimate Essence
Chapter 16: Daivāsura Sampad Vibhaga Yoga – Divine and Demoniac Nature
Chapter 17: Sraddha Traya Vibhaga Yoga – The Threefold Faith
Chapter 18: Moksha Yoga – Liberation

Block Chart on Book Format

Standard Gita Chapters >> Major Topics >> Sub-Topics

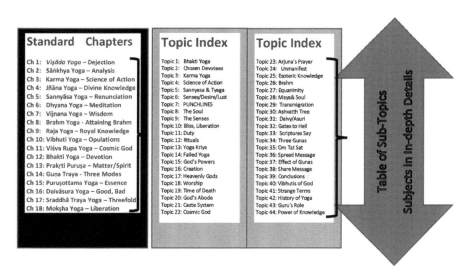

Standard Chapters

- Ch 1: *Viṣāda Yoga* – Dejection
- Ch 2: Sāṅkhya Yoga – Analysis
- Ch 3: Karma Yoga – Science of Action
- Ch 4: Jñāna Yoga – Divine Knowledge
- Ch 5: Sannyāsa Yoga – Renunciation
- Ch 6: Dhyana Yoga – Meditation
- Ch 7: Vijnana Yoga – Wisdom
- Ch 8: Brahm Yoga - Attaining Brahm
- Ch 9: Raja Yoga – Royal Knowledge
- Ch 10: Vibhuti Yoga – Opulations
- Ch 11: Viśva Rupa Yoga – Cosmic God
- Ch 12: Bhakti Yoga – Devotion
- Ch 13: Prakṛti Puruṣa – Matter/Spirit
- Ch 14: Guṇa Traya - Three Modes
- Ch 15: Puruṣottama Yoga – Essence
- Ch 16: Daivāsura Yoga – Good, Bad
- Ch 17: Sraddhā Traya Yoga – Threefold
- Ch 18: Mokṣha Yoga – Liberation

Topic Index

- Topic 1: Bhakti Yoga
- Topic 2: Chosen Devotees
- Topic 3: Karma Yoga
- Topic 4: Science of Action
- Topic 5: Sannyasa & Tyaga
- Topic 6: Senses/Desire/Lust
- Topic 7: PUNCHLINES
- Topic 8: The Soul
- Topic 9: The Senses
- Topic 10: Bliss, Liberation
- Topic 11: Duty
- Topic 12: Rituals
- Topic 13: Yoga Kriya
- Topic 14: Failed Yoga
- Topic 15: God's Powers
- Topic 16: Creation
- Topic 17: Heavenly Gods
- Topic 18: Worship
- Topic 19: Time of Death
- Topic 20: God's Abode
- Topic 21: Caste System
- Topic 22: Cosmic God

Topic Index

- Topic 23: Arjuna's Prayer
- Topic 24: Unmanifest
- Topic 25: Esoteric Knowledge
- Topic 26: Brahm
- Topic 27: Equanimity
- Topic 28: Maya& Soul
- Topic 29: Transmigration
- Topic 30: Ashvatth Tree
- Topic 31: Daivy/Asuri
- Topic 32: Gates to Hell
- Topic 33: Scriptures Say
- Topic 34: Three Gunas
- Topic 35: Om Tat Sat
- Topic 36: Spread Message
- Topic 37: Effect of Gunas
- Topic 38: Share Message
- Topic 39: Conclusions
- Topic 40: Vibhutis of God
- Topic 41: Strange Terms
- Topic 42: History of Yoga
- Topic 43: Guru's Role
- Topic 44: Power of Knowledge

Table of Sub-Topics

Subjects in In-depth Details

Index of Topics

TOPIC N   Arjuna's Questions to Krishna 3

TOPIC W   War Preparation 5

TOPIC 1   Bhakti Yoga (Path of Devotion) 13

TOPIC 2   Types of Devotees Dear to God 23

TOPIC 3   Karma Yoga (Path of Yoga of Action) 25

TOPIC 4   Science of Action 33

TOPIC 5   Karma Sannyasa vs. Karma Yoga (Renunciation vs. Action)... 36

TOPIC 6   Senses, Desires, and Lust 41

TOPIC 7   Gita Mahavakyas (Punchline Verses) 48

TOPIC 8   Sankhya Yoga (The Nature of Soul) 55

TOPIC 9   Philosophy of Samkhya and Practice of Yoga 62

TOPIC 10   The Ladder to Perfection, Bliss, Liberation 66

TOPIC 11   Adhering to Inherent Duties 77

TOPIC 12   Vedic Rituals 80

TOPIC 13   Yoga Kriya 84

TOPIC 14   Fate of Unsuccessful Yogi 93

TOPIC 15   God's Powers – Shakti 96

TOPIC 16   The Creation 103

TOPIC 17   Worship of Celestial Gods – Devatas 107

TOPIC 18   Types of Worship and Offerings 109

TOPIC 19   Remembering God at Death 114

TOPIC 20   God's Abode 117

TOPIC 21   Caste System and Inherent Duties 120

TOPIC 22   Cosmic Form – Universal Darshan 123

TOPIC 23   Arjun's Prayer to the Cosmic Form 132

TOPIC 24   Worship of Unmanifest 134

TOPIC 25   Knowledge of Prakriti, Purush, Kshetra, and Kshetrajna 136

TOPIC 26   Attributes of Brahm 141

TOPIC 27   Signs of Sthitprajna and the One Beyond

                  Triguna (trigunatit) 146

TOPIC 28   Maya, Three Gunas, and the Soul 151

TOPIC 29   Transmigration of Soul 154

TOPIC 30   Ashvatth Tree, Complex Samsara 157

TOPIC 31   Daivy (Divine) and Asuri (Demoniac) Nature 159

TOPIC 32   Gates to Hell 164

TOPIC 33   Follow Scriptural Injunctions 166

TOPIC 34   Manifestation of Three Gunas 168

TOPIC 35   Significance of Om Tata Sat 173

TOPIC 36   Spreading the Divine Message of Gita 175

TOPIC 37   Effect of Three Gunas 176

TOPIC 38   Sharing the Message of Gita 183

TOPIC 39   End of Gita - Conclusions and Impressions 185

TOPIC 40   God's Glories – Vibhutis 188

TOPIC 41   Meaning of few Esoteric Terms 197

TOPIC 42   History of Ancient Knowledge of Yoga Taught in Gita 200

TOPIC 43   Guru's Role According to Gita 202

TOPIC 44   Power of Knowledge 203

Table of Sub-Topics (Four Pages)

INDEX OF SUB-TOPICS	Verses and Topics Containing These Verses
See stated verses/commentaries for these topics	Example - 15.6 (T20) means Verse 6 in original Chapter 15, in Topic 20 of this Book
Abode - Divine - Characteristics of	15.6 (T20)
Abode - Eternal, Spiritual Realm	9.4 (T15), 8.20 (T16)
Abodes - Heaven and Hell	8.16 (T20)
Action With Attachment – Weakness	7.11 (T40)
Ahimsa (Non-Violence)	2.17 (T8)
Arise, Awake, and Fight	2.3 (Topic W)
Arrow Chart - Mind off Senses Leads to Liberation	3.19 (T10)
Arrow Chart - Total Destruction	2.62 (T6)
Ashtang Yoga - Meditation Process	6.11/6.12/6.14/6.15 (T13)
Ashtang Yoga – Pranayam, How Breath Binds Soul to Body	4.29/4.30 (T13),
Ashtang Yoga - Pratyahara, Withdrawal of Mind	6.26 (T13)
Ashtang Yoga - Process	5.27/5.28/8.9/8.10 (T13)
Ashtang Yoga - Qualifications to Receive Knowledge	4.3 (T42)
Ashtang Yoga - Samadhi, Attributes of	18.51 (T10), 6.21/6.22 (T13)
Ashvattha Tree – Similarity With Samsara	15.2 (T30)
Aum - Om	17.24 (T35), 10.25 (T40)

Bhakti Yoga - Shankaracharya Quote	18.54 (T10)
Bhakti Yoga – Guru Nanakdevji Quote	13.19 (T1)
Bliss - Supreme	6.27 (T13)
Bodies - Gross, Subtle, Causal	2.28 (T8)
Body - City of Nine Gates	5.13 (T10)
Brahm, Attaining	14.26 (T1)
Buddhi Yoga	2.39 (T3), 10.10 (T10)
Caste System	4.13/18.41 (T21), 5.18 (T27)
Creation - Physical Elements	14.3/14.4 (T10)
Creation vs. Evolution	3.10 (T16)
Demoniac Prakrity - Fate of People With	16.19/16.20 (T31)
Desires	2.62 (T6)
Desires - Restrain of - a Saibaba Message	2.63 (T6)
Desires and Lust - the Negative Impact of	3.41 (T6)
Devata - Vajra, the Weapon of Indra	10.28 (T40)
Devatas - Adityas, Maruts, Rudras, Vasus, Yakshas	10.22 (T40)
Devatas - Celestial Deities	3.11/4.12 (T12)
Devatas - Spiritual Standing of	7.20/7.22/7.23 (T17)
Devatas - Worship of	9.23 (T17)
Devotees God Likes - Traits*	14.21 (T27)T
Devotion - Ecstasy	18.74 (T39)
Devotion - Physical Symptoms of	11.14 (T22)
Devotion - Strength	9.30 (T1)
Devotion - the Essence of	9.3 (T1)
Dharma - meaning	3.35 (T3), 4.8 (T7), 18.66 (T1)
Diet - Vegetarian vs Non-Vegetarian	17.8/17.10 (T33)
Dissolution - Four Pralayas	8.18 (T16)
Divine Calendar - Brahma's Life Calculations	8.17 (T16)

Divine Calendar - Manus and Manvantara	10.6 (T16)
Divine Knowledge - Qualifications to Receive	4.3 (T42)
Divine Vision - Kaurava's Death	11.26/27/28/29 (T22)
Duality	7.27 (T6)
Duty - Allotted - Prescribed	3.8 (T3)
Faith - Innate	17.2/17.3/17.4 (T33), 4.39 (T42)
Faith - Lack of	4.40 (42)
Faith - What Is It?	17.28 (T35)
Family Traditions - Result of Abandoning	1.44 (Topic W)
Gita - All Arjuna's Questions to Krishna in	Topic N
Gita - Heart of	18.66 (T1)
Gita - Its Essence	18.65/18.66 (T18)
Gita - Spreading its Message	18.68/18.69/18.70 (T38)
Gita - Study and Listening, Sankaracharya Story	18.70/18.71 (T38)
God - Avatara - God's Descension in Human Form	4.7 (T7)
God - Contradicting Attributes of	13.15/13.16/13.17 (T26)
God - Cosmic Form of	11.5/6/7, 11.10/11/12, 11.15 to 11.21,11.26/27 (T22)
God - Cosmic Form, Terrifying	11.31 (T22)
God - Glories of and the Essence of	10.29/10.42 (T40)
God - His Instrument	11.33/11.34 (T22)
God - Jeev Shakti of, Soul Energy	7.5/7.6 (T15)
God - Kaal Swarup, Destructive Form	11.32 (T22)
God - Krishna, the Nirguna Brahm, His Attributes	11.38 (T20), 14.27/15.12 (T26),
God - Maya Shakti (Creative Power of God)	2.16 (T8), 7.4/7.6/7.13/7.14 (T15)
God - Paramatma vs. Atma, Super Soul vs. Soul	4.5 (T42)

God - Prayer to Cosmic Form	11.39/11.40 (T23)
God - Ridicule of Human Form by the Ignorant	9.11/9.12 (T31)
God - the Best in Class, Krishna	7.8 (T40)
God - the Origin of	10.2 (15)
God - the Unique Qualities of	10.14 (T15)
God - the Unique Descriptions of Brahm in Sanskrit	15.18 (T26)
God – Yoga Maya Shakti of	7.25 (T15), 11.47 (T15)
God, Supreme - How He manifests?	15.19 (T1)
Guru's Role	2.7/2.8 (Topic W), 4.34 (T7), 6.14 (T13)
Happiness - Types of	6.28 (T13)
Happiness- Sattvic, Rajasic, and Tamasic	18.37/18.38/18.39 (T37)
Heaven - Celestial Abodes - Life There	9.20/9.21 (12)
Hinduism - Not Mentioned in Gita	3.13 (T18), 13.5 (T25)
Human and Animals - Difference	2.40 (T3)
Jainism Buddhism - Basis of Non-Vedantic Faiths	2.26 (T8)
Kaal Swarup	11.32 (T7)
Karm Yoga - Danger of Working With Attachment	2.40 (T3)
Karm Yoga - Foundation	2.47 (T3)
Karma - Action and Inaction	4.18/4.20 (T3)
Karma - Excess Baggage of Karma	3.5/4.20/18.12 (T3)
Karma - Reaction That Accrues Karma	4.19 (T3)
Karma Yogi - Characteristics	5.7 (T5)
Karma Yogi - Krishna as One	3.22 (T3)
Knowledge - Types, Which Gita Reveals	9.1 (T1)
Leadership - Setting Examples	3.20/3.21 (T3)
Liberation, Means of	9.14/9.34/11.55/12.6/12.7,8,9,10,11 (T1)
Meru Mountain	10.23 (T40)
Mind - Control	9.4 (T1), 2.41 (T2), 6.19/20 (T13), 6.36 (T14), 4.27 (T18)

Mind - Meaning	6.5 (T6), 15.8 (T29)
Mind - Practical Way to Restrain	9.14 (T1), 6.6 (T6)
Mind - Purity of	15.11 (T8), 4.10 (T10)
Naam Smaran	11.55 (T1), 8.8 (T10)
Naam Smaran - Remembering God	11.55 (T10)
Nature's Cycle	3.13 (T3)
Nishkam Karma - Selfless work	2.39 (T3)
Ocean Churn - Ucchaishrava, Airavata, Kamdhnu	10.27/10.28 (T40)
Offering - Prasaad - to God	9.26 (T1), 9.27 (T1)
Paths of Light and Darkness	8.23/8.24 (T19)
Prahlad - Devotee	10.30 (T40)
Prakriti - Manifest and Unmanifest	2.28 (T8)
Prakriti - Nature - How Does it Function?	9.7/9.8 (T16)
Prayers - Before Eating Your Food	3.13/4.24/9.27/15.14 (T7)
Reincarnation	Topic 29 Introduction, Verse 2.22 (T8)
Sacrifices, Summary of Various	4.29/4.30 (T18)
Sages - Their Mission	18.10 (T11)
Sankhya Yoga	2.39 (T3), 3.3 (T3)
Scriptures - Brihad Sama Mantra in Samaveda	10.35 (T40)
Scriptures - Extreme Austerity Against	17.5/17.6 T(33), 17.19 (T34)
Scriptures - Follow Injunctions	16.23/16.24/17.1/17.11 (T33)
Scriptures - Gayatri Mantra	10.35 (T40)
Scriptures - Sanatana Dharma	13.5 (T25)
Senses - Control of	2.59/2.60 (T6), 6.8 (T27)
Senses - Forced Restrain of - a Herman Hess Story	3.6 (T6), 4.26 (T18)
Senses - Purpose	2.64 (T11)
Siddhi - Perfection - Spiritual Powers	7.3 (T15)
Similarity of Traits of Three Types Identified With *	14.21 (T27)
Sin - Root Cause	3.37 (T6), 16.21 (T32)

Sinners, Reform How	9.30 (T1)
Soul - Destination of	9.25 (T17)
Soul - Its Bondage and Delusion	2.23 (T8), 3.28 (T34)
Soul - Liberated, Its Characteristics	5.26 (T10)
Soul - Reincarnation and Transmigration of	2.22 (T8), 9.7/9.8 (T16)
Sthitprajna - Traits*	2.58 (T27), 6.9 (T27)
Surrendering to God - What Does It Mean?	18.62/7.29 (T1), 9.27 (T1), 10.9 (T1)
Terminology - Adhibhuta, Adhidaiva, Adhiyagna	7.30 (T19)
Terminology - Ajnana, Jnana, Vijnana	6.8 (T 27)
Terminology - Prakriti, Purush, Kshetra, Kshetrajna	13.2/13.3/13.21/2/3 (T25)
Terminology - Terms Synonymous to Sthitprajna	2.58 (T27)
Thoughts Lead to Destiny	17.16 (T34)
Trigunatit - Beyond the Gunas - Traits*	14.21/14.24/14.25 (T27)
Universe - Physical and Divine - Relative Size of	8.21 (T20)
Unsuccessful Yogi - the Fate of	6.40/6.41/6.42/6.43/6.44/6.45 (T14)
Vedas, Sections of, the Sama Veda Hymns	2.42/2.43 (T12), 10.22 (T40)
Virtues - a Practical Suggestion for Cultivation of	16.1/2/3 (T31)
Work - Skillful (Karmeshu Kaushalam)	2.50 (T3)
Work is Worship - Vyadh Gita Story	18.46/18.47 (T7)
Worship - of Form or Formless	12.20 (T1), Topic 2 In
Yajna or Sacrifice - Meaning	3.9 (T3), 3.10 (T16), 4.31 (T18), 18.70 (T38)
Yogi - Traits at Advance Stage	6.4 (T13)

Quantitative Summary of Gita's Verses

Gita has 701 verses, counting verse 13.1 or 700 without verse 13.1. Some versions have 13.1, while some do not. A detailed look at the verses revealed the number of verses spoken by Krishna, Arjuna, and Sanjay each. Arjuna spoke altogether 80 verses in which he asks the 16 questions and expresses his observations and prayers. Krishna spoke 580 verses covering a wide range of subjects to answer Arjuna's 16 questions. Sanjay spoke 40 verses to relay the status of the war and his observation to the blind king Dhritarashtra, the father of the Kauravas. Sanjay was an assistant of Dhritarashtra and an observer of the war proceedings. He remotely saw the battle by the vision gifted by his Guru Ved Vyas.

Arjuna addresses Krishna respectfully by several titles, frequently as Achyuta (infallible one), Bhagawan (Supreme Lord), Janardan (he who looks after the public), Keshav (killer of the Keshi demon), Mahabaho (mighty-armed), Mahatman (Greatest of all beings), Krishna, Rishikesh (Master of the senses), Varshneya (belongs to Varshni clan), Vasudeva (son of Vasudev), Madhusudan (Slayer of demon Madhu), Devesh (Lord of Lords).

Krishna uses the following names to address Arjuna: Parth (the son of Pritha), Arjuna, Bharat (descendent of Bharat), Kaunteya (son of Kunti), Parantapa (scorcher of enemies), Dhananjaya (winner of wealth), Pandavah (son of Pandu), Gudakesh (conqueror of sleep), Kurunandana (descendent of Kuru), Mahabaho (mighty-armed one).

Interestingly, the particular titles Krishna and Arjuna used to address each other relate to the message of the verse containing these names. Because of space constraints, we exclude an explanation of how a title relates to a verse.

Introduction

The Bhagavad Gita means the song of God. It is one of the most famous ancient books from India on spiritual philosophy and the right way to live your life. Gita is a practical guide to discover the essence of life, more profound than the pleasure and pain experienced by our senses. It reveals multiple paths of yoga, which aims to unite the individual soul (Atma) with the super soul (Paramatma). Gita unveils various paths to reach the Supreme Essence, the chief objective of a spiritual quest, together with the pros and cons of each path, including permissible and prohibited actions. It guides the spiritual aspirants on a journey from darkness to light, ignorance to enlightenment. It explains who we really are and our relationship with Brahm, the conscious reality according to Upanishad, and infinity (satyam jnanam anantam Brahm).

This revered handbook is embedded in a vast scripture known as Mahabharata, which has voluminous contents similar to Greek Mythology, in depth and in classification. Gita has been translated into all major languages of the world. Thousands of expert commentators have written interpretations of it, collectively more than any other scripture. It captures the essence of the four Vedas, one hundred and eight Upanishads, and the six systems of Sanatana Dharma philosophy into Sanskrit poetry, 700 verses long with 18 chapters. The author of Mahabharat and Gita is believed to be the illumined sage Ved Vyasa, whose date is unknown.

Gita is a dialogue between Krishna (the king of Dwarka) and Arjuna (one of the five Pandava brothers) that took place on the Kurukshetra battleground before the war began between the righteous Pandavas and their evil cousins Kauravas, 5,000 years ago. The Pandavas were the rightful owners of half of the Hastinapur kingdom, but the Kauravas usurped their share and adamantly refused to part with it. The Pandavas tried diplomacy, with the help of Krishna, to resolve the dispute peacefully and establish the legal ownership of the kingdom. However, the Kauravas rejected all peaceful proposals, unfortunately leaving no option other than war. This war was one of the most colossal and cataclysmic battles in the ancient history of India. It engaged virtually all Indian kingdoms, aligning themselves either on the side of the Pandavas or the Kauravas. Duryodhana (the oldest of the 100 Kaurava brothers) and Arjuna each solicited Krishna's help, who offered two choices: they can have either his trained army with weapons or Krishna himself. However, he stated that he will not carry any weapons and thus will not actively take part in the fight as a commander or a soldier. Arjuna happily chose the unarmed Krishna as the advisor to the Pandavas. Duryodhana selected Krishna's army to join the Kauravas; he was happy with his choice, convinced that Krishna would be of no help without his weapons. The history proved that Duryodhana was ignorant of Krishna's divine powers. The fearsome war ended with everyone dead on the Kaurava and Pandava sides except the five Pandava brothers and few others.

When the battle was about to start, Arjuna lost his nerves on seeing his elders, teachers, and friends arrayed on the enemy side, all ready to fight on behalf of the Kauravas. He was horrified and depressed at the thought of having to kill people whom he worshipped. Arjuna dropped his weapons and sat down in his chariot. He disclosed to Krishna, serving as Arjuna's chariot driver, that he will not fight. He declared he would have no use for the kingdom and prosperity, and would gladly give up his life instead of killing the elders.

In the state of confusion, Arjuna surrendered to Krishna and supplicated for his guidance for the proper course of action. Krishna came forward, willing to enlighten Arjuna. He reminded Arjuna of his moral obligations, his duty as a 'Kshatriya', and the consequences of neglecting the duties. The divine dialogue of Gita started from this point forward when Arjuna asked Krishna altogether 16 questions on a variety of spiritual subjects. Krishna answered the questions elaborately, covering the practical science of Karma Yoga, Bhakti Yoga, and Jnana Yoga in incredible depth. He gave Arjuna inspiring instructions about the characterization of the soul and its relationship with the super soul (God), who we really are, consciousness and reality, and the structure of the material and spiritual worlds. Krishna also displayed to Arjuna his astounding supernatural Cosmic form, the God of life and death, which impressed, dazzled, and ultimately terrified Arjuna beyond description.

The prominent ancient sage Veda Vyasa recorded the sacred conversation between Krishna and Arjuna, which came to be known as Bhagavad Gita (this book calls it Gita). It has served humanity in their pursuit of spirituality and paths to liberation over the centuries. Gita is by far the most famous Indian scripture which condenses the lessons of the Vedas and Upanishads. It is a guiding light that has enlightened people of the righteous way of living. Though mistakenly construed by some as a "Hindu" scripture, Gita's message has a universal appeal and application, as clear from its worldwide popularity in the past few hundred years. People of all backgrounds and faiths can apply its teaching to experience permanent happiness.

Originally spoken and written in Sanskrit, Gita has been translated in many Indian and European languages. Charles Wilkins first translated it in English around 1795. Thousands of authors worldwide have written books interpreting it in their distinct styles ever since. The contents of Gita address complex subject matters and philosophy. Moreover, translating Sanskrit is not straightforward. Both issues together made writing about Gita a challenging endeavor. No wonder the interpretations by experts vary significantly in their meaning. Also, the background of the author can introduce differing views, reflecting beliefs of their ideology in their translation. Admittedly, some books on Gita are very detailed and lengthy, often written in a complex language for the benefit of literal minds. However, most people interested in learning Krishna's teaching would not understand and be frustrated by big words and lengthy sentences. These interpretations occupy enormous volumes, perhaps harder to read and understand than the original Gita.

The author of this version of Gita, wherever possible, has attempted to write an interpretation of Gita verses in conversational English, making it easier to read and understand. The Sanskrit verses originate from standard Gita books. The author used his knowledge of Sanskrit and also reached out to draw from a few prominent Gita books disclosed in the bibliography and combined it with his own translation to reflect the actual meaning without sectarian spin. Though a difficult goal, the author made sincere efforts to compile unbiased English translation and offer simple interpretations. Along with the followers of Gita, this book should attract and benefit the younger generation and devotees lacking philosophical background.

Did Krishna Pronounce in Gita He Was Brahm?

Whether Krishna was Brahm (Formless God) or he was only a God's messenger is one of the recurring questions raised through the ages. This subject has stirred never-ending debates and individual opinions and judgments from people of varied backgrounds and philosophies. Most people answer the question by suggesting it is a matter of faith. Instead of engaging in intuitive speculation and providing a (blind) faith-based answer, this book adopts a quantitative approach to address this question. A thorough analysis of Gita meticulously organized and presented here would (should) allow you to draw your conclusion whether Krishna declared himself as God or he was referring to a third-party divine entity.

The in-depth exploration of all topics shows that Krishna mentions Brahm or God in altogether 210 of the 580 verses he spoke. Now, out of these 210 verses, Krishna unequivocally announces himself as God in 177 of them. In the remaining 33 verses, he refers to God as a third-party divine entity, different from him. The people who maintain that Krishna was merely a human, not God, ask, "If that divine entity is separate from Krishna, then who is he?" Notably, a quick review would reveal that in the verses where he mentions (a third-party) God, he invariably comes back in the following verse(s) to assert that he is the Brahm, the ultimate absolute.

For example, in verse 15.17 in Topic 26, Krishna mentions God, implying a power other than him, "The indestructible Lord differs from these mortal and immortal beings. He pervades the three worlds and supports them." Hence, the question, "Since he mentions God, then, who is he?" However, in the next verse 15.18, he makes the clarification and emphasizes that he is the Brahm, "I transcend the perishable world, and am superior to the imperishable (meaning Atma, the soul); hence, I am celebrated in the world and Vedas as the highest Purush or supreme God (Purushottam)." Consider a few more examples where Krishna declares himself as God. In verse 14.27 (Topic 26), he emphasizes that he is the Brahm, "I am the basis of the formless Brahm, the immortal, the imperishable, the eternal dharma, and of absolute bliss." In 15.12 (Topic 26), he says, "I am like the light of the sun that illuminates the world. I am the source of the light of the moon and the brightness of the fire." Consider another instance, Verse 15.13 where Krishna says, "I nourish all living beings by my energy by permeating the earth. Becoming the moon, I feed all plants with the juice of life." To summarise, there are 177 such verses in all where Krishna declares in no uncertain terms that he is the Ultimate Supreme.

Here are a few more examples of verses in which Krishna enunciates himself as God: verses 3.30/12.6/12.7/12.20/13.19/14.26 in Topic 1, verses 3.22/3.24 in Topic 3, verses 4.7/4.8 in Topic 7, verses 8.7/8.8/8.15/9.13 in Topic 10, verses 6.15/6.15 in Topic 13, verse 4.6 in Topic 15, verse 3.32 in Topic 32, verse 7.8 in Topic 40, verses 4.1/4.5 in Topic 42.

Examples of verses in which Krishna refers to God or Brahm as a third-party divine entity: verse 18.62 Topic 1, verse 18.61 Topic 11, verse 3.15 Topic 12, verse 6.28 Topic 13, verse 6.44 Topic 14, verses 13.14/13.15 Topic 26, verses 15.3/15.4 Topic 30, verse 5.14 Topic 34, verses 8.9/8.10 Topic 41. For additional examples, refer to this book or any standard book on Gita.

The 177 verses, as mentioned above, are drawn from an elaborate review of the entire Gita. The analysis confirms with no doubt that Krishna declared himself as the formless Nirguna Brahm. Upanishads and Shrimad Bhagwat also reinstate that the eternal essence is none other than Krishna. He is a form of Parabrahm. Brahm is worshipped by other names depending on one's faith. The unique names and forms of the same One God (Ek Omkaar) should not raise controversy. It is understandable that people of different faiths in this world can visualize Brahm by unique names and forms or the Formless (Nirakar).

Can One who carries the entire universe with an ounce of his energy (verse 10.42) assume unique names and forms or no names and no forms? Unquestionably, yes. Gita promotes inclusiveness, which means we all can (and should) accept the philosophies of all faiths.

The aim of this book is to interpret Gita factually and present to the readers a simplified guidebook, not to debate those having differing views. The ancient Indian thought is based on an extraordinarily broad-minded philosophy that is always receptive and respectful to other ideas. We leave the readers to their discrimination and let them draw their conclusions about whether Krishna was God or a human medium of communication, based on the factual information provided here.

TOPIC N

Arjuna's Questions to Krishna

On the Kurukshetra battlefield, before the war started, Arjuna asked Krishna sixteen questions. Krishna addressed these questions in incredible detail about the soul, God, the mind, intellect, and body, including the origin of the universe. Veda Vyas, a reputable sage and author of several scriptures, recorded Krishna's elaborate answers and embedded them in a colossal Indian scripture called Mahabharat. This dialogue between Krishna and Arjuna is known as the Bhagavad Gita, also called Gitopanishad. Krishna discloses the real secrets of a variety of spiritual subjects listed in the Index of Topics extracted and compiled from Gita as included in this book.

The questions Arjuna asked Krishna are available in Sanskrit verses in any book on Gita; the following is the list of questions and requests for enlightenment from Arjuna.

1. Verse 2.54 – What is the characteristic of Sthitprajna, the one in the state of equanimity?

2. Verse 3.1 – You said knowledge is superior to actions, then why do you want me to fight?

3. Verse 3.36 – What are the factors which compel one to sin despite reluctance to engage in such actions?

4. Verse 4.4 – You say you were born after Vivasvan many years ago, how could you have taught him spirituality? Arjuna is thinking Krishna was not there when Vivasvan was born.

5. Verse 5.1 – You are praising renunciation and also doing work in the state of devotion. Tell me with certainty which path is best of the two?

6. Verse 6.33 – The mind is always very agitated and impossible to control any more than the wind. How can one manage the mind?

7. Verse 6.37 – What is the fate of a failed yogi after he follows the path of yoga sincerely, but distracted by passions later, never reaches the absolute perfection in this life?

8. Verse 10.16 – What are these (esoteric) terms – Brahm, Karma, Adhibhūta, Ādhidaiva, and Ādhiyajña? How can one unite with you after death?

9. Verse 10.16 – Arjuna is requesting Krishna to tell him about Krishna's divine opulence (Vibhuti).

10. Verse 11.3 – Another request from Arjuna - show me your universal form (Vishwarup Darshan).

11. Verse 11.31 – You have been here always, even before "creation". Who are you? Your ways and background are mystifying.

12. Verse 12.1 – Which of the two paths is better in pursuit of liberation – the devotion to your personal form or the formless Brahm?

13. Verse 13.1 – What are - Prakṛiti (Nature or Maya), Purush (the soul), the field of activities, the knower of the field, the nature of knowledge, and the purpose of knowledge?

14. Verse 14.21 – How can I identify people who have risen above (detached from) the three Gunas? And how do they act? How do they go beyond the three Gunas?

15. Verse 17.1 – What is the outcome of people who do not follow scriptural commands but still follow you with faith?

16. Verse 18.1 – What is the difference between Sannyasa (renunciation), and Tyaga (renouncing the results of actions)?

TOPIC N - Arjuna's Questions to Krishna

4

TOPIC W

War Preparation

Krishna's discourse on Gita took place on the Kurukshetra battlefield before the war between the Pandavas and their cousins Kauravas started. Kurukshetra is located in the present Indian state of Haryana, about 100 miles north of New Delhi. Saint Ved Vyasa, a renowned author of several Indian scriptures, recorded the dialogue narrated by Sanjaya to his blind king Dhritrashtra, the father of the Kauravas. Sanjaya received the power of remote vision and hearing from his Guru Ved Vyas. Consequently, he could hear the words spoken and see the fighters as well as Krishna while speaking to the king in his palace far away from the battlefield.

The war became inevitable as several attempts to find a peaceful solution for the dispute about the legal ownership of the kingdom failed. The Kauravas usurped the kingdom, denying the Pandavas their fair share. Krishna, out of his love for Arjuna, agreed to be his charioteer but pledged to carry no weapons. Krishna also offered Duryodhana, the oldest of the Kauravas, a choice between the weaponless Krishna and all of Krishna's army. Duryodhana out of his ignorance of Krishna's divinity picked his army, thinking the armless Krishna would be of no use in winning the war. The events as they unfolded later showed Duryodhana's choice was wrong as Krishna's guidance helped the Pandavas win the war. Just before the battle was about to start, Arjuna asked Krishna to move the chariot in the middle of the two armies as he wanted to behold the leaders in both armies.

Note that some people speculate the war between the Pandavas and Kauravas never transpired, but rather symbolizes a war between the good and bad qualities within us. This book avoids debating unproven speculations and attempts to stick with a set of events as Vyasa reported in Gita and Mahabharata.

Gita is an ancient scripture and a nonsectarian philosophical work. The teachings therein apply universally to all humans, regardless of their religious faith, in their pursuit of a spiritual and blissful way of life. Gita serves as an excellent guide for aspirants in their pursuit of enlightenment.

1.1 धृतराष्ट्र उवाच धर्मक्षेत्रे कुरुक्षेत्रे समवेता युयुत्सवः मामकाः पाण्डवाश्चैव किमकुर्वत सञ्जय   **The blind king Dhritrashtra, the father of Kauravas inquires:** Sanjay, tell me what are my sons and Pandu's (Dhritarashtra's younger brother) sons doing on the battlefield?

Instead of stopping the war, which Dhritrashtra (the king of the Kurus) could have, he wanted the war to go on and his sons to win.

The following verses are Sanjay's narration (to Dhritrashtra) as the events unfold on the battlefield. He starts with Duryodhana, who is in conversation with Acharya Dron:

1.2 सञ्जय उवाच दृष्ट्वा तु पाण्डवानीकं व्यूढं दुर्योधनस्तदा आचार्यमुपसङ्गम्य राजा वचनमब्रवीत्   Looking at the Pandava army, Duryodhana is talking to Acharya Drona.

Duryodhana sounds afraid of the outcome of the war.

1.3 पश्यैतां पाण्डुपुत्राणामाचार्य महतीं चमूम् व्यूढां द्रुपदपुत्रेण तव शिष्येण धीमता   He is asking Acharya Dron to look at Pandava's army, arranged by Acharya's disciple Drupada's son.

1.4 and 1.5 and 1.6 शूरा महेष्वासा भीमार्जुनसमा युधि युयुधानो विराटश्च द्रुपदश्च महारथ: धृष्टकेतुश्चेकितान: काशिराजश्च वीर्यवान् पुरुजित्कुन्तिभोजश्च शैयश्च नरपुङ्गव: युधामन्यु विक्रान्त उत्तमौजाश्च वीर्यवान् सौभद्रो द्रौपदेयाश्च सर्व एव महारथा:
Duryodhana is appealing to Acharya (teacher) to look at all Maharathis (great fighters), by name, on the Pandava side.

1.7 तु विशिष्टा ये तान्निबोध द्विजोत्तम नायका मम सैन्यस्य संज्ञार्थं तान्ब्रवीमि ते   Now, Duryodhana is pointing out to Drona, the principal generals on his side.

1.8 कर्णश्च कृपश्च समितिञ्जय: अश्वत्थामा विकर्णश्च सौमदत्तिस्तथैव च   Next, Duryodhana is bringing to attention 'those who always win', like Drona, Bhishma, Karna, Krupa, Vikarna, etc.

In verses 1.8 and 1.9, Duryodhana displays over-confidence and pride in the capability of the great warriors on his side by saying, "They always win." Duryodhana concludes he will win.

1.9 च बहव: शूरा मदर्थे त्यक्तजीविता: नानाशस्त्रप्रहरणा: सर्वे युद्धविशारदा:   Duryodhana is asking Drona to look at all other warriors who are prepared to die for him; skilled in the art of warfare and well equipped with weapons.

1.10 अपर्याप्तं तदस्माकं बलं भीष्माभिरक्षितम् पर्याप्तं त्विदमेतेषां बलं भीमाभिरक्षितम्

He is asserting that the strength of his army led by Bhishma is unlimited, while the resilience of the Pandava army led by Bhima is limited.

Again, Duryodhana displays optimism about the superiority of his army over Pandava's, and again, clearly disregarding Krishna's powers.

1.11 अयनेषु च सर्वेषु यथाभागमवस्थिता: भीष्ममेवाभिरक्षन्तु भवन्त: सर्व एव हि   He wants all generals on his side to support Bhishma besides defending their positions

Outwardly, Duryodhana is projecting his confidence, but deep within, he seems to be panicking.

Next, Sanjay directs his attention to the other events on the battleground and narrates to Dhritrashtra through the following verses:

1.12 स्य सञ्जनयन्हर्षं कुरुवृद्ध: पितामह: सिंहनादं विनद्योच्चै: शङ्खं दध्मौ प्रतापवान्

Bhishma (granduncle of the Pandavas and Kauravas, fighting for the Kauravas) is blowing his conch loudly, giving joy to Duryodhana.

The presence of Bhishma, the undefeatable warrior, on his side boosted the confidence of Duryodhana.

1.13 तत: शङ्खाश्च भेर्यश्च पणवानकगोमुखा: सहसैवाभ्यहन्यन्त स शब्दस्तुमुलोऽभवत्

Following Bhishma, many conches, kettledrums, bugles, trumpets, and horns have suddenly started blowing on the Kaurava side with an overwhelming sound.

1.14 तत: श्वेतैर्हयैर्युक्ते महति स्यन्दने स्थितौ माधव: पाण्डवश्चैव दिव्यौ शङ्खौ प्रदध्मतु:

Seated in a glorious chariot in the middle of the armies, Krishna and Arjuna are also blowing their divine conches.

1.15 पाञ्चजन्यं हृषीकेशो देवदत्तं धनञ्जय: पौण्ड्रं दध्मौ महाशङ्खं भीमकर्मा वृकोदर:

Krishna is blowing his conch Panchajanya, Arjuna is blowing Devdutta, and Bhim, his huge conch Paundra.

Duryodhana had the first choice to pick weaponless Krishna or Krishna's army as his allies, and he chose the army, thinking Krishna would be of no help without his weapons.

1.16 and 1.18 अनन्तविजयं राजा कुन्तीपुत्रो युधिष्ठिर: नकुल: सहदेवश्च सुघोषमणिपुष्पकौ काश्यश्च परमेष्वास: शिखण्डी च महारथ: धृष्टद्युम्नो विराटश्च सात्यकिश्चापराजित: द्रुपदो द्रौपदेयाश्च सर्वश: पृथिवीपते सौभद्रश्च महाबाहु: शङ्खान्दध्मु: पृथक् पृथक्

Yudhisthir is blowing his conch Anantavijay, Nakul - Sughosha, and Sahdev - Manipushpak. The expert archer and the king of Kashi, the great warrior Shikhandi, Dhrishtadyumna, Virat, and the indomitable Satyaki, Drupad, the five sons of Draupadi, and the mighty-armed Abhimanyu, son of Subhadra, all are blowing their respective conch shells too.

Yudhisthir is the eldest Pandava, and Nakul and Sahadev are the youngest. The other generals of the Pandava army blew their conches, following Krishna and the five Pandava brothers.

1.19 स घोषो धार्तराष्ट्राणां हृदयानि व्यदारयत् नभश्च पृथिवीं चैव तुमुलो नुनादयन्   The booming sound originating from the Pandava side has shattered the hearts of your (Dhritarashtra's) sons, i.e., the Kauravas.

The evil element is aggressive but restless and fearful of the uncertainty and lacks the calm confidence of the righteous.

1.20 अथ व्यवस्थितान्दृष्ट्वा धार्तराष्ट्रान् कपिध्वज: प्रवृत्ते शस्त्रसम्पाते धनुरुद्यम्य पाण्डव: हृषीकेशं तदा वाक्यमिदमाह महीपते   Arjuna is carrying a flag with Lord Hanuman's symbol on top of his chariot. Seeing the Kaurava army, Arjuna begins to speak.

Sages interpreted the presence of Krishna and the symbolic presence of Lord Hanuman as a victory in the making for the Pandavas. Dhritarashtra should have called a truce and accepted the peace treaty had he an ounce of wisdom. Instead, he wanted the war to begin.

1.21 and 1.22 अर्जुन उवाच सेनयोरुभयोर्मध्ये रथं स्थापय मेऽच्युत यावदेतान्निरीक्षेऽहं योद्धुकामानवस्थितान् कैर्मया सह योद्धव्यमस्मिन् रणसमुद्यमे   Arjuna is asking Krishna to take the chariot in the middle of the battlefield so that he can see the warriors of the Kaurava side confronting him in the war.

1.23 योत्स्यमानानवेक्षेऽहं य एतेऽत्र समागता: धार्तराष्ट्रस्य दुर्बुद्धेर्युद्धे प्रियचिकीर्षव: Arjuna is saying, "I want to see those who have come to fight for the evil-minded son of Dhritrashtra."

1.24 सञ्जय उवाच एवमुक्तो हृषीकेशो गुडाकेशेन भारत सेनयोरुभयोर्मध्ये स्थापयित्वा रथोत्तमम्   Accepting Arjuna's request, Krishna has driven the magnificent chariot between the two armies.

Krishna willingly undertook the humble task of being a chariot driver for his friend.

1.25 भीष्मद्रोणप्रमुखत: सर्वेषां च महीक्षिताम् उवाच पार्थ पश्यैतान्समवेतान्कुरूनिति   In the presence of Bhishma, Dron, and other generals, Krishna has advocated Arjuna to behold the Kurus gathered there.

1.26 तत्रापश्यत्स्थितान् पार्थ: पितृ नथ पितामहान् आचार्यान्मातुलान्भ्रातृ न्पुत्रान्पौत्रान्सखींस्तथा श्वशुरान्सुहृदश्चैव सेनयोरुभयोरपि   Arjuna is observing, stationed in the armies, his elders, grandfathers, teachers, uncles, brothers, cousins, sons, nephews, friends, fathers-in-law, and friends.

1.27 तान्समीक्ष्य स कौन्तेय:सर्वान्बन्धूनवस्थितान् कृपया परयाविष्टो विषीदन्निदमब्रवीत्
Seeing all his relatives overwhelms Arjuna with compassion. With deep sorrow, he puts forward his thoughts to Krishna.

All verses from 1.27 to 2.10 describe the depressed state of Arjuna's mind, facing the prospect of killing his close relatives. In the end, he sets aside his weapons, showing his refusal to fight.

❧ *Sanjay tells Dritrashtra that Arjuna is saying:*

1.28 अर्जुन उवाच दृष्ट्वेमं स्वजनं कृष्ण युयुत्सुं समुपस्थितम् सीदन्ति मम गात्राणि मुखं च परिशुष्यति   I am looking at my relatives in the battlefront; my limbs are giving way, and my mouth has turned dry.

1.29, 1.30, and 1.31 वेपथुश्च शरीरे मे रोमहर्षश्च जायते गाण्डीवं स्रंसते हस्तात्वक्चै व परिदह्यते न च शक्नोम्यवस्थातुं भ्रमतीव च मे मन: निमित्तानि च पश्यामि विपरीतानि केशव न च श्रेयोऽनुपश्यामि हत्वा स्वजनमाहवे   My entire body is shaking, and my hair is standing up. My bow, the Gāṇḍīv, is sliding off my hand, and my skin is scorching. My mind is in a dilemma and spinning in confusion; I am unable to stand any longer. O Krishna, I only see signs of calamity. I do not envision any good outcome by destroying my close relatives in this war.

1.32 and 1.33 न काङ्क्षे विजयं कृष्ण न च राज्यं सुखानि च किं नो राज्येन गोविन्द किं भोगैर्जीवितेन वा येषामर्थे काङ्क्षितं नो राज्यं भोगा: सुखानि च त इमेऽवस्थिता युद्धे प्राणांस्त्यक्त्वा धनानि च   I don't want triumph, monarchy, and pleasure. What good is the kingdom, joys, and life, when you are ready to fight the people you love?

1.34 and 1.35 आचार्या: पितर: पुत्रास्तथैव च पितामहा: मातुला: श्वशुरा: पौत्रा: श्याला: सम्बन्धिनस्तथा एतान्न हन्तुमिच्छामि घ्नतोऽपि मधुसूदन अपि त्रैलोक्यराज्यस्य हेतो: किं नु महीकृते   Closely related teachers, seniors, and the young generation are ready to die for riches. I don't want to fight them back even if they attack me. How would the dominion over the kingdom satisfy me?

1.36 and 1.37 निहत्य धार्तराष्ट्रान्न: का प्रीति: स्याज्जनार्दन पापमेवाश्रयेदस्मान्हत्वैता नाततायिन: तस्मान्नार्हा वयं हन्तुं धार्तराष्ट्रान्स्वबान्धवान् स्वजनं हि कथं हत्वा सुखिन: स्याम माधव   What enjoyment comes from killing the Kauravas? Even if they attack me, it is an act of sin to kill them. How can we be happy by killing our cousins?

1.38 and 1.39 यद्यप्येते न पश्यन्ति लोभोपहतचेतस: कुलक्षयकृतं दोषं मित्रद्रोहे च पातकम् कथं न ज्ञेयमस्माभि: पापादस्मान्निवर्तितुम् कुलक्षयकृतं दोषं प्रपश्यद्भिर्जनार्दन   Greed has overpowered the Kauravas, and they believe it is OK to kill their relatives. We think it is evil to destroy a family, so why should we not stay away from this sin?

1.40 कुलक्षये प्रणश्यन्ति कुलधर्मा: सनातना: धर्मे नष्टे कुलं कृत्स्नमधर्मोऽभिभवत्युत   When a royal family is destroyed, its religious traditions are lost, pushing the family into irreligious and corrupt acts.

When the elders of the family die, no one is left behind to pass on traditions to the younger generation. Consequently, the descendants may develop a corrupted character. Therefore, Arjuna says it is not right to kill the elders.

TOPIC W - War Preparation

1.41 सङ्करोनरकायैवकुलघ्नानांकुलस्यचपतन्तिपितरोह्येषांलुप्तपिण्डोदकक्रिया:   From
the prevalence of vices, the women of the family become corrupt and produce
unwanted progeny of mixed castes.

*Irresponsible men take advantage of women and produce unwanted children who
inherit similar vices.*

1.42 सङ्करो नरकायैव कुलघ्नानां कुलस्य च पतन्ति पितरो ह्येषां लुप्तपिण्डोदकक्रिया:
Unwanted children ruin the lives of those who abandon virtuous life. Ancestors of
the corrupt families fall as no one performs the sacrificial ritual (pind kriya).

1.43 दोषैरेतै: कुलघ्नानां वर्णसङ्करकारकै: उत्साद्यन्ते जातिधर्मा: कुलधर्माश्च शाश्वता:
The evil deeds of those who destroy family traditions and produce unwanted progeny
ruin a variety of social and family activities as a result of their corrupt acts.

This verse depicts the so-called "free" lifestyle of modern society with little personal discipline.

1.44 उत्सन्नकुलधर्माणां मनुष्याणां जनार्दन नरकेऽनियतं वासो भवतीत्यनुशुश्रुम   The
enlightened sages say the people who abandon family traditions and spiritual
practices dwell in hell indefinitely.

*Among the most unfortunate outcomes of the uncontrolled lifestyle and "abandoning the
family traditions" are unwanted newborn babies whose lives are terminated because the
father and the mother of these unfortunate souls are unwilling to take responsibility for
their sustenance and upbringing.*

1.45 and 1.46 अहो बत महत्पापं कर्तुं व्यवसिता वयम् यद्राज्यसुखलोभेन हन्तुं स्वजनमुद्यता:
यदि मामप्रतीकारमशस्त्रं शस्त्रपाणय: धार्तराष्ट्रा रणे हन्युस्तन्मे क्षेमतरं भवेत्   Motivated
by the desire for pleasures, we are getting ready to kill our kin and commit sin. It is
better to die on the hands of the enemy – unarmed and submissive.

❧ *Sanjay tells Dhritrashtra:*

1.47 सञ्जयउवाचएवमुक्त्वार्जुन:सङ्ख्येरथोपस्थउपाविशत्विसृज्यसशरंचापंशोकसंविग्नमानस:
Now, Arjuna has dropped his weapons, and is sitting back upset and stunned with
grief.

2.1 सञ्जय उवाच तं तथा कृपयाविष्टमश्रुपूर्णाकुलेक्षणम् विषीदन्तमिदं वाक्यमुवाच मधुसूदन:
He is in a pitiable position, overcome by grief with tears in his eyes. Krishna is now
speaking to Arjuna.

*Through the following verses, Sanjay transcribes to Dhritrashtra what Krishna is
explaining to Arjuna:*

2.2 श्री भगवानुवाच कुतस्त्वा कश्मलमिदं विषमे समुपस्थितम् अनार्यजुष्टमस्वर्ग्यमकीर्तिकरमर्
जुन   How is the delusion taking the possession of you at the hour of danger? Such
behavior is not honorable and will close the gates of heaven for you.

Krishna chastises Arjuna by calling him an Anarya (crude person). He points out to Arjuna that the state of confusion is dishonorable for an Aryan. Now, some critics blame Krishna for the war and conclude he should have stopped the war when Arjuna was ready to drop his weapons. Some others speculate that the war between the Pandavas and Kauravas never occurred, it just denotes a symbolic war between the good and bad qualities in us. Here, we offer no comments on such speculations and prefer to stick with a set of events as Vyasa reported in Gita and Mahabharata.

2.3 क्लैब्यं मा स्म गम: पार्थ नैतत्तवय्युपपद्यते क्षुद्रं हृदयदौर्बल्यं त्यक्त्वोत्तिष्ठ परन्तप   Do not yield to unmanliness. It does not become of you. Shake off this base faint-heartedness and arise, O punisher of enemies. (This translation is from Swami Vivekananda and is chosen for inclusion here as it is one of the best).

Embedded here is Krishna's entire message of the Gita for Arjuna and the human world. Krishna says to Arjuna, "You talk like a wise man, but your action and negligence to your duty makes you look like a coward. Wake up from the sleep of ignorance and darkness, recognize the divinity within you, drop fear and weakness, and fiercely go after the mission without the distraction provoked by uncertainty of the outcome. Do not let the negativity cloud your rational thinking and strength you are born with."

Does this not sound like a brilliant lesson we all can apply in our lives to overcome fear, uncertainty, and negativity we often encounter while in the middle of our essential tasks?

❧ To this, Arjuna replies or rather questions Krishna in the following verses:

2.4 अर्जुन उवाच कथं भीष्ममहं सङ्ख्ये द्रोणं च मधुसूदन इषुभि: प्रतियोत्स्यामि पूजार्हावरिसूदन
How can I shoot arrows to Bhishma and Drona, who are worthy of worship?

Bhishma is Arjuna's granduncle, highly regarded for his many virtues. Drona is Arjuna's teacher, from whom he learned the art of warfare and archery.

2.5 गुरूनहत्वा हि महानुभावान् श्रेयो भोक्तुं भैक्ष्यमपीह लोके हत्वार्थकामांस्तु गुरूनिहैव भुञ्जीय भोगान् रुधिरप्रदिग्धान्   It is better to live my life by begging than killing respectable elders and teachers. The wealth I acquire by killing them will be stained with their blood.

The kingdom gained by killing people worthy of worship can turn into a haunting experience and deprive one of all mental peace.

2.6 न चैतद्विद्म: कतरन्नो गरीयो यद्वा जयेम यदि वा नो जयेयु: यानेव हत्वा न जिजीविषाम स्तेऽवस्थिता: प्रमुखे धार्तराष्ट्रा:   I am not sure what is preferable - to defeat the enemies or allow them to overcome me? By killing them, I will lose the desire to live. Yet the enemy army has allied with Dhritarashtra, and now confront us in the war.

Bhishma, Drona, and Kripacharya received livelihood from the Kauravas so out of obligation, they chose to fight for them. However, these noblemen knew the Kauravas were evil characters, and would lose the war due to Krishna's presence among the Pandavas.

2.7 कार्पण्यदोषोपहतस्वभाव: पृच्छामि त्वां धर्मसम्मूढचेता: यच्छ्रेय: स्यान्निश्चितं ब्रूहि तन्मे शिष्यस्तेऽहं शाधि मां त्वां प्रपन्नम्   I am no longer sure about my responsibility and am plagued with apprehension and weakness of my resolve. I am your devotee, and I surrender to you. Please guide me to the decision that is best for me.

Arjuna, overcome by cowardice (karapanya dosha), is requesting Krishna to be his guide (guru) to point him to the right path. Upanishad says, "Approach a Guru who knows the scriptures and has attained God-realization; he can lead you to Absolute Essence."

2.8 न हि प्रपश्यामि ममापनुद्याद् यच्छोकमुच्छोषणमिन्द्रियाणाम् अवाप्य भूमावसपत्नमृद्धं राज्यं सुराणामपि चाधिपत्यम्   I don't know how to get rid of the pain that is burning up my senses. The victory, sovereignty, and the vast kingdom on the earth will not dispel my grief.

Spiritual knowledge can resolve our problems in life, and a qualified Guru can show us the right way, as Arjuna desires from Krishna.

❧ *Sanjay tells Dhritrashtra:*

2.9 सञ्जय उवाच एवमुक्त्वा हृषीकेशं गुडाकेश: परन्तप न योत्स्य इति गोविन्दमुक्त्वा तूष्णीं बभव ह   Arjuna has told Krishna that he will not fight and has gone into silence.

2.10 तमुवाच हृषीकेश: प्रहसन्निव भारत सेनयोरुभयोर्मध्ये विषीदन्तमिदं वच: Now Krishna, with a smile on his face, is speaking to the devastated Arjuna.

Krishna displays his balance of mind in such a testing situation, willing to help Arjuna. The spiritual teaching of Gita starts from this point onwards until the end of Krishna's discourse, which marks the culmination of Gita.

TOPIC 1

Bhakti Yoga (Path of Devotion)

Many paths lead you to God, but the "easiest" and favored route is one of devotion with deep love, surrender, and selfless worship of God. Krishna emphasizes Bhakti Yoga or the path of devotion frequently in over 50 verses spread across different chapters within Gita. A bhakti yogi worships and loves God with a form. Krishna often says, "Constantly think of Me, meditate on Me, be free from desires, surrender to my will, understand that ultimate beneficiary of your actions is Me, and I promise you will easily attain Me. Do not let your ego mislead you; you are not the doer, but just my instrument. Do not fear and doubt." Gita states that even the jnanis and yogis resort to devotion for achieving union with Krishna or Brahm. It is noteworthy how Krishna keeps reverting to emphasize devotion in several chapters on other subjects. In fact, towards the end of Gita, Krishna concludes his preaching through the two verses 18.65 and 18.66, both glorifying the path of devotion.

"Always think of Me, be devoted to Me, worship Me, and offer obeisance to Me. By doing so, you will undoubtedly come to Me; in other words, you will be liberated. I promise (pratijane) this to you because you are dear to Me. Abandon all varieties of dharmas and simply surrender unto Me alone. I will redeem you from all sins. Be free of grief, doubt, and fear." These two verses at the end of Krishna's sermon summarize Bhakti Yoga.

The following verses on Bhakti Yoga from different chapters are compiled below. Notably, the chapter on Bhakti Yoga in the classical Gita has 20 verses, however, the total number of verses on Bhakti Yoga scattered across Gita is more than 50, as presented below. Note, Krishna repeats his crucial points about devotion multiple times to emphasize their importance. Although several verses carry the same message, they are all listed here, unedited, as they show up in the original Gita.

◆ *Krishna says to Arjuna:*

3.30 मयि सर्वाणि कर्माणि संन्यस्याध्यात्मचेतसा निराशीर्निर्ममो भूत्वा युध्यस्व विगतज्वरः: Work as an offering to Me, always meditate on Me, and be free from desire, selfishness, and grief.

Bhakti yoga combined with karma yoga makes a potent spiritual path.

4.11 ये यथा मां प्रपद्यन्ते तांस्तथैव भजाम्यहम् मम वर्त्मानुवर्तन्ते मनुष्याः: पार्थ सर्वशः: In whatever way people surrender unto Me, I reciprocate with them accordingly. Everyone follows My path, knowingly or unknowingly.

Surrendering to God's will is a foundation of bhakti yoga. See the commentary under Verse 18.62 in the current topic for the meaning of the term surrender.

5.29 भोक्तारं यज्ञतपसां सर्वलोकमहेश्वरम् सुहृदं सर्वभूतानां ज्ञात्वा मां शान्तिमृच्छति A selfless and faithful person who realizes that God is the supreme and the ultimate enjoyer of sacrifices and austerities, attains peace and bliss.

Whatever the motive for charities and sacrifice, cultivate faith and understanding that the ultimate beneficiary is God.

6.47 योगिनामपि सर्वेषां मद्गतेनान्तरात्मना श्रद्धावान्भजते यो मां स मे युक्ततमो मतः: The highest Yogis are always engrossed in Me and worship Me faithfully.

Yogis may experience bliss and see God's light in Karma Yoga, jñānayoga, and Aṣṭāṅg Yoga. Krishna mentions at several places in Gita that ultimately, everyone turns to the path of devotion and love to reach God.

7.1 श्रीभगवानुवाच मय्यासक्तमनाः: पार्थ योगं युञ्जन्मदाश्रयः: असंशयं समग्रं मां यथा ज्ञास्यसि तच्छृणु Have no doubt; you will know Me if you attach the mind to Me and surrender to Me through the practice of Yoga.

The essential element of Bhakti Yoga is one-pointed devotion with surrender. Singing the glory of God (naam smaran) fixes the mind on God.

7.19 बहूनां जन्मनामन्ते ज्ञानवान्मां प्रपद्यते वासुदेवः: सर्वमिति स महात्मा सुदुर्लभ: After many births, the Jnani surrenders to Me, knowing that all this is Vasudevah (Krishna).

Jnanis also resort to bhakti yoga ultimately, as stated earlier. Love and devotion to God impart humility. Without bhakti, Jnanis are likely to develop ego.

7.29 जरामरणमोक्षाय मामाश्रित्य यतन्ति ये ते ब्रह्म तद्विदुः: कृत्स्नमध्यात्मं कर्म चाखिलम्
Those who take shelter in Me, striving for liberation from old age and death, come to know the Brahm, the individual self, and the entire field of karmic action.

A devotee receives God's grace by surrendering. Kathopanishd states, "You cannot know God by spiritual discussion and preaching, nor through the intellect, nor by teachings. Only when He bestows His grace upon someone, does that fortunate soul comes to know Him."

8.8 अभ्यासयोगयुक्तेन चेतसा नान्यगामिना परमं पुरुषं दिव्यं याति पार्थानुचिन्तयन्
Constantly engaging the mind in Me without deviating, you will attain Me.

Krishna has frequently emphasized constantly engaging the mind in God, for example, in verses 8.14, 12.8, and 10.10 under Topic 1 on Bhakti Yoga. In reality, it is not easy to keep the mind on God, however, Krishna suggests in verse 6.20 that by practice and detachment, the mind can be made steady and engaged in God. Sangat (the company of spiritual people) also helps in turning to God.

8.14 अनन्यचेता: सततं यो मां स्मरति नित्यश: तस्याहं सुलभ: पार्थ नित्ययुक्तस्य योगिन:
A focused Yogi who always remembers Me for long without deviation can "easily" attain Me (by bhakti yoga).

The most significant message of this verse is Krishna says he can be attained "easily" by bhakti.

8.22 पुरुष: स पर: पार्थ भक्त्या लभ्यस्त्वनन्यया यस्यान्त:स्थानि भूतानि येन सर्वमिदं ततम्
God is greater than anything that exists, and though he is everywhere and in everyone, he can "only" be realized by "one-pointed bhakti."

Again, realizing God requires one-pointed devotion, faith, and love.

9.1 श्रीभगवानुवाच इदं तु ते गुह्यतमं प्रवक्ष्याम्यनसूयवे ज्ञानं विज्ञानसहितं यज्ज्ञात्वा मोक्ष्यसेऽशुभात् I will impart to you this extremely secret knowledge (relating to Bhakti Yoga) combined with wisdom, because you are without any fault, and not envious of Me. This secret knowledge will liberate you from existence in the material world.

Gita mentions three types of confidential knowledge that can liberate the soul. Chapter 2 talks about Guhya (secret) knowledge revealing that "the Atma is distinct from the body." Chapters 7 and 8 mention Guhyatar (more secret) knowledge about various powers of God. Chapter 9 onwards describe Guhyatam (most secret) knowledge relating to bhakti marg.

9.2 राजविद्या राजगुह्यं पवित्रमिदमुत्तमम् प्रत्यक्षावगमं धर्म्यं सुसुखं कर्तुमव्ययम् This knowledge is the most superior knowledge. It is a royal secret and purifies those who hear it. It can be realized by direct intuitive experience; it is very easy to perform and practice and will have an everlasting effect.

Purifying knowledge means it destroys sins accumulated over lifetimes. If the royal knowledge is so easy to master, then why do people not practice it? The next verse has the answer.

9.3 अश्रद्दधाना: पुरुषा धर्मस्यास्य परन्तप अप्राप्य मां निवर्तन्ते मृत्युसंसारवर्त्मनि People lacking faith in this path of the knowledge of the self (Atma Jnana), again and again, come back to this world of death without attaining Me.

Devotion inspires faith, according to scriptures. Anything you do right is based on the faith in yourself that it is worth doing and you can do it. Devotion and faith are enhanced by 1. a company of faithful people (Satsang), 2. internal purity (Atmshuddhi), 3. service of humanity and God (Seva), and 4. chanting God's glories (Naam Smaran).

9.13 महात्मानस्तुमांपार्थदैवींप्रकृतिमाश्रिता:भजन्त्यनन्यमनसोज्ञात्वाभूतादिमव्ययम्   The great souls who take refuge in my divine energy know Me as the origin of all creation; they engage in my devotion with their mind fixed wholly on Me.

Again, Krishna emphasizes devotion by saying the great souls engage in the devotion of God.

9.14 सततं कीर्तयन्तो मां यतन्तश्च दृढव्रता: नमस्यन्तश्च मां भक्त्या नित्ययुक्ता उपासते
Great souls (sages or Sant Mahatmas) always worship Me with devotion and determination, singing my glories and bowing down to Me.

One way to restrain the wandering mind is to engage it in thoughts of God - reading, hearing, and singing God's glories, and keeping the company of spiritual people (Satsang). Great bhakti yogis like Surdas, Tulsidas, Meera, Nanak, Kabir, Tukaram, Ekanath, Narsi Mehta, Jayadev, Tyagaaraj, and many others composed and sang bhajans as part of their bhakti yoga process towards God. Ramayan says, "In Kali Yug, the most effective means of liberation is singing the glories of God."

9.22 अनन्याश्चिन्तयन्तो मां ये जना: पर्युपासते तेषां नित्याभियुक्तानां योगक्षेमं वहाम्यहम्
Those devotees whose minds are absorbed in Me, I provide them with their material needs and preserve resources they already have.

This verse provides powerful reassurance for the livelihood and maintenance of faithful devotees. Sankaracharya says, "God maintains the devotees even if they do not make any effort."

9.26 पत्रं पुष्पं फलं तोयं यो मे भक्त्या प्रयच्छति तदहं भक्त्युपहृतमश्रामि प्रयतात्मन: If one offers Me with devotion and a pure mind, a leaf, a flower, a fruit, or even water, I accept it from a pure-hearted devotee.

God is the source of everything in the universe and needs nothing from us. Offering to God with a pure heart and complete surrender stimulates devotion; hence, you are the beneficiary, not God. God accepts small offerings given with pure heart.

9.27 यत्करोषि यदश्नासि यज्जुहोषि ददासि यत् यत्तपस्यसि कौन्तेय तत्कुरुष्व मदर्पणम्
Whatever you do, eat, offer in sacrifice, give in charity, and practice as penance; do it as an offering to Me!

Krishna says in Verse 9.26, all objects should be offered to him; in 9.27, he says that all actions should also be offered to him. A related prayer expressing surrender to God is Kaayena Vaacaa Manase indriyairvaa; Buddhy-Aatmanaa Va prakrite-Svabhaavaat; Karomi Yad-Yat-Sakalam Parasmai; Naaraayannayeti Samarpayami. The meaning of this Sanskrit expression is, whatever I do with the body, speech, mind, or the sense organs, either by the intellect, or through feelings, or by the mind, I do them all without the sense of ownership, and I surrender them to God.

TOPIC 1 - Bhakti Yoga (Path of Devotion)

9.29 समोऽहं सर्वभूतेषु न मे द्वेष्योऽस्ति न प्रिय: ये भजन्ति तु मां भक्त्या मयि ते तेषु चाप्यहम्
I am 'equal' to all, do not hate or favor anyone. BUT those who worship Me with devotion are in Me, and I am in them.

Krishna bestows his grace on the devotees even though he is impartial.

9.30 अपि चेत्सुदुराचारो भजते मामनन्यभाक् साधुरेव स मन्तव्य: सम्यग्व्यवसितो हि स:
Even the worst sinners who reform themselves by worshipping Me with exclusive devotion are on a righteous path because they have made the right decision to worship God with steady faith.

Bhakti (devotion) is potent as it can reform even the vilest of the sinners like Valmiki, who was a violent robber, later transformed into a close devotee of Lord Ram. He saw the Ramayan story in his vision and wrote the brilliant scripture called Ramayan before Ram was born.

9.31 क्षिप्रं भवति धर्मात्मा शश्वच्छान्तिं निगच्छति कौन्तेय प्रतिजानीहि न मे भक्त: प्रणश्यति   The sinners referred to in verse 9.30 quickly become virtuous and peaceful. Avow it that no devotee of mine is ever lost.

This verse highlights a significant reassurance of God to everyone, including the sinners, that His devotees will never be lost and achieve peace and virtues.

9.32 and 9.33 मां हि पार्थ व्यपाश्रित्य येऽपि स्यु: पापयोनय: स्त्रियो वैश्यास्तथा शूद्रास्तेऽपि यान्ति परां गतिम् किं पुनर्ब्राह्मणा: पुण्या भक्ता राजर्षयस्तथा अनित्यमसुखं लोकमिमं प्राप्य भजस्व माम्   If sinners can attain my grace, surely you can too. Therefore, having come to this mortal and transient world, engage in my devotion.

9.34 मन्मना भव मद्भक्तो मद्याजी मां नमस्कुरु मामेवैष्यसि युक्त्वैवमात्मानं मत्परायण:
Always be devoted, think of Me, worship Me, offer obeisance to Me, and dedicate your mind and body to Me. Then you will undoubtedly come to Me.

Krishna guarantees there should be "no doubt" that all followers of bhakti yoga will reach him. Swami Shivanand, a prominent spiritual leader, says, "A complete, unreserved surrender to God brings a marvelous transformation. The devotee will have the vision of God everywhere, all his sorrows will disappear, his mind will merge with God, and he will live in God forever."

10.9 मच्चित्ता मद्गतप्राणा बोधयन्त: परस्परम् कथयन्तश्च मां नित्यं तुष्यन्ति च रमन्ति च
With their mind absorbed in Me, their life force is immersed in Me, educating one another, and talking to one another about Me daily, they will find contentment and delight.

Surrender promotes contentment. The mind drifts to what it likes. Devotees of God are always thinking of God. They admire him and surrender to him. They gladly accept good and bad outcomes in their life as the will of God, thus remaining calm and contented.

10.10 तेषां सततयुक्तानां भजतां प्रीतिपूर्वकम् ददामि बुद्धियोगं तं येन मामुपयान्ति ते   To those who are connected with Me and worship Me faithfully with love, continually thinking of Me; I grace them with discrimination by which they can reach Me.

God's grace of discrimination and the ability to understand him is a superior form of a gift, more valuable than material gifts.

10.11 तेषामेवानुकम्पार्थमहमज्ञानजं तम: नाशयाम्यात्मभावस्थो ज्ञानदीपेन भास्वता
Out of compassion, I, who reside in their hearts, destroy the darkness of ignorance with the light of knowledge.

God's grace destroys ignorance with his divine energy called Yoga Maya Shakti. The divine power dispels the darkness of the material energy called Maya Shakti. Later in Topic 15 entitled God's Powers, the various energies of God are explained.

11.54 भक्त्या त्वनन्यया शक्य अहमेवंविधोऽर्जुन ज्ञातुं द्रष्टुं च तत्वेन प्रवेष्टुं च परन्तप   Only with single-minded devotion, one can see my cosmic, four-handed, and two-handed forms and merge with Me.

Vedas state devotion alone will - help us see God, enable us to attain him, and unite with him.

11.55 मत्कर्मकृन्मत्परमो मद्भुक्त: सङ्गवर्जित: निर्वैर: सर्वभूतेषु य: स मामेति पाण्डव   The one who regards Me as the Supreme, is devoted to Me, and is free from attachment and enmity, comes to Me.

This verse virtually summarizes the complete teaching of the Gita, according to Swami Shivananda. Here, Krishna emphasizes devotion, again. Saibaba said, "The one who wants to get rid of the cycle of births and deaths should lead a righteous life with a calm, composed, and fearless mind, do good deeds, do their duties, and surrender themselves to God faithfully; such a person is sure to attain self-realization.

12.6, 12.7 ये तु सर्वाणि कर्माणि मयि संन्यस्य मत्पर: अनन्येनैव योगेन मां ध्यायन्त उपासते तेषामहं समुद्धर्ता मृत्युसंसारसागरात् भवामि नचिरात्पार्थ मय्यावेशितचेतसाम्   Those who dedicate their actions to Me, make Me their goal, worship Me, and meditate on Me; I "swiftly" deliver those from the cycles of birth and death because their consciousness is united with Me.

Krishna's emphasis displays the power of bhakti and karma yoga, "I swiftly (nachirat) deliver those devotees."

12.8, 12.9, 12.10, 12.11 मय्येव मन आधत्स्व मयि बुद्धिं निवेशय निवसिष्यसि मय्येव अत ऊर्ध्वं न संशय: अथ चित्तं समाधातुं न शक्नोषि मयि स्थिरम् अभ्यासयोगेन ततो मामिच्छासुं धनञ्जय अभ्यासेऽप्यसमर्थोऽसि मत्कर्मपरमो भव मदर्थमपि कर्माणि कुर्वन्सिद्धिमवाप्स्यसि अथैतदप्यशक्तोऽसि कर्तुं मद्योगमाश्रित: सर्वकर्मफलत्यागं तत: कुरु यतात्मवान्   "No doubt," you will unite with Me if you fix your mind on Me or practice remembering Me by withdrawing the mind from the world, or work for Me in devotional service (Seva).

However, if you are unable to follow any of these paths, surrender to Me with a steady mind renouncing fruits of actions.

Krishna suggests several options to reach him from the most difficult to the easiest. He says, "no doubt," you will merge with Me with the practice of bhakti yoga and karma yoga. The phrase 'NO DOUBT' is Krishna's guarantee that the suggested options are all definite paths to liberation.

12.12 श्रेयो हि ज्ञानमभ्यासाज्ज्ञानाद्ध्यानं विशिष्यते ध्यानात्कर्मफलत्यागस्त्यागाच्छान्तिरनन्तरम्   Knowledge (wisdom born of yoga practice) is superior to yoga practice, meditation is better than the possession of knowledge, and renouncing fruits of actions (karma yoga) is better than meditation because peace immediately follows the renunciation of the result of your work.

Karma yoga and bhakti yoga bestow lasting peace instantaneously.

12.20 ये तु धर्म्यामृतमिदं यथोक्तं पर्युपासते श्रद्दधाना मत्परमा भक्तास्तेऽतीव मे प्रिया:
Those devotees who follow this preaching as declared here, have faith in Me, and make Me their goal; they are extremely dear to Me.

Krishna's answer to Arjuna's question, who is superior between the two - the worshipper of form or formless? Krishna says the worshippers of form are dear to him. Bhakti yoga, as described in Chapter 12, is a more natural path to God.

13.19 यो मामेवमसम्मूढो जानाति पुरुषोत्तमम् स सर्वविद्भजति मां सर्वभावेन भारत
Only my devotees can understand the nature of the field (body), the meaning of knowledge, and the object of knowledge; and only they are eligible to attain my character.

Krishna says, "Undistracted by diverse paths and thoughts, my devotees worship Me as their goal." The holy Guru Granth Sahib reaffirms the power of bhakti, "Hari sama jaga mahan vastu nahin, prem panth soñ pantha; sadguru sama sajjan nahin, gita sama nahin grantha." Translation - there is no personality like God; there is no path equal to the path of devotion; there is no human equal to the Guru, and there is no scripture that can compare with the Gita. Krishna says in Shrimad Bhagawat, "Uddhav, I am not attained by ashtang-yoga or by the study of sankhya or by the cultivation of scriptural knowledge or by austerities or by renunciation. It is by bhakti alone that I am won over."

14.26 मां च योऽव्यभिचारेण भक्तियोगेन सेवते स गुणान्समतीत्यैतान्ब्रह्मभूयाय कल्पते
Those who worship Me with unwavering devotion, having risen above the three Gunas, become fit for attaining Brahm.

Krishna says that unwavering devotion and rising above the three Gunas (the modes of material nature) can lead to the level of Brahm. Note the word "avyabhicharen" or unwavering; it means avoiding the tendency to jump from one path to another.

15.3, 15.4 न रूपमस्येह तथोपलभ्यते नान्तो न चादिर्न च सम्प्रतिष्ठा अश्वत्थमेनं सुविरूढमूल मसङ्गशस्त्रेण दृढेन छित्वा तत: पदं तत्परिमार्गितव्यं यस्मिन्गता न निवर्तन्ति भूय: तमेव चाद्यं पुरुषं प्रपद्ये यत: प्रवृत्ति: प्रसृता पुराणी   The real form of this tree, its beginning, end, and continuity are not apparent. However, this vast tree must be slashed with a strong weapon of detachment. Then one can find the base of the tree, which is the Supreme Lord, who is the source of all activities of the universe. By surrendering to God, one will not be reborn.

The massive tree of Samsara blocks the vision of God. The base of the tree is the Supreme Lord, as Krishna said in Verse 10.8 (Topic 7): "I am the source of the universe. Everything emanates from Me. The wise who know this, worship Me with great faith and devotion."

15.19 यो मामेवमसम्मूढो जानाति पुरुषोत्तमम् स सर्वविद्भजति मां सर्वभावेन भारत
Those who have no doubt I am the Supreme Personality, have complete knowledge. The doubtless Jnanis worship Me whole-heartedly.

Jnanis say the Supreme Entity is ultimately One (Ek Omkar, as Sikhism says), and he manifests in three ways: 1. Brahm - formless and all-pervading, 2. Paramatma - resides in the hearts of all beings as the super soul, and 3. Bhagavan - a personal form such as Ram, Shiv, Durga, etc. Note verses 15.12 and 15.13 in Topic 26 on Brahm refer to Brahm, 15.15 refers to the Paramatma aspect, and 15.17 and 15.18 are relating to Bhagawan. Topic 26 contains all these verses.

18.6 एतान्यपि तु कर्माणि सङ्गं त्यक्त्वा फलानि च कर्तव्यानीति मे पार्थ निश्चितं मतमुत्तमम्
Austerities, charities, and penance must be done without attachment and expectation for rewards.

Whatever the action may be, what binds the soul is not the action but attachment to the action and expectation of a reward.

18.55 भक्त्या मामभिजानाति यावान्यश्चास्मि तत्वत: ततो मां तत्वतो ज्ञात्वा विशते तदनन्तरम्   One knows what and who I really am only by devotion, knowing which my devotee unites with Me.

18.56 सर्वकर्माण्यपिसदाकुर्वाणो मद्व्यपाश्रय:मत्प्रसादादवाप्नोति शाश्वतं पदमव्ययम्   My devotees surrender to Me while doing all work. By my grace, they attain the eternal and imperishable state or abode.

18.57 चेतसा सर्वकर्माणि मयि सन्न्यस्य मत्पर: बुद्धियोगमुपाश्रित्य मच्चित्त: सततं भव
Dedicating all actions to Me mentally, keeping Me as the goal, and resorting to Buddhi yoga (the yoga of discrimination, what is good for us and what is not), always fix your mind on Me.

Accepting everything as a gift from God, believing he is the owner of everything, considering the work we do is for the pleasure of God, using the sense of discrimination as a guide; these are the attributes of bhakti yoga and buddhi yoga.

18.58 मच्चित्त: सर्वदुर्गाणि मत्प्रसादात्तरिष्यसि अथ चेत्त्वमहङ्कारान्न श्रोष्यसि विनङ्क्ष्यसि

If you remember Me always, you will be able to tackle all obstacles and difficulties, by my grace. But if you do not listen to my advice, due to ego, you will perish.

God promises to remove obstacles of his devotees if they listen to him and accept him.

18.62 तमेव शरणं गच्छ सर्वभावेन भारत तत्प्रसादात्परां शान्तिं स्थानं प्राप्स्यसि शाश्वतम्   Surrender exclusively unto him with your whole being; by his grace, you will attain perfect peace and the eternal abode.

Surrender completely and solely to God with your whole being. The meaning of surrender, the term used frequently in Gita:

1. Be happy with what you get. 2. Do not complain. 3. Keep faith that God is protecting you. 4. Be thankful to God. 5. See everything as God's possession. 6. Be humble. The Ramayan also says: "The moment the soul surrenders to God, His grace destroys that soul's account of sinful deeds in endless past lifetimes."

18.63 इति ते ज्ञानमाख्यातं गुह्याद्गुह्यतरं मया विमृश्यैतदशेषेण यथेच्छसि तथा कुरु

Thus, I have explained to you this knowledge that is more secret than all secrets. Ponder over it deeply and then do as you wish.

God gave us the freedom to choose, and He gave us choices. God does not force the soul to surrender to him; this decision has to be made by the soul itself. Here, Krishna is calling Arjuna's attention to his free will and asking him to choose. Refer to comments under verse 9.1 earlier in this section for an explanation of various types of knowledge that Krishna calls a secret.

18.64 सर्वगुह्यतमं भूय: शृणु मे परमं वच: इष्टोऽसि मे दृढमिति ततो वक्ष्यामि ते हितम्   Hear again my supreme instruction, the most confidential of all knowledge. I am revealing this for your benefit because you are very dear to Me.

Krishna gradually imparted knowledge to Arjuna in eighteen chapters to turn his grief into faith and obedience. Again, Krishna repeats some points to make sure Arjuna gets them without any doubt.

18.65 मन्मना भव मद्भक्तो मद्याजी मां नमस्कुरु मामेवैष्यसि सत्यं ते प्रतिजाने प्रियोऽसि मे   Always think of Me, be devoted to Me, worship Me, and offer obeisance to Me. By doing so, you will undoubtedly come to Me; in other words, you will be liberated. I "promise (pratijane)" this to you, because you are dear to Me.

For Krishna to "promise liberation," to his sincere devotee accentuates the power of bhakti yoga. Verse 18.65 and 9.34 convey a similar message about the glory of Bhakti Marga. He reveals the supreme secret in the next verse.

18.66 सर्वधर्मान्परित्यज्य मामेकं शरणं व्रज अहं त्वां सर्वपापेभ्यो मोक्षयिष्यामि मा शुच:

Abandon all varieties of dharmas and simply surrender unto Me alone. I will liberate you from all sins. Be free of grief, doubt, and fear.

Verse 18.66 and 18.65 comprise the essence of Gita. Krishna is instructing Arjuna to simply and completely surrender and promises to liberate him from all sins. At the end of the dialogues, Krishna tells Arjuna not to allow himself to be confused but simply follow the path of devotion. Verse 18.66 says leave all "dharma" and simply surrender. The word dharma in this verse has a broader meaning than the various religions people follow. The literature on Gita contains multiple definitions of "dharma", depending on the individual philosophies of each writer. Krishna preaches a variety of "dharmas" or paths such as Karma Yoga, Bhakti Yoga, and Jnana Yoga and says that all these paths can lead one to the ultimate goal of liberation if his instructions are followed with dedication and single-pointed focus. Like a man standing on the top of the mountain can see many trails coming to the top, but the one at the bottom only sees his path and thinks that is the only way to the top.

Arjuna whole-heartedly and unconditionally surrenders to Krishna in the end, does his duty as a Kshatriya, uses his weapons as Krishna orders him to do, and wins the colossal war against the evil elements of the society. A question may arise whether Arjuna will incur sin by having engaged in the ghastly war. Krishna reassures Arjuna again in verse 18.66 and asks him to be free of fear, promising to exonerate him from all sins and liberate him from the unending cycles of birth and death.

TOPIC 2

Types of Devotees Dear to God

This topic stresses the significance of devotion, love, and faith in spiritual life. Arjuna asks Krishna which one of the two paths is superior – the worship of God with the name and form, or the eternal, indefinable Brahm. Both paths lead one to him, Krishna says, although the worship of the one with name and form is easier as humans are accustomed to identification by name and form similar to them. Worship of Brahm is beyond the reach of the imagination of people. Once the mind is calm and experiences blissfulness by devotion to a personal God, the devotee will transition automatically into the worship of "that" (Tat, in Sanskrit), the formless divinity, the eternal essence.

Krishna tells Arjuna he likes devotees free of malice, the sense of ownership, ego, and desires. He likes devotees who are compassionate, satisfied, dedicated, steady in meditation, equanimous in pleasure and pain, and same with friends and foes. The following Gita verses describe in further detail who Krishna likes.

❧ *Krishna says to Arjuna:*

12.13 & 12.14 अद्वेष्टा सर्वभूतानां मैत्र: करुण एव च निर्ममो निरहङ्कार: समदु:खसुख: क्षमी सन्तुष्ट: सततं योगी यतात्मा दृढनिश्चय: मय्यर्पितमनोबुद्धियों मद्भक्त: स मे प्रिय: Those devotees are very dear to Me who are 1. without malice towards all beings, 2. friendly to all, 3. compassionate, 4. without the sense of ownership and egoism, 5. same in sorrow and joy, 6. self-controlled with firm conviction, 7. ever-contented, 8. steady in meditation 9. dedicated to Me with the mind and intellect.

12.15 यस्मान्नोद्विजते लोको लोकान्नोद्विजते च य: हर्षामर्षभयोद्वेगैर्मुक्तो य: स च मे प्रिय:
Those devotees are very dear to Me who: 1. give no trouble to anyone and are not

agitated by anyone, 2. react the same in pleasure and pain, 3. are free from joy, envy, fear, and anxiety.

12.16 अनपेक्ष: शुचिर्दक्ष उदासीनो गतव्यथ: सर्वारम्भपरित्यागी यो मद्भक्त: स मे प्रिय:
Those devotees are very dear to Me who are free from wants, who are pure, expert, unconcerned, and untroubled, and renounce all undertakings or commencements.

12.17 यो न हृष्यति न द्वेष्टि न शोचति न काङ् क्षति शुभाशुभपरित्यागी भक्तिमान्य: स मे प्रिय:　　　Those devotees are very dear to Me who do not: 1. rejoice in worldly pleasures, 2. despair in sorrows, 3. grieve for losses, 4. desire gain.

12.18 & 12.19 सम: शत्रौ च मित्रे च तथा मानापमानयो: शीतोष्णसुखदु:खेषु सम: सङ्गविवर्जित: तुल्यनिन्दास्तुतिर्मौनी सन्तुष्टो येन केनचित् अनिकेत: स्थिरमतिर्भक्तिमान्मे प्रियो नर:　　　Those devotees are very dear to Me who are: 1. similar to friends and foes; in honor and dishonor; in heat and cold; in pleasure and pain; in criticism and praise; 2. free from attachment, 3. silent, 4. content with everything, 5. homeless, 6. steady in mind; 7. full of devotion.

12.20 ये तु धर्म्यामृतमिदं यथोक्तं पर्युपासते श्रद्दधाना मत्परमा भक्तास्तेऽतीव मे प्रिया:
Those devotees are incredibly dear to Me, who: 1. follow this immortal dharma declared here, 2. have faith in Me, 3. intend to make Me their supreme goal.

To summarize Krishna's answer to Arjuna's question (between the two types of devotees, who are superior: the one who worships form or the one who worships the formless?), Krishna says the steadfast worship of form is easier for spiritual aspirants.

TOPIC 3

Karma Yoga (Path of Yoga of Action)

Arjuna now wants to know what he is supposed to do next in the battlefield after Krishna's mystical discourse on the soul called Sankhya Yoga. Krishna replies Arjuna should do his duty selflessly. He should work for the welfare of everyone, not just himself, to loosen the bonds of karma. The latter reflects the basis for the theory of karma.

Everything we do and the results thereof relate to some action in the past. Actions formulate destiny. If wrong happens to us, that is because we must have done something wrong in the past. Similarly, good work done in the past results in spiritual and material rewards in the present life. All karmas either tighten or loosen the bondage of the soul. Actions done with the intention of satisfying physical desires are binding, but performing duties without selfish attachment to their outcome loosens the binding. Detached karma will loosen and eventually eliminate the accumulated bondage of the soul. As long as the soul is in bondage, the cycles of birth and death will continue. Only with the complete release from the bondage, one can reach the supreme goal. Do not stop working, rather work selflessly to progress on the path leading to liberation. The intent of this verse can be misunderstood and prompt a question. Why would anyone work without purpose? The selfless work done as a God-given duty does not have to be purposeless work. Gita contains many verses on Karma yoga in several chapters besides chapter three on Karma Yoga. All related verses are extracted and grouped under Topic 3, as follows. Collectively, these verses impart an appreciation of the enormous power of Karma yoga and why Krishna frequently mentions it.

❦ *Krishna says to Arjuna:*

2.39 एषा तेऽभिहिता साङ्ख्ये बुद्धियोंगे त्विमां शृणु बुद्ध्या युक्तो यया पार्थ कर्मबन्धं प्रहास्यसि   Previously, I imparted to you the knowledge regarding the nature of the soul (the Sankhya yoga). Now hear about the way of action (Karma yoga). Understanding this frees you up from bondage due to Karma.

Sankhya yoga is the analytical knowledge about the nature of the soul, discussed in Topic 8. The definitions of the new terms Sankhya yoga, Buddhi yoga, and Nishkam karma are as follows. 1. Sankhya yoga – gaining knowledge through the study of the nature of the soul and its distinction from the body. 2. Buddhi yoga or yoga of intellect - working without desire for rewards and detachment from enjoying the results of actions. Detachment comes from discrimination by the intellect. 3. Nishkam Karma – Work that is done without selfish motives does not bind the soul to karma.

2.40 नेहाभिक्रमनाशोऽस्ति प्रत्यवायो न विद्यते स्वल्पमप्यस्य धर्मस्य त्रायते महतो भयात्
In this path of karma yoga (working without attachment to results), you lose nothing by unfinished efforts for realization. Even a small effort saves you from great fear (the suffering in the repeated cycles of birth and death).

What danger is Krishna talking about? Like humans, the lower species also eat, sleep, defend, and mate. Unlike animals, humans have the unique talent to acquire and utilize knowledge for spiritual elevation. As the karmas in this life determine the next birth, the danger Krishna refers to is the possibility of spiritual degradation and rebirth in the lower class or species in the next life. Krishna says, however, even a small effort to practice karma yoga saves one from such a danger.

2.41 व्यवसायात्मिका बुद्धिरेकेह कुरुनन्दन बहुशाखा ह्यनन्ताश्च बुद्धयोऽव्यवसायिनाम्   The intellect of karma yogis is firm, and their aim is one-pointed. However, the aim of those with irresolute or wavering intellect is branched.

The uncontrolled mind is the root cause of attachment to pleasures. How do you overcome the weak mind? The intellect (buddhi) can control the mind as the mind follows the intellect. Firm intelligence can inspire the mind to do karmas as a matter of duty and detach it from the focus on worldly enjoyment.

2.47 कर्मण्येवाधिकारस्ते मा फलेषु कदाचन मा कर्मफलहेतुर्भूर्मा ते सङ्गोऽस्त्वकर्मणि   You have the right to perform prescribed duties, but "you are not entitled to results" (see comments below about this translation). You are never the cause of the results of your activities. However, don't be attached to inaction.

The popular English translation of this verse as "you are not entitled to the results" is confusing and perhaps incorrect. No one works without a goal in mind. Arjuna fought to win, not lose. Then what does the practical-thinking Krishna mean? A more meaningful translation is that do your work as a duty but do not use the results for selfish gain, without being grateful to God. Also, share your success and abundance with those who are in need, and don't just hoard it strictly for your consumption.

Also, understand that everyone has to do something, even Krishna, so never fall in the trap and get into the "Do Nothing" mode out of hopelessness if you fail. If you do not succeed, rise again, and try harder. In the end, gracefully accept success or failure.

2.48 योगस्थ: कुरु कर्माणि सङ्गं त्यक्त्वा धनञ्जय सिद्ध्यसिद्ध्यो: समो भूत्वा समत्वं योग उच्यते   Be absorbed in yoga; do all work giving up attachment to the results; remain steady in success and failure. Such equanimity is called yoga.

This verse has a practical appeal. Success is a likely outcome anytime you do your work with total focus without letting the mind drift away in the anxiety of whether you will succeed or fail. Putting all your energy in the work instead of worries about the outcome will enhance the chances of success, that is common sense.

2.49 दूरेण ह्यवरं कर्म बुद्धियोगाद्धनञ्जय बुद्धौ शरणमन्विच्छ कृपणा: फलहेतव: The work done to fulfill your (worldly) desires is far inferior to that done through wisdom. The miserly seek to enjoy the fruits of their labor (for their selfish motives).

Selfish people use prosperity strictly for their enjoyment only; they do not share their earnings with those who need help and never be grateful for God's grace for their wealth.

2.50 बुद्धियुक्तो जहातीह उभे सुकृतदुष्कृते तस्माद्योगाय युज्यस्व योग: कर्मसु कौशलम्   Any allotted work, done skillfully without expectation of rewards, does not bind; it can eliminate good and adverse reactions in this life itself.

Nishkam Karma, done ideally, will free you from the bondage. Karmeshu Kaushalam - this is a compelling and practical message. It means 1. Do your work with full enthusiasm, not haphazardly, 2. Do the best, high-quality, and perfect work, never lazily 3. Be very efficient, not wasteful, 4. The message applies to all types of work 5. Accept the fact; everyone has to do some work anyway. A perfect job done enthusiastically will make you feel happy. Japan's economy was destroyed after World War II, but the Japanese people restored the wealth in a few years, mainly by doing the best quality work, which spread their reputation for quality and, as a result, the demand for their products.

2.51 कर्मजं बुद्धियुक्ता हि फलं त्यक्त्वा मनीषिण: जन्मबन्धविनिर्मुक्ता: पदं गच्छन्त्यनामयम्
The wise people with balanced intellect are **not** attached to the results of their work, which bind one to the cycle of life and death. As a positive result (working in a detached mode and getting out of the cycle of birth and death), you can rise above all suffering.

Working in the true spirit of Karma yoga relieves or eliminates the load of karma. Krishna says Nishkam Karma can help you avoid the infinite cycles of birth and death.

2.52 यदा ते मोहकलिलं बुद्धिर्व्यतितरिष्यति तदा गन्तासि निर्वेदं श्रोतव्यस्य श्रुतस्य च
When intellect overcomes delusion due to duality, you reach the state of indifference to what you hear and what you have heard.

It is easy to understand and accept that the actual owner is God, and you are doing work assigned by him. Once you know this simple truth, the ignorance and delusion will vanish, and you will enter the enlightened mode.

2.53 श्रुतिविप्रतिपन्ना ते यदा स्थास्यति निश्चला समाधावचला बुद्धिस्तदा योगमवाप्स्यसि
When intellect cannot be dominated by selfish thoughts of rewards from your work,

TOPIC 3 - Karma Yoga (Path of Yoga of Action)

and when it remains firmly in divine consciousness, then you can move to the state of perfect Yoga.

One who is in the higher consciousness and not moved by material allurements attains the state of Samādhi (the highest step in Ashtang yoga) or perfect Yoga. Verses 5.27 and 5.28 under Topic 13 on Yoga Kriya discusses the Ashtang yoga process in detail.

❧ Here, Arjuna interrupts Krishna and asks:

3.1 & 3.2 अर्जुन उवाच ज्यायसी चेत्कर्मणस्ते मता बुद्धिर्जनार्दन तत्किं कर्मणि घोरे मां नियोजयसि केशव व्यामिश्रेणेव वाक्येन बुद्धिं मोहयसीव मे तदेकं वद निश्चित्य येन श्रेयोऽहमाप्नुयाम्   If knowledge is higher than action, then why are you asking me to engage in the war? Your cryptic stand is confusing, so clearly explain to me the one path leading to the end goal.

Arjuna is asking which path takes you to the highest goal - knowledge or action. Krishna has been saying that activities should not be abandoned, but hankering for the rewards from the results be abandoned.

❧ Krishna replies to Arjuna:

3.3 श्रीभगवानुवाच लोकेऽस्मिन्द्विविधा निष्ठा पुरा प्रोक्ता मयानघ ज्ञानयोगेन साङ्ख्यानां कर्मयोगेन योगिनाम्   Two paths that take you to the enlightenment are Jnan Marg or the knowledge route for those who like contemplation and meditation, and Karma yoga, which means working selflessly for people who are action-oriented (virtually a vast majority of people).

Jnana marg, referred to as Sankhya yoga in this verse, is knowledge gained from the study of characteristics of the soul and knowing that the soul is not the same as the body. Karma yoga or buddhi yoga in Gita's terminology is working on the mission as allotted by God in the spirit of devotion to the supreme. The prerequisite for both Karma yoga and Sankhya yoga is action and knowledge. Mere Bhakti (devotion) without knowledge is blind faith, and Jnan Marg (the path of knowledge) without devotion is mere intellectual speculation, that can inflate ego.

3.4 न कर्मणामनारम्भान्नैष्कर्म्यं पुरुषोऽश्नुते न च संन्यसनादेव सिद्धिं समधिगच्छति   Not doing any work does not end the accumulation of karmic reactions. Physical renunciation of actions (work) does not lead to the perfection of knowledge.

Bondage to karma cannot end by renouncing actions. Leaving your job and family does not relieve one from the bondage due to accrued Karma. Not doing any work also does not let you rise on the path of knowledge either.

3.5 न हि कश्चित्क्षणमपि जातु तिष्ठत्यकर्मकृत् कार्यते ह्यवश: कर्म सर्व: प्रकृतिजैर्गुणै:   No one can ever survive without doing any work. Everyone is forced to do some work according to their inherent nature as driven by the three Gunas.

No one spends a single second without doing some work by the body or the mind to "seek happiness", which is the single goal of all activities. However, we don't find permanent happiness because our past karma is strong.

The power of the three Gunas you inherit from your previous lives compels you to work. The three Gunas - Satv, rajas, and tamas - impose the "excess baggage" the soul has accumulated over the many past births, specifically, from the inclinations and impressions the soul has experienced. Whatever work you are doing in this life is a result of the state of the three Gunas inherent in you. The only way to reduce the load of the "excess baggage" is by following Krishna's preaching on Karma Yoga.

3.7 यस्त्विन्द्रियाणि मनसा नियम्यारभतेऽर्जुन कर्मेन्द्रियै: कर्मयोगमसक्त: स विशिष्यते   The karma yogis who restrain their Jnanendriyas (knowledge senses) with mind control and occupy their working senses in doing work without attachment are superior to renunciants.

Karma yogis abiding by the science of karma are superior to renunciants dwelling on sense objects. The five Jnanendriyas or the faculties of perception are ears, skin, eyes, tongue, and nose. The five sense perceptions are hearing, touch, sight, taste, and smell.

3.8 नियतं कुरु कर्म त्वं कर्म ज्यायो ह्यकर्मण: शरीरयात्रापि च ते न प्रसिद्ध्येदकर्मण: Do your allotted work as the action is superior to inaction. By not working, you cannot even maintain the needs of your body.

"Allotted" means as assigned by God. God does not physically come to dictate your lifestyle, so what does the word "allotted" signify? Everyone is born in a particular environment, family, and country, according to past Karma. No one has the control or freedom to choose the body or the family. God has already assigned the work you do, whether you stick with your work or switch it. That is what "allotted" means. Driven by ego, you may disagree and think you can exercise the freedom of choice to select your work, but that is delusionary.

3.9 यज्ञार्थात्कर्मणोऽन्यत्र लोकोऽयं कर्मबन्धन: तदर्थं कर्म कौन्तेय मुक्तसङ्ग: समाचर   This world is bound by actions other than those that are done as a sacrifice (Yajna). Perform activities as a sacrifice and without attachment.

Actions performed to satisfy your desires and without the spirit of offering bind the soul. Krishna uses the word Yajna frequently to mean different things depending upon the context. Many writers translate Yajna as "sacrifice" in English. Some have defined Yajna as "to worship, adore, honor, revere, act." One typical interpretation of the word Yajna is the Vedic rituals (fire ceremonies) involving offerings of food and certain material to celestial gods via fire. The broader meaning of Yajna, as Krishna uses, is any rite, ceremony, devotion, austerity, and charity actions done as a noble mission without attachment and ego.

3.14 अन्नाद्भवन्ति भूतानि पर्जन्यादन्नसम्भव: यज्ञाद्भवति पर्जन्यो यज्ञ: कर्मसमुद्भव: All people (the beings) survive on food. In turn, food is produced by rains, and the rains fall as God's grace for their good acts, such as sacrifice, Yajna. Sacrifice materializes by performing prescribed duties (karma yoga).

This verse discusses the continuous cycle of NATURE, which sustains life. Nature's cycle is expressed in the following arrow chart:

Rains >> Grains >> Human food >> Transformed in blood >> semen or the seed for creating another body >> Performance of Yajna (sacrifice) >> Pleases the heavenly gods >> the rains are produced >> the cycle repeats

3.19 तस्मादसक्त: सततं कार्यं कर्म समाचर असक्तो ह्याचरन्कर्म परमाप्नोति पूरुष: Take action (do your work) without being attached to or preoccupied with the results. Because by working without attachment to results, one can attain the Supreme.

Note, Krishna has repeated the principle of selfless work many times within the Gita for the immense spiritual and practical benefits. Refer to related verses 3.8 and 3.9 in the current topic Karma Yoga.

3.20 and 3.21 कर्मणैव हि संसिद्धिमास्थिता जनकादय: लोकसंग्रहमेवापि सम्पश्यन्कर्तुमर्हसि यद्यदाचरति श्रेष्ठस्तत्तदेवेतरो जन: स यत्प्रमाणं कुरुते लोकस्तदनुवर्तते   By doing their allocated or prescribed duties, King Janak and others were successful in reaching the state of perfection. You should do the work you are assigned to set a leadership example for the betterment of all people because whatever actions the leaders perform, all people will follow. Whatever work ethics and standards the leaders abide by, everyone will pursue.

True leaders lead by example, by performing Karma yoga rather than passive preaching. Examples of good deeds by the leaders have lasting effects on the citizens. Rogue leaders just inundate people with lectures, which they do not follow themselves, nor do the people. They talk for hours, but the audience gets confused.

3.22 न मे पार्थास्ति कर्तव्यं त्रिषु लोकेषु किञ्चन नानवाप्तमवाप्तव्यं वर्त एव च कर्मणि   I have no duty to perform in all three worlds, nor anything to gain or attain by working or not working. Yet I am busy doing my mission.

Krishna played his Kshatriya role as a karma yogi, not karma sannyasi. He did an enormous amount of work for the welfare and protection of others; while living the perfect life of a householder. A significant point here is even an ideal Avatar did prescribed duties to set an example. Many prominent spiritual leaders are also engaged in various selfless service projects for the benefit of people, besides teaching spirituality.

3.24 उत्सीदेयुरिमे लोका न कुर्यां कर्म चेदहम् सङ्करस्य च कर्ता स्यामुपहन्यामिमा: प्रजा:   If I failed to do my duties, the world would perish, and I would be held responsible for the incredible chaos as a result of my inaction. The resulting chaos and disorder would destroy the whole human race.

This verse summarizes what would happen if the leaders and everyone else abandoned their work.

3.25 सक्ता: कर्मण्यविद्वांसो यथा कुर्वन्ति भारत कुर्याद्विद्वांस्तथासक्तश्चिकीर्षुर्लोकसंग्रहम्
Ignorant people perform duties with attachment to results, but wise people perform their work with no selfish expectation from their work (detached mode) to lead ignorant people on the right path.

Note, Krishna in his characteristic style is repeating his message about selfless work or Nishkam karma because it is one of the key messages he wants to deliver and make sure people grasp it.

3.26 न बुद्धिभेदं जनयेदज्ञानां कर्मसङ्गिनाम् जोषयेत्सर्वकर्माणि विद्वान्युक्त: समाचरन्
Wise people should not create disharmony among the ignorant people, who are attached to results, by inspiring them to abandon their work (Karma sannyasa). Instead, wise people should do their duties in a detached mode, which will encourage ignorant people to do their allotted duties.

Working for rewards is far superior to not working at all. Therefore, the wise should never push people to abandon their work for any reason. The wise should not lecture the ignorant for expecting rewards from their work, but they should gradually lead people by example to do their work in the detached mode.

3.30 मयिसर्वाणि कर्माणि संन्यस्याध्यात्मचेतसा निराशीर्निर्ममो भूत्वा युध्यस्व विगतज्वर:
Do all actions as an offering to Me and continuously meditate on Me as the Supreme. Become free from desire and selfishness, and with your mental grief departed, do your duty and fight.

Krishna summarizes the science of karma yoga by emphasizing Bhakti or devotion and then comes back to his goal of motivating Arjuna to do his work, i.e., fight the evil side for establishing righteousness.

3.31 ये मे मतमिदं नित्यमनुतिष्ठन्ति मानवा: श्रद्धावन्तोऽनसूयन्तो मुच्यन्ते तेऽपि कर्मभि:
Those who abide by my instructions faithfully and without argument and objection are released from the bondage of Karma.

Follow Krishna's preaching with faith to release yourself from the bondage.

3.35 श्रेयान्स्वधर्मो विगुण: परधर्मात्स्वनुष्ठितात् स्वधर्मे निधनं श्रेय: परधर्मो भयावह: It is better to do your assigned duty, even if it is erroneous, than to do someone else's, even though the latter may seem flawless and perfect for you. It is preferable to die doing your own duty than to follow another's path full of danger.

This verse suggests to be yourself and carry out your mission, even though people may consider your work inferior and less prestigious. Don't copy someone else out of the inferiority complex. NOTE, Krishna emphasizes the message of this verse by repeating the word dharma four times. Righteousness is a more common translation of dharma from Sanskrit to English. However, righteousness does not convey fully the meaning of the word dharma. Dharma is several attributes such as responsibilities, duties, thoughts, and actions appropriate for us. See the discussion under verse 18.66 in topic 1 on Bhakti yoga for further explanation of dharma.

4.14 न मां कर्माणि लिम्पन्ति न मे कर्मफले स्पृहा इति मां योऽभिजानाति कर्मभिर्न स बध्यते   Activities don't bind Me, and I have no desires for the results of action by people. Karmic effects do not bind those who understand this.

Work does not bind God with a karmic reaction. God is born as a human by his Yoga Maya Shakti - the divine power. God is selfless and compassionate. God's avatars also come for specific missions, but they are not affected by any karmic reactions. God's work is NOT motivated by selfishness. Although he does a lot of work as a human, karmic reactions do not taint him. Ramayan states "Pure personalities are never tainted by defects even in contact with impure situations and entities." Verse 4.9 under Topic 10 conveys a similar message.

4.15 एवं ज्ञात्वा कृतं कर्म पूर्वैरपि मुमुक्षुभि: कुरु कर्मैव तस्मात्त्वं पूर्वै: पूर्वतरं कृतम्   Knowing this truth (that selfless action does not bind the soul), even the ancient sages seeking liberation performed actions (selflessly). You should follow the sages and perform your duty.

The sages carry out their mission to preach, teach, and elevate the spirituality of people; they do so selflessly and as service to God. Therefore, they are free from the karmic reaction.

4.21 निराशीर्यतचित्तात्मा त्यक्तसर्वपरिग्रह: शारीरं केवलं कर्म कुर्वन्नाप्रोति किल्बिषम्
Without expectation and the sense of ownership, and with the mind and intellect under control, a sage incurs no sin, even though he does his work by his body.

Sages are working in divine consciousness, thus not incurring sin.

4.22 यदृच्छालाभसन्तुष्टो द्वन्द्वातीतो विमत्सर: सम: सिद्धावसिद्धौ च कृत्वापि न निबध्यते
They are happy with whatever they gain, free of envy, beyond dualities, and unmoved by success and failure. Therefore, they are not bound by their actions, although they do many activities.

To remain steady and undisturbed in success and failure, do your work diligently in service of God and be detached. Joyfully accept positive and negative results.

4.23 गतसङ्गस्य मुक्तस्य ज्ञानावस्थितचेतस: यज्ञायाचरत: कर्म समग्रं प्रविलीयते   They are freed from the bondage of Maya, and their intellect is set in divine knowledge. They work for the sake of God; therefore, they are not bound by the karmic reaction.

Those who know the soul is subservient to God, do their work in the spirit of serving God. They are released from sinful reactions to their work.

18.17 यस्य नाहङ्कृतो भावो बुद्धिर्यस्य न लिप्यते हत्वापि स इमाँल्लोकान्न हन्ति न निबध्यते   Those with intellect, not tainted by good or evil, do not have the ego of being the doer. Though they slay these (wicked) people, they never kill and nor are bound by sinful reactions.

Those with pure intellect do their work as a duty and not to enjoy the results. They are free from sinful reactions from their work. Note, verse 5.10 under Topic 5 also says that those who are detached from results are not incurring sins from their work.

TOPIC 4

Science of Action

Krishna vividly simplified the complexity of the principle of Karma and how it works. At any time, both the body and mind are engaged in doing karmas. Abandoning bodily actions is not necessarily renunciation if the mind remains engrossed in the thoughts of pleasure. It is impossible to stop working entirely as the influence of the Gunas compels one to work. Topics 28, 34, and 37 discuss the three Gunas. Let it be said here, that each person is born with a mix of three Gunas based on past karmas, as established by Maya Shakti.

Krishna introduces unique terms in this topic, "action in inaction" and "inaction in action", which are tricky to grasp. A simplified definition of action in inaction can be when you lay back giving up actions, thinking you are renouncing actions, but your mind is busy thinking about worldly pleasures. Inaction in action means when you are working as an instrument of God, free of the thought that you are the doer, and free of the desire to enjoy the results. Further clarification of these terms is covered by verses 4.16, 4.17, and 4.18 in this topic.

Also discussed is what type of actions trigger a "karmic reaction" that increases the balance of karmas or strengthens the "bondage" of the soul, and what actions do not. Any work done by adhering to Karma Yoga principles does not produce a reaction and will lighten the load of the accrued karma. Any work done in expectation of selfish outcome for personal benefit will increase the balance of accrued karma.

🐚 Krishna further explains to Arjuna:

3.4 न कर्मणामनारम्भान्नैष्कर्म्यं पुरुषोऽश्रुते न च संन्यसनादेव सिद्धिं समधिगच्छति   Not doing any work does NOT lead to freedom from karmic reactions. Renunciation (sannyasa) does not lead to perfection.

The mind remains active even if one gives up action. By mere renouncement of action, one cannot achieve perfection or freedom from action. Therefore, physical renunciation does not free one from bondage when thoughts of pleasure and passions continue to dwell in the mind.

3.5 न हि कश्चित्क्षणमपि जातु तिष्ठत्यकर्मकृत् कार्यते ह्यवश: कर्म सर्व: प्रकृतिजैर्गुणै:   No one can remain even for a moment without working. Everyone is forced to work and act helplessly due to his Gunas born out of nature, i.e., the influence of the three Gunas.

The power of the three Gunas compels you to work. The three Gunas - Sattva, rajas, and tamas - are also defined as the product of Maya, which impose the "excess baggage" on the soul, accumulated over the many past births. The past inclinations and impressions the soul has experienced compel you to do the work you are doing in the present life. This "baggage" gets heavier or lighter from one birth to the next and will not release the soul from the bondage until the accumulated karma is burned out by karma yoga.

4.16 किं कर्म किमकर्मेति कवयोऽप्यत्र मोहिता: तत्ते कर्म प्रवक्ष्यामि यज्ज्ञात्वा मोक्ष्यसेऽशुभात् "What is action, and what is inaction?" Even the wise are confused by this question. Now, let me explain to you the mystery of action. After knowing this, you can attain freedom from bondage.

"What is the right action and what is not," is a difficult question even for the celestial gods and sages. Only God knows right from wrong. The correct understanding of the difference between action and inaction can free one from the clutches of Maya Shakti.

4.17 कर्मणो ह्यपि बोद्धव्यं बोद्धव्यं च विकर्मण: अकर्मणश्च बोद्धव्यं गहना कर्मणो गति:   You must understand the nature of all three types of actions —recommended action (Karmanah), prohibited action (vikarmanah), and inaction (akarmanah). The exact nature of the action is hard to understand.

Three types of actions mentioned here are 1. Recommended actions that restrain the senses and clean the mind 2. Prohibited actions are those that degrade the soul 3. Inaction is the karma done merely as a duty without attachment to the outcome. Note that Krishna uses the term "boddhavyam", which means "must understand," in this verse three times to emphasize that a correct understanding of the three types of karmas is crucial.

4.18 कर्मण्यकर्म य: पश्येदकर्मणि च कर्म य: स बुद्धिमान्मनुष्येषु स युक्त: कृत्स्नकर्मकृत्   Those who see action in inaction and inaction in action are truly wise amongst humans. They are Yogis and performers of all actions.

Inaction in Action: It is the thought "I am the doer" that binds a human being to the material world. In the absence of such an idea, the action becomes no action at all. However, if you are working believing that you are merely an instrument of God, the work you do does not bind you; in other words, that work is like inaction. Actions performed with only the desire to please God is thus considered "inaction," or nonbinding action.

Action in Inaction: Some people give up their social duties misunderstanding it as renunciation, but their mind remains on the sense objects. They may appear inactive, and they may think they are inactive, but their mind is busy (working). When Arjuna wanted to abandon his duty, Krishna explained to him that it would be a sin, and he would go to the infernal regions for such inaction.

4.19 यस्य सर्वे समारम्भा: कामसङ्कल्पवर्जिता: ज्ञानाग्निदग्धकर्माणं तमाहु: पण्डितं बुधा:

The self-realized sages call those people wise, whose actions are free of the desire for pleasures, and whose works are burnt in the fire of knowledge.

The soul is bound in karmic reaction when it thinks that it is the body, while its actions remain attached to desire. The soul is not bound in karmic reactions when it is enlightened and realizes it is not the body and dedicates all activities as service to God. Then, the work will result in no karmic reactions or is said to be "burnt in the fire of knowledge." Refer to a related verse 9.27 (Topic 1) in which Krishna says, "Whatever you do and eat, offer as oblation to the sacred fire, bestow as a gift; and austerities you perform, do them as an offering to Me."

4.20 त्यक्त्वा कर्मफलासङ्गं नित्यतृप्तो निराश्रय: कर्मण्यभिप्रवृत्तोऽपि नैव किञ्चित्करोति स:

Having abandoned attachment to the fruit of the action, ever content, depending on nothing, he does not do anything though engaged in the activity. Their actions are called inaction or "akarma".

Actions cannot be judged by the outward looks of them but by what is in your mind. The minds of sages are always in the Supreme. In such a mode, all their actions are said to be akarma or inactions. The ancient sage Durvasa once ate a full dinner offered by his devotees, yet he could show by his powers (siddhi) that mentally he only ate a piece of grass, and his stomach was empty.

TOPIC 4 - Science of Action

TOPIC 5

Karma Sannyasa vs. Karma Yoga (Renunciation vs. Action)

Krishna explains the difference between renunciation (sannyasa) and the life of detached action (karma yoga). Sannyasa, to most, means going away from regular life in preference for austere life, and wandering without a home. Sannyasi has no family or society. Krishna does not recommend Arjuna to pursue the life of a Sannyasi. He says everyone has to do some work. Gita recommends renouncing selfish actions done to gratify personal desire. He advises Arjuna to abide by his duties, but without a selfish purpose. Krishna reminds Arjuna that he should never give up virtuous actions, such as sacrifice, charity, and spiritual discipline.

Both renunciation and karma tyaga require a detached state of mind, which is very hard to achieve. The mind is hard to control; no force can ever control the mind either. Instead of forced restraining, the scriptures suggest developing an attachment to God to "divert" the mind away from sensual pleasures and idle pursuits. Jnanis (those who have attained the state of purified knowledge) use the strength of intellect (the higher mind) to dissuade the fickle mind (the lower mind) and direct it away from sense objects.

Gita does not promote asceticism (sannyasa) as defined by the scriptures. Although Krishna does not disapprove of sannyasa to reach the spiritual goal, he says the life of selfless action is a better path than no work. However, he makes it clear that ultimately both roads lead to the same supreme goal.

❦ *Krishna says to Arjuna:*

3.17 यस्त्वात्मरतिरेव स्यादात्मतृप्तश्च मानव: आत्मन्येव च सन्तुष्टस्तस्य कार्य न विद्यते   But the person who is delighted in the Self, satisfied with the Self, and contented in the Self, has no duties to fulfill.

'Karma yoga' is working as a service to God and it is prescribed for the material-oriented humans. 'Karma sannyasa' is not working but entirely dedicating oneself to God. Karma sannyasa is more suitable for a self-illumined person whose consciousness has united with God. A true Sannyasi has already attained the ultimate supreme goal and has no duty to perform.

3.18 नैव तस्य कृतेनार्थो नाकृतेनेह कश्चन न चास्य सर्वभूतेषु कश्चिदर्थव्यपाश्रय: The enlightened souls gain or lose nothing by working or not working. They do not need to rely on others to fulfill their needs.

For the self-realized, to do or not do does not matter. Examples of Karma sannyasis are Sankaracharya, Madhavacharya, etc. Notably, not even the Karma sannyasis remained idle but were very busy doing the spiritual work. Examples of karma yogis from scriptures are Prahlad, Vibhishan, Hanuman, Kabir, Nanak, etc. Krishna says later that everybody has to do something. Although Krishna did not 'need' to work, he nonetheless did so, as a Kshatriya and a spiritual leader.

❧ Here, Arjuna asks:

5.1 अर्जुन उवाच संन्यासं कर्मणां कृष्ण पुनर्योगं च शंससि यच्छ्रेय एतयोरेकं तन्मे ब्रूहि सुनिश्चितम् You praised Karma sannyasa, but you also advised performing Karma yoga. Tell me decisively which one is better karma sannyasa or karma yoga?

Arjuna may be thinking that karma yoga and sannyasa are opposite and cannot be followed simultaneously.

❧ Krishna replies:

5.2 श्रीभगवानुवाच संन्यास: कर्मयोगश्च नि:श्रेयसकरावुभौ तयोस्तु कर्मसंन्यासात्कर्मयोगो विशिष्यते Both karma sannyasa and karma yoga lead to the supreme goal. Of the two paths, karma yoga (performance of selfless action) is superior to karma sannyasa.

Karma sannyasi abandons his social duties and devotes his time entirely to spiritual responsibilities. A caution with this path is their mind must be free of worldly thoughts, and their senses must be under control. If their mind dwells on sense objects, the karma sannyasis cannot succeed in their spiritual goal. Karma yogis do both worldly and spiritual duties without expectation for reward and dedicate them to God, so, karma yoga is more natural for most people.

5.3 ज्ञेय: स नित्यसंन्यासी यो न द्वेष्टि न काङ्क्षति निर्द्वन्द्वो हि महाबाहो सुखं बन्धात्प्रमुच्यते
The karma yogis, who are devoid of desire or hatred, should be considered in renounced mode already. Free from all dualities, they are easily liberated from the bonds of Maya– the material energy.

Karma yogis do their work as a duty while remaining detached. They remain undisturbed with good and bad results and accept them as God's will. Swami Shivananda's commentary is "a man does not become a Sannyasin (renunciant) by merely giving up actions due to laziness, ignorance, some family quarrel or calamity or unemployment. A true Sannyasin is one who has neither attachment nor aversion to anything. Physical renunciation of objects is no renunciation at all. What is required is the renunciation of egoism and desires."

5.4 साङ्ख्ययोगौ पृथग्बाला: प्रवदन्ति न पण्डिता: एकमप्यास्थित: सम्यगुभयोर्विन्दते फलम्
Only those lacking knowledge (ajnani) say that sānkhya (giving up actions or karma sanyāsa) and karma yoga (working with detachment and dedication to God) are different. Those who are genuinely knowledgeable say that by following either of these paths, you can achieve the same results.

Karma sannyasa is renouncing actions, remaining established in jnana (knowledge), looking at everything as the energy of God, and believing God owns everything, and ultimately, he is the enjoyer. Karma yoga is acting for the pleasure of God selflessly as servants of God. The internal state of karma yogis and karma sannyasis is the same.

5.5 यत्साङ्ख्यै: प्राप्यते स्थानं तद्योगैरपि गम्यते एकं साङ्ख्यं च योगं च य: पश्यति स पश्यति
The supreme state is attained by karma sannyasa or karma yoga, which is working in a detached and dedicated mode. Those knowing that both paths are identical are the ones who know the truth.

The karma sannyasi and karma yogi have their minds in God, and their goal is common, i.e., self-realization, so both paths are the same.

5.6 संन्यासस्तु महाबाहो दु:खमासुमयोगत: योगयुक्तो मुनिर्ब्रह्म नचिरेणाधिगच्छति   Perfect renunciation or karma sannyasa is difficult to attain without Karma Yoga (performing action). Nonetheless, the wise who follow the path of selfless service (Karma Yoga) can quickly reach the Supreme.

By doing prescribed duties without expectation, it is possible to conquer anger, greed, and desire. However, if one first gives up responsibilities, it is difficult to purify the mind; and without a pure mind, true detachment is not possible.

5.7 योगयुक्तो विशुद्धात्मा विजितात्मा जितेन्द्रिय: सर्वभूतात्मभूतात्मा कुर्वन्नपि न लिप्यते   One who is established in yoga, who has conquered the mind, body, and senses, and who sees his Self in all beings, can perform all kinds of actions but is not influenced (tainted) by them.

The karma yogis with the mind, body, and senses under control engage in selfless work. The intellect of such yogis is purified. They see God in all living beings and behave respectfully toward everyone.

Karma yogi is 1. vishuddhatma or who has purified intellect; 2. vijitatma or who has conquered the mind 3. jitendriya or who has controlled senses.

5.8 and 5.9 नैव किञ्चित्करोमीति युक्तो मन्येत तत्ववित् पश्यञ्श्रृण्वन्स्पृशञ्जिघ्रन्नश्नन्गच्छन् स्वपञ्श्वसन् प्रलपन्विसृजन्गृह्णन्नुन्मिषन्निमिषन्नपि इन्द्रियाणीन्द्रियार्थेषु वर्तन्त इति धारयन्
Those steadfast in karma Yoga always think they are not the doers, even when

engaged in seeing, hearing, touching, smelling, moving, sleeping, breathing, speaking, excreting, grasping, opening/closing the eyes. With divine knowledge, they see the senses moving among their objects.

The sage Vashisth advised Ram, his student, "O Ram, externally do all your work diligently, but internally have the attitude that you are non-doer, and God is the doer of all your activities."

5.10 ब्रह्मण्याधाय कर्माणि सङ्गं त्यक्त्वा करोति यः लिप्यते न स पापेन पद्मपत्रमिवाम्भसा
Those who dedicate their actions to God and give up attachment are not touched by sin – just like a lotus leaf in water.

Krishna reiterates the essential message. The work done as dedication and without attachment does not incur sin and does not accumulate "the balance of karma."

5.11 कायेन मनसा बुद्ध्या केवलैरिन्द्रियैरपि योगिनः कर्म कुर्वन्ति सङ्गं त्यक्त्वात्मशुद्धये
Yogis do their work with their body, senses, mind, and intellect, giving up attachment to the work and the results, only to purify themselves.

The yogis work to purify the mind and intellect. To illustrate this point, before the battle with Ravan, Sugreev (the head of the army helping Ram) was nervous. Ram told him he could destroy Ravan and all demons merely by moving his finger. Sugreev asked, "Why do you need the army to help you, then?" Ram replied, "I do not need anyone's help, but I want to let you and everyone else offer devotional service and purify your mind."

6.1 श्रीभगवानुवाच अनाश्रितः कर्मफलं कार्यं कर्म करोति यः स संन्यासी च योगी च न निरग्निर्न चाक्रियः   Those who do their allotted work without selfish desire are real sannyasis (renunciates) and yogis, not those who have merely stopped doing their work and stopped doing Yajna such as the Agnihotra yajna (fire ritual).

Krishna repeats the message of this verse several times. Renouncing work, as some sannyasis do, does not make anyone a sannyasi. Those who do obligatory work selflessly are true renunciants and yogis.

6.3 आरुरुक्षोर्मुनेर्योगं कर्म कारणमुच्यते योगारूढस्य तस्यैव शमः कारणमुच्यते   To the sage who wishes for perfection in yoga, the work without attachment is said to be the means; to the sage who has attained perfection in yoga, tranquility is said to be the means.

Karma yoga purifies the mind and ripens spiritual knowledge. The elevated yogi with the purity of the mind can move to Karma sannyasa.

❧ To this, Arjuna puts forward his doubt by asking:

18.1 अर्जुन उवाच सन्न्यासस्य महाबाहो तत्वमिच्छामि वेदितुम् त्यागस्य च हृषीकेश पृथक्केशिनिषूदन   I wish to understand: 1. the nature of sannyasa (renunciation of actions) and tyaga (renunciation of the desire for the fruits of actions); and the distinction between the two.

Earlier, Krishna had talked about sannyasa, and about tyaga. Arjuna is asking this question for clarification, one more time.

❧ Krishna explains to Arjuna:

18.2 श्रीभगवानुवाच काम्यानां कर्मणां न्यासं सन्न्यासं कवयो विदुः सर्वकर्मफलत्यागं प्राहुस्त्यागं विचक्षणाः   Sages say sannyasa is to give up the work by desires. They say tyaga is giving up the desire to enjoy the results.

Sannyasis continue daily activities to maintain the body, but give up Kamya Karma - activities relating to wealth, progeny, prestige, status, and power. Tyaga is renouncing the desires for enjoying the outcome, but not giving up the prescribed duties.

18.3 त्याज्यं दोषवदित्येके कर्म प्राहुर्मनीषिणः यज्ञदानतपःकर्म न त्याज्यमिति चापरे   Some people say all actions should be given up as evil, while others maintain that acts of sacrifice, charity, and penance should never be abandoned.

There are two schools of thought relating to the subject of this verse. Abandoning all work thinking that it is motivated by desire and causes the life-death cycle is the Sankhya school of thought. The Mimansha school of thought declares that we must never give up beneficial activities, such as sacrifice, charity, and penance.

18.7 नियतस्य तु सन्न्यासः कर्मणो नोपपद्यते हात्तस्य परित्यागस्तामसः परिकीर्तितः   Obligatory work, as suggested in scriptures, should never be given up. Such misguided renunciation is said to be in the mode of ignorance (tamas).

Prescribed duties should not be abandoned by anyone, whether a yogi or a beginner.

18.11 न हि देहभृता शक्यं त्यक्तुं कर्माण्यशेषतः यस्तु कर्मफलत्यागी स त्यागीत्यभिधीयते   For all beings, it is impossible to give up work entirely. However, those who are not attached to the rewards of actions are true sannyasis or renunciants.

The primary functions for the maintenance of the body, such as eating, sleeping, and bathing, are necessary and unavoidable.

18.12 अनिष्टमिष्टं मिश्रं च त्रिविधं कर्मणः फलम् भवत्यत्यागिनां प्रेत्य न तु सन्न्यासिनां क्वचित्   The three types of results from work – good, bad, or mixed – accrue when the work is done for personal benefit. However, the one who has no desire to enjoy the results is the true renouncer.

The word accrues here means accumulate in one's balance of karma that accompanies him from birth to birth. The results of unselfish actions do not accrue.

18.49 असक्तबुद्धिः सर्वत्र जितात्मा विगतस्पृहः नैष्कर्म्यसिद्धिं परमां सन्न्यासेनाधिगच्छति
One without selfish attachments, who has controlled the mind and passions, achieves the highest level of freedom from action.

Freedom from action means the action does not accrue the balance of karma. Doing prescribed work as a duty without any desires would detach the mind from events and outcomes. The work done in this manner will not bind the soul.

TOPIC 6

Senses, Desires, and Lust

Many verses in Gita warn that the senses, if allowed to dwell on their objects, create an unquenchable desire for the objects. The senses if continued to let live on the objects, strengthen the power of desires and transform to uncontrollable and destabilizing lust for the objects. Krishna says lust is the root cause of sin and the resulting decline in spirituality, thus undermining the prospect of the liberation of the soul. Continued lust can completely destroy prospects for spiritual progress. Krishna says that control of desires for sensual enjoyment is essential for progress on a spiritual journey. The following verses sourced from Gita, relating to this critical topic, carry a similar message that has been often repeated by Krishna throughout his discourse. Krishna, as seen before, repeats crucial messages multiple times. When you come across a message repeated multiple times, consider it very important. The verses with a repeated message are left unedited as they are in the original Gita for the reader's appreciation of what Krishna considers crucial.

❧ *Krishna says to Arjuna:*

2.14 मात्रास्पर्शास्तु कौन्तेय शीतोष्णसुखदुः खदाः आगमापायिनोऽनित्यास्तांस्तितिक्षस्व भारत   The perceptions of hot and cold, pleasure and pain, are a result of the contact between senses and sense objects. Such ideas have a beginning and an end. They are not permanent; bear them patiently.

The body has five senses—sight, smell, taste, touch, and hearing. When the senses dwell on the sense objects, perceptions are created, leading to the desire to enjoy the objects. Contact between the senses and objects causes transient cycles of happiness and distress. Here, Krishna encourages Arjuna to rise above the dualities of pleasure and pain.

2.59 विषया विनिवर्तन्ते निराहारस्य देहिन: रसवर्जं रसोऽप्यस्य परं दृष्ट्वा निवर्तते   You can prevent senses from pursuing objects, but the taste of objects remains. The feeling ceases for those who realize the Supreme.

The senses are impossible to control. Forced restraining of the senses does not cease the taste and memory of the objects. Forcing control of senses (Indriyas) does not work even for renunciants who abandon worldly responsibilities. So, Arjuna is curious about how the senses can be controlled. Krishna illustrates, "By directing the senses to God." On its own merits, that instruction is even harder. However, Krishna does offer many suggestions to acquire control of the senses. A complete list of his ideas can be overwhelmingly long and may frustrate the well-meaning practitioner. Realized gurus suggest that just follow one or two suggestions, but do so firmly and master them; then, the other ideas become easier to practice.

2.60 यततो ह्यपि कौन्तेय पुरुषस्य विपश्चित: इन्द्रियाणि प्रमाथीनि हरन्ति प्रसभं मन:
Senses are keen and turbulent, and can forcibly carry away the mind even for a person of discrimination and self-control.

Krishna says the senses can overpower even a person having a high degree of self-control. The power of senses is so intense, it has even stumbled highly elevated sages like the Great Rishi Vishvamitra, who was deeply attracted by beautiful Menka and fell in love with her. You can force senses to behave, but your mind will continue to dwell on the object. The more you repress the mind, the more it will think of the object.

2.61 तानि सर्वाणि संयम्य युक्त आसीत मत्पर: वशे हि यस्येन्द्रियाणि तस्य प्रज्ञा प्रतिष्ठिता
Those who subdue their senses and keep the mind always focused on Me are established in perfect knowledge.

Subduing the senses would mean restraining consciously and preventing one from being out of control. Diverting the mind to God is an effective method of suppressing the senses; that would keep the mind occupied in a desirable object.

2.62 ध्यायतो विषयान्पुंस: सङ्गस्तेषूपजायते सङ्गात्सञ्जायते काम: कामात्क्रोधोऽभिजायते
Dwelling on sense objects causes attachment to them. Attachment breeds desires; desires breed anger.

The desire can never be controlled by fulfilling it and continuing to dwell on the objects. Desires multiply and get stronger each time. No matter how much of whatever object you have had, you will keep on wanting more, not less, like feeding the fire with fuel. The trap of unrestrained senses is impossible to avoid by ordinary means.

2.63 क्रोधाद्भवति सम्मोह: सम्मोहात्स्मृतिविभ्रम: स्मृतिभ्रंशाद् बुद्धिनाशो बुद्धिनाशात्प्रणश्यति
When anger clouds the judgment, you end up with the loss of memory (of the Self). The next thing that happens is the intellect or the faculty of discrimination is destroyed. Thereupon, one is ruined permanently.

How you can get on to the downward spiral to destruction by dwelling on sense objects is explained in this verse beautifully.

TOPIC 6 - Senses, Desires, and Lust

The following combines the thoughts expressed in verses 2.62 and 2.63 in a cause-and-effect arrow chart.

Dwelling on Sense Objects >> Attachment >> Desire >> ANGER if the object not achieved or >> GREED if the object is achieved >> Hazy judgment >> Destruction of Intelligence >> Complete Destruction when one is overwhelmed with many evil qualities.

To further elaborate the point, consider one of Saibaba's discourses to his disciples about restraining the senses, quoted from Sai Satcharita Chapter 49. When Nanasaheb Chandorkar, an educated follower of Saibaba, was once visiting Baba, a beautiful lady from Bijapur (in Madhya Pradesh) came to see Baba. Seeing the veiled lady, Nanasaheb wanted to go away, but Baba prevented him from doing so. When the lady removed her veil in saluting Baba and then resumed it again, Nanasaheb, who saw her face, was so much smitten with her rare beauty that he wished to see her face again. Detecting restlessness of Nana's mind, Baba spoke to him after the lady had left the place as follows - "Nana, why are you getting agitated in vain? Let the senses do their allotted work or duty; we should not meddle with their work. God has created this beautiful world, and we have to appreciate its beauty. The mind will get steady and calm slowly and gradually. When the heart is pure, there is no difficulty whatsoever. The eyes may do their work; why should you feel shy and tottering?"

Saibaba continued, "Our mind is fickle by nature; it should not be allowed to get wild. The senses may get restless, the body, however, should be held in check and not allowed to be impatient. Senses run after objects, but we should not follow them and crave for their objects. By slow and gradual practice, the restlessness can be conquered. The senses should not be allowed to sway us; make note they cannot be completely controlled. We should curb them rightly and properly according to the need of the occasion. Beauty is the subject of sight; we should fearlessly look at the beauty of objects. Only we should never entertain evil thoughts. Making the mind desireless, observe God's works of beauty. In this way, the senses will be easily and naturally controlled, and even in enjoying objects, you will be reminded of God. If the outer senses are not held in check and if the mind is allowed to run after objects and be attached to them, our cycle of births and deaths will not come to an end. Objects of sense are harmful things. With Viveka (discrimination) as our charioteer, we will control the mind and not allow the senses to go astray. With such a charioteer, we reach the final abode, our real and permanent Home from which there is no return."

❦ Krishna says to Arjuna:

2.67 इन्द्रियाणां हि चरतां यन्मनोऽनुविधीयते तदस्य हरति प्रज्ञां वायुर्नावमिवाम्भसि
Discrimination goes off the tangent from its intended course when the mind is allowed to give in to the wandering senses, just as a boat on the waters is carried off course by the heavy winds.

Attachment to just one of the senses can cause a total loss of control, as clear from the following example. A deer hunter releases sweet sounds from his cabin to attract deer that is attached to soft tones. The sounds tempt and draw the deer near to the hunter's cabin. Subsequently, the hunter kills the deer.

2.68 तस्माद्यस्य महाबाहो निगृहीतानि सर्वश: इन्द्रियाणीन्द्रियार्थेभ्यस्तस्य प्रज्ञा प्रतिष्ठिता
The one who controls the senses from objects is firmly in the state of perfect wisdom and divine knowledge.

Control of senses leads to knowledge (jnana), which leads one on the way to the supreme.

2.69 या निशा सर्वभूतानां तस्यां जागर्ति संयमी यस्यां जाग्रति भूतानि सा निशा पश्यतो मुने:
What everyone considers as the day is the night of ignorance for the wise. What everyone regards as the night is the day for the introspective saint.

The words Day and Night are used as a figure of speech, not to be taken literally, as these words can be confusing. For spiritually elevated saints, the sense of enjoyment is night or darkness or ignorance; victory over the sense objects is the day or light or enlightenment.

3.33 सदृशं चेष्टते स्वस्या: प्रकृतेर्ज्ञानवानपि प्रकृतिं यान्ति भूतानि निग्रह: किं करिष्यति
Even the wise work within the limitation of their own prakriti (nature). All beings are under the influence of prakriti. So, what is the reason for repression (why repress)?

The accumulated tendencies (Samskaras) from the past lives force you to act in a certain way. Instead of forcibly repressing the inherent tendencies, one should accept what we are and then sincerely try to improve on it.

❧ *Now Arjuna asks Krishna:*

3.36 अर्जुन उवाच अथ केन प्रयुक्तोऽयं पापं चरति पूरुष: अनिच्छन्नपि वार्ष्णेय बलादिव नियोजित: What causes one to commit sins unwillingly? What power (shakti) moves us against our own will as if forcing us?

Arjuna recognizes that attraction and aversion can lead to devastation, and wants to know the root cause of sin.

❧ *Krishna replies to Arjuna:*

3.37 श्रीभगवानुवाच काम एष क्रोध एष रजोगुणसमुद्भव: महाशनो महापाप्मा विद्ध्येनमिह वैरिणम्   Lust born from a mode of passion forces one to sin, then the lust turns into anger. Know lust to be the sinful and all-devouring enemy in the world.

Lust compels humans to commit sins and stops spiritual progress. It leads you in the downward spiral. Unsatisfied desire turns into anger.

3.38 धूमेनाव्रियते वह्निर्यथादर्शो मलेन च यथोल्बेनावृतो गर्भस्तथा तेनेदमावृतम्   Just as a fire is covered by smoke, a mirror is masked by dust, and the womb conceals an embryo, one's inherent knowledge gets covered by desire.

TOPIC 6 – Senses, Desires, and Lust

The desire for sensual enjoyment envelops knowledge and diminishes the power of discrimination. As a result, we cannot tell the right from the wrong.

3.39 आवृतं ज्ञानमेतेन ज्ञानिनो नित्यवैरिणा कामरूपेण कौन्तेय दुष्पूरेणानलेन च   Desires cover the knowledge of the most discerning individuals. Desires can never be satisfied; they burn like fire.

As Krishna said before, desires to satisfy the senses multiply each time you fulfill them. Lust is the enemy of spiritual progress and further binds the soul.

3.40 इन्द्रियाणि मनो बुद्धिरस्याधिष्ठानमुच्यते एतैर्विमोहयत्येष ज्ञानमावृत्य देहिनम्
Senses, mind, intellect (under the influence of the three Gunas, the modes) produce desires. Through them, the desire clouds one's knowledge and deludes the soul.

Lust clouds knowledge and causes delusion.

3.41 तस्मात्त्वमिन्द्रियाण्यादौनियम्यभरतर्षभपाप्मानंप्रजहिह्येनंज्ञानविज्ञाननाशनम्   So, bring the senses under control right in the beginning and destroy the enemy called desire, which is the precursor to sin and destroys knowledge and self-realization.

The two greatest enemies of the human race are desire and lust.

The following summarizes the negative impact of desire and lust as described in verses 3.37 through 3.41:

Desire: 1. clouds knowledge; 2. breeds lust; 3. burns like a fire; 4. can never be satisfied; 5. destroys self-realization or AtmJnan.

Lust: 1. the ultimate, destructive enemy; 2. hides knowledge; 3. drives you crazy and forces you to sin; 4. makes you angry when unsatisfied.

Krishna recommends to Arjuna to use the higher instruments to control desire, as stated in the next verse.

3.43 एवं बुद्धे: परं बुद्ध्वा संस्तभ्यात्मानमात्मना जहि शत्रुं महाबाहो कामरूपं दुरासदम्
Thus, knowing the soul to be superior to the intellect, let the strength of the soul (higher self) rule the lower self, i.e., ego (senses, mind, and intellect) and kill this fierce enemy called selfish desire.

Kill desire and lust by using the power of the soul. Slay this enemy called lust through knowledge of the self. Train the intellect to think in this manner. The trained intelligence is called Sanmati or Sadbuddhi in Sanskrit. Use Sanmati to bring the mind and the senses under control, to kill the powerful enemy - lust.

3.6 कर्मेन्द्रियाणि संयम्य य आस्ते मनसा स्मरन् इन्द्रियार्थान्विमूढात्मा मिथ्याचार: स उच्यते
Those who restrain (repress) their indriyas or organs of action, but their mind is absorbed in the sense objects; they are under delusion and in a deplorable state of hypocrisy.

Krishna warns Arjuna not to be like a false ascetic hiding in the orange robs. An excellent example to complete the thought of this verse is offered here from a Hermann

TOPIC 6 - Senses, Desires, and Lust

Hesse's book entitled "Goldmund and Narcissus" as it illuminates Krishna's point. The book is based on a story about two German friends living in a monastery in spiritual pursuit. The two were diametrically opposite in nature and their lifestyles. Goldmund leaves the monastery after some time out of boredom and wanders off aimlessly without any specific purpose, spending his time in whatever came his way - gambling, drinking, prostitution, and criminal behavior, but he never enjoyed these activities. Eventually, Goldmund gets saturated with the undisciplined lifestyle. He would then drift into long periods of silence and sit steadily for hours at a time, in no specific posture, and with no particular goals. Thoughts about his past haunted him, but he ignored them. Slowly, the thoughts about the past faded away. His friend Narcissus, on the other end, worked hard and advanced in the monastery hierarchy in his search for "the meaning of life". However, he could not abandon the thoughts of Goldmund and his approach to life. Skipping to the end, Narcissus does not find the meaning of life and bliss, which he struggled all his life to discover; he decides to visit Goldmund. In the meantime, Goldmund becomes very peaceful and undisturbed in all situations. He experiences bliss.

The moral of the story is that the forced control of the mind does not work. Desires vanish naturally if the mind remains detached with actions and anticipations.

5.22 ये हि संस्पर्शजा भोगा दुःखयोनय एव ते आद्यन्तवन्तः कौन्तेय न तेषु रमते बुधः   The pleasures that are born from contacts only arouse pain. Such desires are temporary as they have a beginning and an end. The wise do not go for such pleasures.

Sensual pleasures may appear enjoyable but the satisfaction derived from undisciplined acts is a source of misery. In comparison, the divine bliss is infinite and eternal.

5.23 शक्नोतीहैव यः सोढुं प्राक्शरीरविमोक्षणात् कामक्रोधोद्भवं वेगं स युक्तः स सुखी नरः:   The devotees who can withstand (and fight off) the urge arising from passion and anger are real yogis and the only ones who are happy.

With a sense of discrimination (understanding of what is right and what is wrong) and elevated consciousness, desire and anger can restrained.

6.5 उद्धरेदात्मनात्मानं नात्मानमवसादयेत् आत्मैव ह्यात्मनो बन्धुरात्मैव रिपुरात्मनः:   Elevate through the power of the mind and not degrade because the mind can be a friend or an enemy of the self (the soul).

A controlled mind elevates consciousness, whereas an uncontrolled mind can degrade the consciousness with wrong thoughts.

The word mind has multiple synonyms in the context of this verse. 1. When it creates thoughts, we call it "mana"; 2. When it analyzes and decides, we call it "Buddhi" or intellect; 3. When attached to objects or a person, we call it "Chitta"; 4. When it identifies with wealth, status, beauty, and learning, we call it "Ahankar" or ego.

The intellect is higher than the mind. Krishna suggests, use the higher mind (he means "buddhi" - intelligence) to control the lower mind.

Again, mind control is possible only if the lust is controlled.

TOPIC 6 - Senses, Desires, and Lust

6.6 बन्धुरात्मात्मनस्तस्य येनात्मैवात्मना जित: अनात्मनस्तु शत्रुत्वे वर्ते तात्मैव शत्रुवत्

For those who have conquered the mind, it is their friend. For those who have failed to do so, the mind works as their enemy.

In essence, the mind is the gate to liberation, heaven, or hell. The mind can be the best friend or the worst enemy. Lust, anger, greed, envy, illusion, and ego all arise from the uncontrolled mind and are the enemies that torment us. The mind is unstable but can be controlled by the logical ability of intellect, combined with detachment and diligence. A common question the Gita students raise is why God would give us all faculties to enjoy if we are not supposed to; they misunderstand Krishna's message.

Krishna's life was full of enjoyment in many ways, which confuses the students. However, Krishna was never a slave of enjoyment and could walk away from the experience of pleasure without any regret. For instance, once, he quietly left a lavish dinner in Duryodhan's palace when the Kauravas insulted him. As if nothing happened, he went to the house of Vidur (a poor devotee). All Vidur had to offer Krishna was some boiled spinach, which Krishna relished and blessed Vidur for the delicious dinner. Another instance of Krishna's detachment is when his golden city of Dwarika sunk in the ocean towards the end of his era. Krishna just quietly moved from there without looking back and without a single word of regret or grief, as if nothing happened.

7.27 इच्छाद्वेषसमुत्थेन द्वन्द्वमोहेन भारत सर्वभूतानि सम्मोहं सर्गे यान्ति परन्तप   The dualities of desire and aversion arise from illusion. People in the world are deluded from birth by these dualities.

A spiritual aspirant on the path of progress moves above the dualities of attraction and aversion, likes and dislikes, and accepts both as an integral and inevitable part of God's creation.

7.28 येषां त्वन्तगतं पापं जनानां पुण्यकर्मणाम् ते द्वन्द्वमोहनिर्मुक्ता भजन्ते मां दृढव्रता:

Those whose sins have ended become free from the illusion of dualities. Such people worship Me with determination.

Addiction to pleasure can destabilize us when pleasures come to an end. Those devotees who are free of the influence of desire and hatred can retain their focus on God. Working for a higher ideal in the spirit of karma yoga is an effective means of dealing with dualities.

TOPIC 7

Gita Mahavakyas (Punchline Verses)

This topic provides examples of certain prominent verses, like on performing the duty courageously and diligently, the theory of soul, the prayer of thanks to God for the food, importance of a spiritual guide, selfless service, renunciation, the cosmic form of God, and Bhakti Yoga in Gita, that are the punchline of Krishna's teaching to Arjuna. Embedded in these verses is the philosophy of Gita. Students of Gita should take time and guidance from experts to thoroughly understand the meaning of these verses as a must for deciphering Krishna's preaching and advancing in spiritual pursuits. Many Gita fans know these verses by heart.

☙ Krishna says to Arjuna:

2.3 क्लैब्यं मा स्म गम: पार्थ नैतत्तवय्युपपद्यते क्षुद्रं हृदयदौर्बल्यं त्यक्त्वोत्तिष्ठ परन्तप   Do not yield to unmanliness; it does not become of you. Shake off this base of faint-heartedness and arise, you punisher of enemies. (As translated by Swami Vivekanand)

This verse contains Krishna's entire message of the Gita for Arjuna and the human world. Krishna says to Arjuna, "You talk like a wise man, but your action and negligence to your duty makes you look like a coward. Wake up from the sleep of ignorance and darkness, recognize the divinity within you, drop fear and weakness, and fiercely go after the mission without the distraction and uncertainty of the outcome. Do not let the negativity cloud your rational thinking and strength you are born with."

Does this not sound like a brilliant lesson we all can apply in our lives to overcome fear, uncertainty, and negativity we often encounter while in the middle of our essential tasks?

2.23 नैनं छिन्दन्ति शस्त्राणि नैनं दहति पावक: न चैनं क्लेदयन्त्यापो न शोषयति मारुत:
The weapons cannot cut it, the fire cannot burn it, water cannot wet it, and the wind cannot dry it (the soul).

The individual soul is a part of Paramatma or super soul, but it is detached from God, not free, and under bondage. When it is liberated, it merges with the source. Regardless, the soul does not lose its divinity even under the bondage. Its divine characteristics are that it is eternal and cannot be slain by any means.

2.47 कर्मण्येवाधिकारस्ते मा फलेषु कदाचन मा कर्मफलहेतुर्भूर्मा ते सङ्गोऽस्त्वकर्मणि.   You are entitled to do your prescribed duties, but not to the results. You are never the cause of the results of your activities. Don't be attached to inaction. (NOTE: This verse is also included in Topic 3 on Karma Yoga).

The literal translation of this verse as "you are not entitled to the results" is confusing and perhaps incorrect. No one works without a goal in mind. Arjuna fought to win, not lose. Then what does the practical-thinking Krishna mean? A more meaningful interpreation is that do your work as a duty but do not use the results for selfish gain, and be grateful to God. Share your success and abundance with those who are in need, and don't just hoard it strictly for your consumption.

Also, understand that everyone has to do something, even Krishna, so never fall in the trap and get into the "Do Nothing" mode out of hopelessness. If you fail, rise again, and try harder. In the end, gracefully accept success or failure.

2.50 बुद्धियुक्तो जहातीह उभे सुकृतदुष्कृते तस्माद्योगाय युज्यस्व योग: कर्मसु कौशलम्.
Any allotted work done skillfully without expectation of rewards does not bind; it can eliminate good and bad reactions in this life itself. Doing your work skillfully is yoga. (This verse is also included in the topic Karma Yoga.)

Nishkam Karma done diligently will free you from the bondage. Concentrate on the task and do it well. Karmeshu Kaushalam - this is a compelling and practical message. If practiced, it will significantly improve the quality of life. It means 1. Do your work with full enthusiasm, 2. Do the best, high-quality, and perfect work, never haphazardly and lazily, 3. Be very efficient, not lethargic.

The message applies to all types of work. No job is superior or inferior. Accept the fact that everyone has to do some work anyway, Krishna says even he has to do some work. Perfect work done enthusiastically will make you feel happy. Very rarely, the work done well goes unrewarded.

3.13 यज्ञशिष्टाशिन: सन्तो मुच्यन्ते सर्वकिल्बिषै: भुञ्जते ते त्वघं पापा ये पचन्त्यात्मकारणात्
The devotees who eat food only after it is offered in sacrifice are released from sin. Those who prepare food only for their consumption and enjoyment, verily incur sin.

Offer food to God before you eat to avoid sin. Offering and consuming the remnants of food offered to God is a devotional act. It relieves you from the karma involved in growing and making the food. Not offering is equivalent to not being grateful to God, whose energy makes the food we eat. Guru Nanak said give food to hungry people ("Bukhe ko kuchh do").

TOPIC 7 - Gita Mahavakyas (Punchline Verses)

4.24 ब्रह्मार्पणं ब्रह्म हविर्ब्रह्माग्नौ ब्रह्मणा हुतम् ब्रह्मैव तेन गन्तव्यं ब्रह्मकर्मसमाधिना   The oblation (the offering in the yajna – the fire ceremony) is Brahm, the ladle with which it is offered is Brahm, the act of offering is Brahm, and the sacrificial fire is Brahm. Such people who view everything as God are liberated and reach him.

This verse is chanted commonly while offering food to Divine. One who sees God everywhere and in everyone is the highest sage, according to Srimad Bhagawat. For such people - the one making the sacrifice, the purpose, the instruments, the fire, and the act of conducting yajna, are all the same as Brahm, the Supreme.

4.34 तद्विद्धि प्रणिपातेन परिप्रश्नेन सेवया उपदेक्ष्यन्ति ते ज्ञानं ज्ञानिनस्तत्त्वदर्शिन: Learn spirituality by going to a spiritual expert – a guru. Ask him questions with reverence and sincerity, render loving service unto him. An enlightened guru who has seen the light himself can enlighten you from his success on the path.

Krishna reveals the importance of Guru, the spiritual master, in the process of acquiring knowledge. Sankaracharya says, "Until you surrender to a Guru, you cannot be liberated from Maya. Past karma, the intensity of desire, and God's grace will bring you in contact with a Sadguru who is "tatvadarshinah" (a self-realized) and Jnani (capable of imparting knowledge). The one trapped in the complex "tree" of samsara will have difficulty finding his way out without a competent Guru.

4.7 यदा यदा हि धर्मस्य ग्लानिर्भवति भारत अभ्युत्थानमधर्मस्य तदात्मानं सृजाम्यहम्
Whenever there is a decline in the dharma or when righteousness diminishes, and when adharma or unrighteousness dominates, at that time I reincarnate or take avatar; meaning, I descend on the earth in human form or as other beings, as necessary.

Note that the word dharma here is translated as righteousness; see discussion under verse 3.35 in topic 3 on karma yoga for a broader meaning of dharma.

Regarding the avatars: some of God's incarnations accompany his full, unlimited powers, some with partial powers (ansh).

1. *Scriptures mention ten significant avatars of God.*
2. *Srimad Bhagavat also enumerates 24 total avatars.*
3. *Vedic scriptures mention that infinite avatars come on earth constantly, some for a short time for a specific mission, and some for many years, in the form of humans or other beings. The avatar with partial powers is described in scriptures as God's ansh – a Sanskrit term for a minuscule power.*
4. *The fact that God comes in various forms for specific missions can mean God may be present on the earth anytime and may not reveal his divine identity to everyone but only to some people. Be respectful to everyone.*
5. *An avatar has six divine qualities - splendor, virtue, glory, opulence, knowledge, and dispassion.*

4.8 परित्राणाय साधूनां विनाशाय च दुष्कृताम् धर्मसंस्थापनार्थाय सम्भवामि युगे युगे
To protect the righteous, to annihilate the wicked, and to re-establish the Dharma (righteousness), I appear from one yug (an era) to the next or from one time period to the next. This verse is a continuation of the previous verse 4.7 regarding why God takes an avatar.

The following is a summary of the reasons for God's avatar from verses 4.7 and 4.8.

The avatar comes when there is a decline in the dharma (righteousness), and an increase in adharma (unrighteousness) to protect good people, eliminate the wicked, and re-establish Dharma - righteousness. Again, the broader meaning of dharma is duty, virtue, justice, morality, spiritual beliefs, and law and order. As mentioned earlier, the significant avatars occur every yug (an era), and an avatar as an ansh (a part of God) occurs frequently. A yug is an epoch or period within a four-yug cycle. A complete cycle includes the Satya Yug, Treta Yug, Dvapar Yug, and Kali Yug. Our present time is said to be and agreed by most authorities on scriptures is ascending Kali yug. See Verse 8.17 under topic 16 on the Creation for more details regarding the four yugas.

9.26 पत्रं पुष्पं फलं तोयं यो मे भक्त्या प्रयच्छति तदहं भक्त्युपहृतमश्रामि प्रयतात्मन: If one offers Me with devotion and a pure mind, a leaf, a flower, a fruit, or even water, I accept it from a pure-hearted devotee.

God is the source of everything in the universe and needs nothing from us. Offering to God with a pure heart and complete surrender stimulates devotion; hence, you are the beneficiary, not God. God accepts small offerings given with pure heart.

9.27 यत्करोषि यदश्नासि यज्जुहोषि ददासि यत्तपस्यसि कौन्तेय तत्कुरुष्व मदर्पणम्
Whatever you do, whatever you eat, whatever you offer in sacrifice, whatever you give, and whatever you practice as penance, do it as an offering unto Me!

This verse is chanted as a prayer before meals. Krishna says in verse 9.26, all objects should be offered to Him. Now He says that all actions should also be offered to Him. A related popular prayer expressing surrender to God is Kaayena Vaacaa Manase indriyairvaa; Buddhy-Aatmanaa Va prakrite-Svabhaavaat; Karomi Yad-Yat-Sakalam Parasmai; Naaraayannayeti Samarpayami. Meaning: Whatever I do with the body, speech, mind, or the sense organs, either by the intellect, or by the feelings of the heart, or by tendencies of the mind, I do them all without ownership, and I surrender them at the feet of Narayana (God). The attitude of surrender is an integral part of devotion to God, and it transforms all your work into an ego-free service of God.

10.8 अहं सर्वस्य प्रभवो मत्त: सर्वं प्रवर्तते इति मत्वा भजन्ते मां बुधा भावसमन्विता:
I am the source of everything; all creation emerges from Me. Realizing this, the wise is impressed and adores Me.

The devotees understand that God is the origin of everything, the supreme truth, and the ultimate goal. Refer to verses 7.7 under Topic 15 on God's Powers, and verse 15.15 under Topic 26 on Brahm.

10.42 अथवा बहुनैतेन किं ज्ञातेन तवार्जुन विष्टभ्याहमिदं कृत्स्नमेकांशेन स्थितो जगत् But of what benefit is it to you, the knowledge of these details (about Krishna's splendors)? I exist pervading this entire universe by a fraction of myself.

Krishna describes his glories and splendors in detail in reply to the request of Arjuna. See Topic 40 on God's Glories for the details. Then he summarizes by asking Arjuna, "Why you want to know these trivial things? What is the use?"

"The entire creation of countless universes is held merely within a fraction of my being. Counting and naming my unlimited extraordinary manifestations is impossible and unnecessary. I am the ancient seed, the origin of all creation that comes into existence. I am the seed, and the self in everyone and nothing can exist without Me, the soul of everything. Anytime anywhere you see magnificence in anyone or anything in the entire universe, know that to be Me."

11.32 कालोऽस्मि लोकक्षयकृत्प्रवृद्धो लोकान्समाहर्तुमिह प्रवृत्त: ऋतेऽपि त्वां न भविष्यन्ति सर्वे येऽवस्थिता: प्रत्यनीकेषु योधा: I am the Time (Kal), a seasoned annihilator of the worlds, the source of destruction that annihilates the worlds, engaged in destroying all these people. Even without your participation, all these warriors will cease to exist.

Krishna shows Arjuna his Kaal Swaroop - the destroyer of the worlds. God, as a kaal swaroop, displayed a tiny preview of his power when the experimental atom bomb was detonated at the Trinity site in New Mexico, the USA, in 1945. The inventor and maker of these bombs, Robert Oppenheimer, was reminded of Verse 11.32, after seeing the phenomenal and horrific result of the blast. A permanent sign as shown was posted on the New Mexico Highway 380 near the entrance to the site which is open to visitors on certain days.

The US government designated this sign as the Official Scenic Historical Marker. Soon after the experiment, two bombs were dropped by the US Airforce on Hiroshima and Nagasaki in Japan, which ended World War II. The two cities were almost completely destroyed instantly, a sad reminder of the human history.

> **Official Scenic Historic Marker**
>
> **TRINITY SITE**
>
> The nuclear age began with the detonation of the world's first atomic bomb at the Trinity Site on July 16, 1945. The site may have been named Trinity by J. Robert Oppenheimer, director of the Los Alamos Nuclear Physics Laboratory, who said at the blast, "Now, I have become Death, the destroyer of worlds", quoting from the *Bhagavad Gita*. The detonation of the bomb marked the culmination of the Manhattan Project.

15.14 अहं वैश्वानरो भूत्वा प्राणिनां देहमाश्रित: प्राणापानसमायुक्त: पचाम्यन्नं चतुर्विधम् Residing in the bodies of beings as the digestive fire (vaishvanarya), combined with prana and apana (incoming and outgoing breaths), it is I who digests the four kinds of food.

This verse is chanted as a prayer before meals. It is God's energy – Jeev Shakti, which digests food in our stomach. The Bṛhadāraṇyak Upaniṣhad also states: "God is the fire inside the

TOPIC 7 – Gita Mahavakyas (Punchline Verses)

stomach that enables living beings to digest food." To summarize, God supports life, powers the earth to make it habitable, provides energy to the moon to nourish vegetation, and acts as a gastric fire to digest the four kinds of food.

18.46 यत: प्रवृत्तिर्भूतानां येन सर्वमिदं ततम् स्वकर्मणा तमभ्यर्च्य सिद्धिं विन्दति मानव:

By doing your particular duty, you worship the Creator who dwells in every being. By doing your work as worship, you will easily attain perfection. ("Work is Worship")

This verse says that doing the allotted work in dedication to God itself is a form of worship. If we discharge our essential duty - swadharma – competently and selflessly, we will automatically purify ourselves. When done in divine consciousness, our work automatically becomes a form of worship, whether one is a high caste brahmin or a low caste butcher.

If we perform our natural duty selflessly, whether it is viewed as good or bad, that will clean our mind and inspire devotion. No work is low. Doing our work as a mission of God, the soul gradually evolves from gross to divine consciousness. "Work itself is worship."

18.65 मन्मना भव मद्भक्तो मद्याजी मां नमस्कुरु मामेवैष्यसि सत्यं ते प्रतिजाने प्रियोऽसि मे

Always think of Me, be devoted to Me, worship Me, and offer obeisance to Me. Doing so, you will undoubtedly come to Me; that is my PROMISE to you because you are very dear to Me.

This verse is the essence of Gita along with the next verse 18.66. The instruction to follow the path of devotion is bhakti, wholeheartedly, which is what all the scriptures teach. This verse 18.65 is very similar to verse 9.34, which says, "Always think of Me, be devoted to Me, worship Me, and offer pranaam - obeisance to Me. By offering your mind and body to Me, you will certainly attain Me."

18.66 सर्वधर्मान्परित्यज्य मामेकं शरणं व्रज अहं त्वां सर्वपापेभ्यो मोक्षयिष्यामि मा शुच:

Abandon all varieties of dharmas and surrender unto Me alone. Just surrender to Me completely, and I will liberate you, without any fear and doubt.

Varieties of spiritual paths and total surrendering to God paves the way to liberation. Krishna has given Arjuna many options, including the pros and cons of each. In the end, Krishna is asking Arjuna to transcend all instructions and surrender wholeheartedly and promises him to absolve from all sins. The verse says leave all "dharma" and surrender. The word "dharma" carries many interpretations with no two sources in complete agreement. The root meaning of Sarva dharma (dhri, to support) is all your supports, meaning the external dependencies. The verse can mean, "leave your support on everything, and rely on yourself." Arjuna does surrender, then engages in the ghastly war, and wins it. A question may arise whether Arjuna will incur sin by giving up all "dharmas". Krishna reassures Arjuna and promises to exonerate him from all sins.

18.67 इदं ते नातपस्काय नाभक्ताय कदाचन न चाशुश्रूषवे वाच्यं न च मां योऽभ्यसूयति   This discourse (about Gita) should not be discussed with people who are not austere, not devoted, not interested in listening (to spiritual topics), and envious of Me.

Gita is open for everyone to read; so Krishna is not asking that it be hidden from specific types and disclose it to others. Then why does Krishna say the knowledge of Gita should not be given to unqualified and atheist people? The answer is, why instruct those who have no faith and are ineligible? It is a waste of energy as they will not believe you no matter how hard you argue.

❦ ***Now, at the end, Sanjay says to Dhritrashtra:***

18.78 यत्र योगेश्वर: कृष्णो यत्र पार्थो धनुर्धर: तत्र श्रीर्विजयो भूतिध्रुवा नीतिर्मतिर्मम
Wherever there is Yogaeshvar Krishna, and the supreme archer Arjuna, there will be eternal splendor, victory, prosperity, and virtues. Of this, I am certain.

Sanjay offers his prayer at the end. Regardless of the strengths of the two armies, the only judgment in this war is that triumph will always accompany God and his pure devotee, and so will goodness, supremacy, and prosperity. Wherever the Yogeshwar Krishna and his devotees are present, the light of truth will decidedly defeat the darkness of lies and deceit. Blessed are the faithful listeners of the song of Gita full of nectar.

TOPIC 7 - Gita Mahavakyas (Punchline Verses)

TOPIC 8

Sankhya Yoga (The Nature of Soul)

Krishna begins his discourse on the nature of the soul by stating that the real Self or the Atman (the soul) never dies because it is never born, and it is eternal. The ultimate premise of Gita is that the immortal soul is more important than the mortal world. The soul wears the body as its garment and discards it when it gets old and changes into another new clothing (i.e., a new body). The soul, in its bonded state, travels from life to life. Death of the living body is inevitable, and so is the rebirth of the dead. Krishna says, unless you rise above the dualities – pleasure/pain, hot/cold, success/failure, you cannot realize the truth; you cannot realize the self. Krishna repeats several times that detachment is necessary to acquire the serenity to overcome the notion of the dualities and to free the soul from the bondage by Maya for its union with the super soul (Paramatma). Once liberated, the soul unites with the super soul and is not reborn in the mortal world. All verses mentioned in different chapters of Gita are compiled under this topic as follows, including those with a similar message.

Krishna encourages direct experience instead of the study of scriptures and theoretical knowledge to attain enlightenment. Learn all you want to learn about any subjects, but apply the lessons in practice to gain the first-hand experience; otherwise, the learning may not lead you to the blissful state.

❦ *Krishna says to Arjuna:*

2.12 न त्वेवाहं जातु नासं न त्वं नेमे जनाधिपा न चैव न भविष्याम: सर्वे वयमत: परम्

There was never a time when I or you or other things did not exist. In the future, none of them will cease to exist.

According to Upanishad, the universe is made of three entities: God, soul, and Maya. All three are eternal.

2.16 नासतो विद्यते भावो नाभावो विद्यते सत: उभयोरपि दृष्टोऽन्तस्त्वनयोस्तत्वदर्शिभि:

The unreal has no existence. The real has no non-existence. The eternal does not cease. The material world ends, but the soul does not end. The truth about these two is known to men of wisdom.

Real is eternal and constant; unreal is changing and temporary. "The unreal has no existence" means the unreal physical world of names and forms has no permanent existence as they change, decay, and eventually die. "There is no non-existence of the real" means the soul never ends because the soul is eternal and therefore, real. The physical world, created by Maya, is temporary and unreal, just like other products of Maya, such as the body.

2.17 अविनाशि तु तद्विद्धि येन सर्वमिदं ततम् विनाशमव्ययस्यास्य न कश्चित्कर्तुमर्हति

Know that to be indestructible, by whom all this is pervaded. None can destroy that.

Krishna means the soul is indestructible, and as part of the super soul, it pervades the universe. The soul permeates the body as consciousness, and it remains after the body dies. After the soul and consciousness leave the body, a dead body is left behind. Note that verses 2.17 through 2.30 repeatedly emphasize a crucial point that the soul is eternal and cannot be killed or destroyed. Therefore, Krishna is asking Arjuna, "Then why worry?" It is Himsa to kill without reason, but warriors must fight evil enemies for the protection of the righteous. Defending the innocent and weak is the duty of warriors and not considered a sin. Simply watching and not defending the innocent being tortured by the evil is not Ahimsa.

Ahimsa is not a new concept, but it is a foundational thought of the Sanatana Dharma. The ancient Vedas preach Ahimsa, and it is the first of the six rules of "Yama", the first step of the eight steps in Ashtang Yoga.

2.18 अन्तवन्त इमे देहा नित्यस्योक्ता: शरीरिण: अनाशिनोऽप्रमेयस्य तस्माद्युध्यस्व भारत

Only the physical body is perishable. However, the soul residing in the body is indestructible, immeasurable, and eternal.

2.19 य एनं वेत्ति हन्तारं यश्चैनं मन्यते हतम्   Ignorant thinks the soul can slay or can be slain. The truth is the soul neither kills nor can be killed.

2.20 न जायते म्रियते वा कदाचि नायं भूत्वा भविता वा न भूय: अजो नित्य: शाश्वतोऽयं पुराणो न हन्यते हन्यमाने शरीरे   The soul is never born, nor does it die. Once existed, it will never cease to exist. The soul is without birth; it is eternal, changeless, and ever-same. It is not slain when the body is killed.

Other scriptures, including the Upanishads, contain a similar description of the soul, "The soul is not born, nor does it die; it did not come from something, and nothing emanated from it. It is unborn, eternal, immortal, and ageless. It is not destroyed when the body is destroyed."

TOPIC 8 - Sankhya Yoga (The Nature of Soul)

2.21 वेदाविनाशिनं नित्यं य एनमजमव्ययम् कथं स पुरुष: पार्थं कं घातयति हन्ति कम्   One who knows the soul to be imperishable, eternal, unborn, and immutable, how can he kill or cause anyone to be killed?

Krishna is implying that the eternal essence (the soul) neither acts nor is affected by external actions.

2.22 वासांसि जीर्णानि यथा विहाय नवानि गृह्णाति नरोऽपराणि तथा शरीराणि विहाय जीर्णा न्यन्यानि संयाति नवानि देही   As one discards torn clothes and replaces them with new ones, similarly, the soul leaves behind the dead body and arrives in a new body.

Verse 2.22 introduces the concept of reincarnation, supported by the Vedantic scriptures. The Darshan Shastra (scripture) says, "jātasya harṣhabhayaśhoka sampratipatteḥ." Meaning - infants change their emotions for no apparent reason, happy sometimes, and unhappy the other times because they remember the past life. They lose memories and impressions of the past as the present memories are etched sharply in their minds. The Darshan also says, "stanyābhilāṣhāt." Meaning – infants know no language, but based on the memory from many births, they automatically suck in the milk from the mother's breast as soon as born.

The extreme disparity in the physical, mental, and financial states from birth is quite puzzling. Examples - rich or poor, healthy or unhealthy, virtuous, or promiscuous. Why such extreme diversity from birth? Some explain it is due to God's will. It is illogical to rationalize that fate in the present life is God's will, as God is 'just' and 'compassionate', not random. He is the ultimate witness and impartial chief justice.

Past karmas decide the destination in the new life. After the karmas are burned or destroyed, the soul is liberated and "goes home" to God.

2.23 नैनं छिन्दन्ति शस्त्राणि नैनं दहति पावक: न चैनं क्लेदयन्त्यापो न शोषयति मारुत: Weapons cannot cut it, fire cannot burn it, water cannot wet it, and wind cannot dry it (the soul).

The soul, though part of the super soul, is not free; it is under bondage due to the influence of Maya. When it is released from the bondage or liberated, it merges with the source. Regardless, the soul does not lose its divinity even under the bondage. Its divine characteristics are that it is eternal and cannot be slain by any means.

2.24 अच्छेद्योऽयमदाह्योऽयमक्लेद्योऽशोष्य एव च नित्य: सर्वगत: स्थाणुरचलोऽयं सनातन: The soul cannot be cut, burnt, dampened, or dried. It is eternal, omnipresent (in all places), unalterable, immutable, and primordial.

Krishna often repeats crucial points so the student can grasp the meaning. The things you can cut, burn, dampen and dry are objects made from panch Mahabhoot. However, the soul is spirit, an ansh (part) of the super soul. Therefore, it cannot be destroyed or degraded.

2.25 अव्यक्तोऽयमचिन्त्योऽयमविकार्योऽयमुच्यते तस्मादेवं विदित्वैनं नानुशोचितुमर्हसि

The soul is invisible, inconceivable, and unchangeable. Know this and don't grieve for the body.

The body is mortal and will come to an end. So, Krishna says to Arjuna, why grieve for the inevitable?

2.26 अथ चैनं नित्यजातं नित्यं वा मन्यसे मृतम् तथापि महाबाहो नैवं शोचितुमर्हसि

If you think, however, the soul is born and dies, even then, you should not grieve like this.

According to certain non-Vedantic philosophies, the soul is not eternal. It changes and dies. The view that the soul dies is one of the many opinions and beliefs India has had and still does. Indian philosophy is comprised of 12 Schools of thought, six of which are based on the Vedas and believe that the soul is eternal: 1.Mīmānsā, 2.Vedānt, 3.Nyāya, 4.Vaisheshik, 5.Sānkhya, and 6. Yoga. The remaining six schools do not accept the authority of Vedas and do not believe the soul is permanent; these are Charvak Vaad, the four Buddhist schools - Yogachar vada, Madhyamik vada, Vaibhashik vada, and Sautatrik vada; and Jainism.

Note, Krishna does not criticize or mention other non-vedantic faiths in this verse. In fact, none of the authentic Sanatana dharma scriptures mention or criticize other faiths.

2.27 जातस्य हि ध्रुवो मृत्युर्ध्रुवं जन्म मृतस्य च तस्मादपरिहार्येऽर्थे न त्वं शोचितुमर्हसि

Death is inevitable for the one who has been born, and rebirth is inevitable for the one who has died (regardless of the particular school of thought one believes in, as all Indian philosophies believe in reincarnation).

All vedantic and non-vedantic philosophies in India believe in reincarnation, so a wise person does not lament over the inevitable.

2.28 अव्यक्तादीनि भूतानि व्यक्तमध्यानि भारत अव्यक्तनिधनान्येव तत्र का परिदेवना

All created beings were unmanifest before birth, manifest in life, and unmanifest after death, so why grieve?

The unmanifest state is when the soul leaves the gross body at death and remains with the subtle body. The manifest state is when the soul reincarnates in a different body for another lifetime. The gross body is the manifest physical body; it is made up of gross and subtle elements. The subtle and causal bodies are unmanifest. Just like a tree that is unmanifest in the mango seed, it becomes manifest when the seed grows. The following summarizes the three different bodies.

The gross body consists of the five gross elements of nature—Akash (vacuum), Vayu (air), Agni (fire), Jal (water), and Prithvi (earth). The gross body also contains annamay kosh and a portion of pranmay kosh (sheaths), which provides food, drink, and air to the body.

The subtle body (also known as the astral or ling body) consists of eighteen elements.

1. Five Pranas or life - Air (Pran - respiration), Apan (waste removal), Vyan (blood circulation), Saman (digestion), Udan (sneezing, crying, vomiting, ejecting the subtle body from the gross body on death);
2. Five working senses or karmendriyas or organs of action: mouth (speech), hands, legs, anus, and genitals;
3. Five knowledge senses or jnanendriyas: eyes, ears, skin, tongue, and nose;
4. the mind, 5. the intellect, and 6. ego.

This accounts for the 18 elements.

PLUS the Manomayakosha, which ties to the mind. And the Vigyan and Gyanmayakosh, which link to the intellect; and also a part of the Pranmayakosha, which moves the pranic force (Jeev Shakti) to direct the physical and mental activities, through the nadis or channels which are the conductors of energy controlled by the six chakras.

The causal body consists of the accumulated karmas from countless past lives, including the sanskars (tendencies), inclinations, and unfulfilled desires that are carried forward from the past. The soul is different from the three bodies. At death, the soul discards its gross body and departs in the bonded state that is integral to the subtle and causal bodies. The soul goes to another gross body as determined from the state of the associated subtle and causal bodies, and goes into a particular mother's womb in a specific family and specific environment as determined from the accumulated karma. The soul is reborn anytime within a few seconds to a few years after death.

The soul transmigrates continuously until it is liberated from the bonded state, at which time it unites with the super soul. After liberation, the soul is no longer reborn except as a realized Yogi on a special mission from God, as an "ansh" of God. See 4.7 in Topic 7.

2.29 आश्चर्यवत्पश्यति कश्चिदेन माश्चर्यवद्वदति तथैव चान्य: आश्चर्यवच्चैनमन्य: शृणोति श्रुत्वाप्येनं वेद न चैव कश्च   Some see, describe, or hear of the soul as amazing. While others, after hearing all this, still cannot understand the soul at all.

God's creations are amazing. A rose flower is fantastic, and so is the human body, an incredibly complicated biological, mechanical, chemical, electrical, intellectual, and automatic instrument powered by consciousness, and designed based on the history. The soul is a tiny part of the super soul. Its powers are incredible. With this verse, the topic on the soul is nearing its end; but it is also raising Arjuna's curiosity.

2.30 देही नित्यमवध्योऽयं देहे सर्वस्य भारत तस्मात्सर्वाणि भूतानि न त्वं शोचितुमर्हसि   The embodied soul is immortal, so it is pointless for you to mourn anymore.

This verse summarizes Krishna's discourse on the soul that it is immortal, and it is distinct from the body.

13.30 प्रकृत्यैव च कर्माणि क्रियमाणानि सर्वशः यः पश्यति तथात्मानमकर्तारं स पश्यति
They alone truly see who understand that all actions of the body are performed by the material nature or Prakriti, while the embodied soul does nothing.

The Tantra Bhagawat says, "The soul falsely thinks it is the body and proudly thinks it is the doer; these wrong ideas are the reasons the soul remains bonded in the subtle and causal bodies during the life and death." In reality, the soul does nothing. Physical actions are done by prakriti.

13.33 यथा सर्वगतं सौक्ष्म्यादाकाशं नोपलिप्यते सर्वत्रावस्थितो देहे तथात्मा नोपलिप्यते
Everything is held in subtle space. Space does not get contaminated by what it contains. In the same way, the soul's consciousness occupies the whole body; the soul remains unaffected by the traits of the body.

The soul experiences sleep, waking, tiredness, refreshment, etc., due to the illusion that it is the body. The soul is subtler energy and retains its divinity even while it identifies with the material body.

13.34 यथा प्रकाशयत्येकः कृत्स्नं लोकमिमं रविः त्रं क्षेत्री तथा कृत्स्नं प्रकाशयति भारत   Just as the sun lights up the complete solar system, the soul illumines the entire body (with consciousness).

Although the soul spreads consciousness in the entire body, yet by itself, it is incredibly tiny. Śhwetāśhvatar Upaniṣhad states: "If we divide the tip of a hair into a hundred parts, and then divide each part into further hundred parts, we will come close to the size of the soul."

15.9 श्रोत्रं चक्षुः स्पर्शनं च रसनं घ्राणमेव च अधिष्ठाय मनश्चायं विषयानुपसेवते   Presiding over the ears, eyes, skin, tongue, and nose, and the mind, the soul within the body enjoys the sense objects.

The soul enjoys sense objects, bound by the mind and the senses. The soul is divine and does not directly taste, touch, feel, smell, or hear without the help of the senses and the mind. The senses and mind are insentient but are energized by the consciousness of the soul and become lifelike. Hence, they perceive pleasure and pain from objects, situations, thoughts, and persons. Due to the ego, the soul thinks it is part of the mind and senses and experiences the same pleasures. Tulsidas says in Ramayan, "As a lustful man desires a beautiful woman, may my mind and senses always want Lord Ram."

15.10 उत्क्रामन्तं स्थितं वापि भुञ्जानं वा गुणान्वितम् विमूढा नानुपश्यन्ति पश्यन्ति ज्ञानचक्षुषः   The ignorant fail to see the soul when it resides in the body and even when it leaves the body. They don't see the soul enjoying sense objects or reacting to the Gunas. However, the wise with their eye of wisdom (jnana chakshu) do see.

Ignorant people cannot perceive the soul, but the jnanis do. The soul is divine, not made of material, and the senses cannot see or touch it. The soul energizes the body with consciousness. When the soul departs, the body loses consciousness upon death.

TOPIC 8 - Sankhya Yoga (The Nature of Soul)

Consciousness is a symptom of the soul; it is present as long as the soul is present, and leaves when the soul departs. Only those who possess the eyes of knowledge - jñāna chakṣhu - can see this. Krishna says in this verse that the ignorant or vimūḍh, unaware of their own divine identity, presume the body is the self or the soul.

15.11 यतन्तो योगिनश्चैनं पश्यन्त्यात्मन्यवस्थितम् यतन्तोऽप्यकृतात्मानो नैनं पश्यन्त्यचेतस: The Yogis, who endeavor to follow spirituality, have a complete awareness of the soul seated inside the body. However, those whose minds are impure cannot recognize it, even though they try hard to do so.

Most people are tempered by their own experience, have a cloudy mind, and limited intellect; they reject the existence of the self. They think the body is the soul. However, those aspiring to travel on the spiritual path are open-minded. They acknowledge there must be higher knowledge beyond the limit of their intellects. With faith, they keep on the spiritual path and strive to purify their mind. When their mind becomes cleansed, the presence of the soul is realized. Many verses in Gita emphasize that the purity of the mind is necessary for liberation.

TOPIC 8 - Sankhya Yoga (The Nature of Soul)

TOPIC 9

Philosophy of Samkhya and Practice of Yoga

Samkhya is a philosophical school of thought with many different viewpoints from the experts. Samkhya philosophy is difficult to understand. Yoga is commonly known for its various spiritual practices that can be learned under able guidance, such as Buddhi Yoga, Karma Yoga, Bhakti Yoga, and Ashtang Yoga.

❧ Schools of Astika and Nastika Thoughts

Consider a brief background on the genesis of Samkhya in relation to several other philosophies. There are six schools of astika (believes in God) Sanatana Dharma philosophy—Nyaya, Vaisheshika, Samkhya, Yoga, Mīmāṃsā, and Vedanta. There are also at least five nastika (does not believe in Brahm) schools—Jain, Buddhist, Ajivika, Ajñana, and Charvaka. Samkhya was founded originally by the eminent sage Kapila, however, Gita defines it in simpler terms. The theoretical discussion on various schools of thoughts (and sub-thoughts) have filled countless colossal volumes, very complex and confusing to beginners on the path of the spiritual journey. People very high in their spiritual awareness seem to understand these philosophies, however, there is no unanimous interpretation as all experts who wrote articles and books about these have different views regarding its real meaning and relevance to ordinary aspirants.

❧ Samkhya

It discriminates between Purusha (the soul or Super Soul) and Prakriti (the mind and intellect). According to Gita verses 2.39 and 3.3 (topic 3 on Karma Yoga), Samkhya

Yoga is the knowledge gained through the study of the characteristics of the soul and its distinction from the body. Specifically, it is the knowledge that the souls are eternal and numerous, and not the same as the body. Verse 3.3 refers to Jnana marg as Samkhya yoga. Prakriti is one and divisible into many parts, like the beings and the innumerable physical worlds and its objects. Samkhya, as Krishna defines it, acknowledges God as the creator and the individual souls as his parts, and Prakriti as his dynamic force behind the "creation".

❦ Samkhya in Ancient Vedas

Not to confound the subject, but in the ancient Vedic tradition, the Samkhya thought was non-theistic and did not believe in a Cosmic Being, or a creator God. According to the Vedic experts, creation was caused by Prakriti. Like the proponents of the modern theory of evolution and the followers of the nastic schools of thought, they believed that Prakriti brought forth the worlds and beings when the "right" conditions between the interacting elements manifested as a matter of chance.

❦ Tattvas

According to Gita, the realities (tattvas) of existence are God, the Soul, body, senses, mind, ego, and intelligence. Of them, God and the soul are pure (suddha) and eternal realities, while the rest are impure (asuddha) and finite. Scriptures call the two categories as "sat" and "asat". The following is how Gita defines each of the elements – tattvas.

❦ God (Brahm)

God is the absolute reality not bound by Nature, yet distinct and separate from it. God is Tat Sat (that which is real). God is the highest state of Brahm, attaining which one is liberated.

❦ The Soul

The soul is eternal, indestructible, and immeasurable, and it resides in the body. However, unlike God, the soul is subject to the cycle of births and deaths. The soul neither kills nor is killed, it is neither born nor subject to death, never non-existent in the past, nor will be in the future. The soul is unborn, eternal, permanent, and the most ancient. It transitions from one life to another and changes bodies each time without undergoing any change in itself.

❦ The Body

It is a constantly changing combination of numerous tattvas and is the abode of the soul. Unlike the soul, the body is impure, perishable, and subject to change. The body is unmanifested in the beginning, manifests in the middle, and becomes unmanifested again when the soul attains liberation. The body is alive and sentient because of the presence of the soul that charges it with consciousness.

TOPIC 9 - Philosophy of Samkhya and Practice of Yoga

❦ Buddhi

Per the Samkhya theory, buddhi is the highest element of Prakriti. Although Gita does not define intelligence as the highest tattva, it acknowledges its importance in the hierarchy of elements. When intelligence is pure (sattvic), the light of the soul shines brightly.

❦ Samkhya and Yoga

Samkhya is a philosophical school of thought with varied viewpoints, rather complex. The term Yoga is frequently used to designate various spiritual practices, that can be learned under able guidance, such as Buddhi Yoga, Karma Yoga, Bhakti Yoga, and Ashtang Yoga. Simply stated, Samkhya is knowing the philosophy and Yoga is applying the knowledge.

❦ The Ego (ahm)

It is an egotistical self-sense that I am special and I have everything. Self-consciousness is benign but ego-consciousness invites delusion and desires. Samkhya categorizes ego along with other tattvas like the mind and intellect.

❦ The Mind

The uncontrolled mind is the root of disturbances and instabilities. It drives the activities of the senses. One of the fundamental teachings of Gita is to stabilize the mind and divert it to spiritual elevation. Samkhya considers the mind as the storehouse of thoughts, past impressions, and memories. As part of the subtle body, the mind goes with the soul to the new body after rebirth. According to Samkhya, rationality is the product of a higher mind or intelligence. Krishna emphasizes to Arjuna that he should drive his mind away from desires, attachments, lust, and dualities, and focus it on his duty. Krishna suggests that by wisdom to see the difference between the soul and the body, and by overcoming desires, the mind can be controlled.

❦ The Senses

They are part of the body - the five organs of action, the five organs of perception, and the five subtle senses. Krishna says the changing feelings of cold and heat, pleasure and pain are due to the contact with the sense-objects. Hence, one should bear with them. However, dwelling upon sense-objects can (sequentially) strengthen attachment, desire, anger, delusion, confusion of memory, and loss of intelligence (buddhi). When buddhi is lost, life becomes useless. So, one should withdraw the senses from the sense objects "just as a tortoise withdraws its limbs". The unattached mind remains tranquil even when the senses wander among sense objects.

❦ The Five Elements

They are earth, fire, water, air, and space. They constitute the body and provide the material needs.

❧ The Gunas

They are sattva, rajas, and tamas. They are not elements but aspects of Prakriti that create desires and desire-prone activities. They cause our attitude, thoughts, activities, and likes and dislikes. Everyone carries a unique combination of the three Gunas which change according to karmas.

❧ Buddhi Yoga

Samkhya is the theoretical foundation and Yoga is the applied discipline. The second chapter is devoted to Samkhya and Buddhi Yoga. Buddhi Yoga leads to Brahm by cultivating stable intelligence (sthita prajna). Stable intelligence is achieved by keeping the senses away from absorption in the sense-objects, desires, and lust. In essence, Buddhi yoga or yoga of intellect is working without desire for rewards and detachment from enjoying the results of actions. Detachment comes from discrimination by the intellect.

❧ Ashtang Yoga

The Ashtang Yoga process is described under verse 5.27 in Topic 13 on Yoga Kriya.

TOPIC 9 - Philosophy of Samkhya and Practice of Yoga

TOPIC 10

The Ladder to Perfection, Bliss, Liberation

The goal of spiritual life is to motivate and guide people to attain the liberation of the soul. The latter means the union of the soul with God. Throughout Gita's discourse, Krishna explains multiple alternative processes to attain liberation. The other terms Gita uses that are similar to liberation are perfection, ultimate bliss, absolute peace, and pure, true essence. For the practical purpose of the beginners on the spiritual path, these terms have a similar meaning, to simplify Krishna's discourses. The verses in different chapters that relate to the achievement of liberation, perfection, and bliss are drawn and compiled under this topic as follows. Note, there are over fifty verses that disclose the keys to liberation, and they are scattered across different chapters of Gita. As per this book's unique format, all these are listed under this topic.

❧ Krishna says to Arjuna:

2.15 यं हि न व्यथयन्त्येते पुरुषं पुरुषर्षभ समदुःखसुखं धीरं सोऽमृतत्वाय कल्पत   The one who is not affected by the happiness and unhappiness and who remains steady in both extreme duality is eligible for liberation.

Maya no longer binds the one who is unaffected by the feelings of misery and joy and remains steady. A person must shed desires to achieve steadiness. Freeing from desires and Maya is a step towards liberation.

2.64 रागद्वेषवियुक्तैस्तु विषयानिन्द्रियैश्चरन् आत्मवश्यैर्विधेयात्मा प्रसादमधिगच्छति
But when you move amidst the world of sense, free from attachment and aversion alike, you become peaceful and your sorrows end. You live in the wisdom of the Self.

While tasting, touching, smelling, hearing, and seeing, like the renunciants and the ordinary people, the one with serenity remains free from attachment and aversion. Unfortunately, people are told not to engage in the senses and that the senses are bad news. One of the common questions that students of Gita raise is why God gave us the senses if we cannot enjoy the objects. Nowhere does Gita say you refrain from using the senses. Gita says, just don't let your mind be swayed and consumed by the objects of enjoyment. If you do not obtain those objects, accept the situation cheerfully, and let it roll off your mind. If you do obtain them, do not become a slave of the senses and allow them to haunt and possess you.

2.65 प्रसादे सर्वदुःखानां हानिरस्योपजायते प्रसन्नचेतसो ह्याशु बुद्धिः पर्यवतिष्ठते   By divine grace, peace is experienced, which ends all sorrows. The intellect of one with the tranquil mind becomes established in God.

2.66 नास्ति बुद्धिरयुक्तस्य न चायुक्तस्य भावना न चाभावयतः शान्तिरशान्तस्य कुतः सुखम्   A person with no discipline and uncontrolled mind, and those who allow the senses to pursue their objects freely cannot have a resolute intellect and steady focus on God. The result – their mind is not united with God and they have no peace.

2.70 आपूर्यमाणमचलप्रतिष्ठं समुद्रमापः प्रविशन्ति यद्वत् तद्वत्कामा यं प्रविशन्ति सर्वेस शान्तिमाप्रोति न कामकामी   He is fully contented who absorbs all desires without being moved, just like the ocean absorbs the constant flow of waters from rivers without any disturbance. He is at peace, not the one who constantly lusts after desires.

There are countless objects all over and around in modern life which attract the senses. The sage who is not affected by these is at peace. It is not easy to develop a firm mind control, but with practice and detachment, the mind can be controlled.

2.71 विहाय कामान्यः सर्वान्पुमांश्चरति निःस्पृहः निर्ममो निरहङ्कारः स शान्तिमधिगच्छति   The person who gives up worldly and sensual desires, and lives a life free of greed, sense of ownership, and ego arrives at the state of perfect peace

Some desires originate from insecurity, arising from the complex of lagging behind others in society. Perfect peace is never disturbed by any object or adverse events of life.

2.72 एषा ब्राह्मी स्थितिः पार्थ नैनां प्राप्य विमुह्यति स्थित्वास्यामन्तकालेऽपि ब्रह्मनिर्वाणमृच्छति   Such is the state of a realized soul (as described in previous verses), attaining which one is never again deluded. One who is established in this state at the hour of death, he is liberated and reaches the Supreme Abode of God.

Verses 2.64 to 2.72 above become clear when combined into an arrow chart.

Mind off Senses >> Unmoved by Desirable Objects >> Mind Control >> No Attachment, Aversion, Greed, Ego, Ownership >> No Sorrow >> Steadiness, Equanimity >> Mind in God >> Divine Grace >> Divine Knowledge, Bliss, Perfect Peace >> Liberation of the Soul >> Supreme Abode >> the Soul Merges with Super Soul >> the End of Birth/Death Cycles

3.19 तस्मादसक्त: सततं कार्यं कर्म समाचर असक्तो ह्याचरन्कर्म परमाप्नोति पूरुष:

Therefore, do your work as a prescribed duty without attachment. With no desire for the pleasure or reward from your work, you can reach the supreme.

Again, Krishna suggests Arjuna be a karma yogi. He repeatedly emphasizes Karma yoga as a pure and straightforward path to liberation, to motivate people. Abandoning the society like some sannyasis (renunciants) do may be due to misunderstanding of the principle of karma yoga.

4.9 जन्म कर्म च मे दिव्यमेवं यो वेत्ति तत्त्वत: त्यक्त्वा देहं पुनर्जन्म नैति मामेति सोऽर्जुन

Those who have grasped the divine nature of my birth and activities, their sins are eliminated, and they are not reborn. They are liberated and ascend to my eternal abode.

4.10 वीतरागभयक्रोधा मन्मया मामुपाश्रिता: बहवो ज्ञानतपसा पूता मद्भावमागता:

Having abandoned attachment, fear, and anger; being lost in Me; surrendering to Me, and being purified by knowledge; many have attained Me.

Devotion and surrender purify the mind of the one who is in the detached mode. Mental purity is a prerequisite for liberation.

4.24 ब्रह्मार्पणं ब्रह्म हविर्ब्रह्माग्नौ ब्रह्मणा हुतम् ब्रह्मैव तेन गन्तव्यं ब्रह्मकर्मसमाधिना

The oblation (the offering in the yajna – the fire ceremony) is Brahm, the ladle with which it is offered is Brahm, the act of offering is Brahm, and the sacrificial fire is Brahm. Such people who view everything as God are liberated and reach him.

This verse is commonly chanted before meals. People who view everything as God easily attain him. That is the true spirit of how sacrifice is made. One who sees God everywhere and in everyone is the highest sage, according to Srimad Bhagawat. For such people, the one making the sacrifice, the purpose, the instruments, the fire, and the act of conducting Yajna are all the same as Brahm, the Supreme.

5.12 युक्त: कर्मफलं त्यक्त्वा शान्तिमाप्नोति नैष्ठिकीम् अयुक्त: कामकारेण फले सक्तो निबध्यते   Those whose consciousness is unified are not attached to the results of action and attain ultimate peace. Split desires and attachment to the results cause bondage.

This verse states the principle of karma yoga. An arrow chart summarizes it.

Desires >> Work With Selfish Motive >> Attachment to Results >> Prompts More Desire >> Permanent Entanglement in Maya >> Accumulates Negative Karmik Effect >> The "Excess Baggage" Increases >> The Bondage of the Soul Is Strengthened >> The Prospect of Everlasting Peace and Liberation Diminishes

5.13 सर्वकर्माणि मनसा संन्यस्यास्ते सुखं वशी नवद्वारे पुरे देही नैव कुर्वन्न कारयन्

Mentally giving up all actions and maintaining self-control, people live happily in the human body (city of nine gates). They are content, and neither act nor cause others to work.

Detachment and awareness that they are the instruments and not the doers lead to peace. The enlightened seeker knows he is the soul, resident in the body, and it is the body, mind, and intellect that act. Self-controlled people live in the body as detached observers (saakshibhav). The nine gates mentioned in this verse are two ears, one mouth, two nostrils, two eyes, anus, and genitals.

The Supreme also resides in the body. When the soul is freed from the clutches of Maya, it connects with God. This is when the soul realizes that it is neither the doer nor the cause of anything.

5.15 नादत्ते कस्यचित्पापं न चैव सुकृतं विभुः अज्ञानेनावृतं ज्ञानं तेन मुह्यन्ति जन्तवः   The eternal essence (God) does not accept anyone's sins or virtues. Men are deluded as their knowledge is covered by ignorance.

Lack of real knowledge is the reason things appear to be what they are not, i.e., delusion. God is separate and distinct from actions, the act of doing, its results, the enjoyment caused consequently, and the act or deed of enjoyment. Similarly, the soul also has nothing to do with actions and results. Under the delusion that it is the body, the soul thinks or believes it is doing or is a party to these activities. When ignorance is removed by the right knowledge, the soul comes to realize that it is the three Gunas that act. Krishna offers a subtle point in this verse by referring to ignorant people to "jantavas" or creatures. As long as people misidentify themselves as the body, they are like animals who also operate by instincts in body consciousness.

5.16 ज्ञानेन तु तदज्ञानं येषां नाशितमात्मनः तेषामादित्यवज्ज्ञानं प्रकाशयति तत्परम्

But for those who have overcome ignorance with real knowledge, knowledge lights up the eternal essence (Brahm or God), just as the sun brightens everything in the daytime.

Due to the influence of Maya Shakti (God's energy that created the universe and the beings), the Self or the soul in us thinks it is the body, the doer and enjoyer. Gita removes the delusion due to ignorance by correct knowledge.

5.17 तद्बुद्धयस्तदात्मानस्तन्निष्ठास्तत्परायणाः गच्छन्त्यपुनरावृत्तिं ज्ञाननिर्धूतकल्मषा

The one who gets rid of sin through this knowledge, engrossed in God and keeping him as his goal and refuge, is liberated and not reborn.

TOPIC 10 - The Ladder to Perfection, Bliss, Liberation

After attaining knowledge, the aspirant transcends the duality and sheds all notions of sins and merits.

5.19 इहैव तैर्जित: सर्गो येषां साम्ये स्थितं मन: निर्दोषं हि समं ब्रह्म तस्माद् ब्रह्मणि ते स्थिता:   Here, while living in this body, birth is overcome by those who have overcome the notion of duality; for them, the same flawless Brahm is in everyone.

Attaining eternal essence or Atmajnan is possible here and now, we don't have to wait for many births. Karma yoga purifies the mind and makes it steady, so the mind can concentrate firmly on God. The one who has conquered duality immediately attains the eternal essence.

5.21 बाह्यस्पर्शेष्वसक्तात्मा विन्दत्यात्मनि यत्सुखम् स ब्रह्मयोगयुक्तात्मा सुखमक्षयमश्नुते
Those who are not affected by sense pleasures experience divine bliss in the Self. Being united with God through yoga, they are in a state of perfect happiness.

Bliss is a characteristic of God. With the senses, mind, and intellect in God, you can experience the heavenly bliss.

5.24 योऽन्त:सुखोऽन्तरारामस्तथान्तज्योतिरेव य: स योगी ब्रह्मनिर्वाणं ब्रह्मभूतोऽधिगच्छति
Those who are happy from within themselves (antahsukh), enjoying the delight of God within (antah-aramah), and illumined by inner light (antarjyoti), such yogis attain liberation and become one with Brahm.

The realized seeker turns inward to Atma and lives within himself, by deep meditation, and not attracted by anything external that will give him peace, joy or enlightenment.

5.25 लभन्ते ब्रह्मनिर्वाणमृषय: क्षीणकल्मषा: छिन्नद्वैधा यतात्मान: सर्वभूतहिते रता:   Those whose sins are destroyed, doubts are removed, the mind is disciplined, and the ones devoted to the welfare of all beings, reach God and are liberated from Maya.

Saints use their words, mind, and body for the benefit of others. You feed a hungry person; he is hungry again in four hours. Spiritual well-being ends suffering permanently and provides a path to God. Hence, the sages perform the highest welfare activity of raising god consciousness. Such welfare attracts God's grace.

5.26 कामक्रोधवियुक्तानां यतीनां यतचेतसाम् अभितो ब्रह्मनिर्वाणं वर्तते विदितात्मनाम्
Those sages who are without desire and anger, who have controlled their thoughts, and who have realized the Self, they are liberated here. And, also, hereafter.

Characteristics of those who are liberated as described in verses 5.24, 5.25, and 5.26 are summarized as follows: 1. Happy within, 2. Blissful, 3. Illumined by inner light, 4. Sinless, 5. Doubtless, 6. Whose minds are disciplined, 7. Devoted to the welfare of everyone, 8. Who have conquered anger and lust, 9. Who have subdued their mind.

8.5 अन्तकाले च मामेव स्मरन्मुक्त्वा कलेवरम् य: प्रयाति स मद्भावं याति नास्त्यत्र संशय:
Whoever remembers Me at death will reach my true nature. Krishna says there is no doubt in this statement.

The next birth is determined by the state of consciousness at the time of death. If one is absorbed in God at the end, one attains Him and becomes God-like.

8.7 तस्मात्सर्वेषु कालेषु मामनुस्मर युध्य च मय्यर्पितमनोबुद्धिर्मामेवैष्यस्यसंशयम्
Therefore, remember Me at all times, do your duty (as a Kshatriya) of fighting the war, and surrender the mind and intellect to Me. Then you will definitely attain Me.

Once again, Krishna relates the power of Karma yoga and Bhakti yoga that is - remembering God and doing your duty with complete surrender, by which "you will attain Me undoubtedly."

8.8 अभ्यासयोगयुक्तेन चेतसा नान्यगामिना परमं पुरुषं दिव्यं याति पार्थानुचिन्तयन्
Constantly focusing the mind on Me (the supreme God) steadily, you will achieve Me.

Krishna has emphasized "the mind in thoughts of God", multiple times in Gita. It is challenging to keep the mind on God always. However, with the control of the senses and karma yoga, it is possible. Also, the company of spiritual people (sangat), Naam Smaran (chanting, kirtans, reading scriptures), and Seva (service) will turn the mind towards God.

8.15 मामुपेत्य पुनर्जन्म दुःखालयमशाश्वतम् नाप्नुवन्ति महात्मान: संसिद्धिं परमां गता: After reaching Me, the great souls no longer take birth in this world, which is temporary and full of misery. They have achieved the highest liberation.

Our lives in this world are full of suffering for one reason or another. Our attachment to worldly objects multiplies miseries and guarantees the cycle of birth and death. Once in the state of perfection, there are no more births.

9.28 शुभाशुभफलैरेवं मोक्ष्यसे कर्मबन्धनै: संन्यासयोगयुक्तात्मा विमुक्तो मामुपैष्यसि By surrendering all your works to Me, you will be free from the bondage of good and bad outcomes. With your mind merged in Me by renunciation, you will be liberated and will reach Me.

To avoid karmic reactions, renounce selfishness and dedicate your work to God. Renunciation is abandoning the sense of doership, not giving up actions by avoiding responsibilities. By surrendering actions and results to God, and by accepting that God is the doer and the enjoyer, the feelings of detachment begin to develop.

10.3 यो मामजमनादिं च वेत्ति लोकमहेश्वरम् असम्मूढ: स मर्त्येषु सर्वपापै: प्रमुच्यते Those who know Me as unborn, without beginning, the great lord of all worlds; they among the mortals are free from delusion and are relieved from all sins.

Earlier, Krishna said no one can know him; now, he says, some people do know him. Is he contradicting himself? No. He means that merely by your effort and without his grace, no one can know him. Later one he says he graces devotees with divine knowledge by which they may easily attain him.

10.10 तेषां सततयुक्तानां भजतां प्रीतिपूर्वकम् ददामि बुद्धियोगं तं येन मामुपयान्ति ते

To those who always think of Me, connect with Me, and worship Me faithfully with love, I grace them with Buddhi yoga - the yoga of discrimination, by which they can reach Me.

Buddhi yoga is defined differently by the authors of books on Gita interpretations. For example, Buddhi yoga is construed as the possession of wisdom, the yoga of discrimination, Jnana yoga (Knowledge yoga), divine knowledge, etc. God's grace of discrimination and the ability to understand him through the intellect is a gift.

11.55 मत्कर्मकृन्मत्परमो मद्भक्तः सङ्गवर्जितः निर्वैरः सर्वभूतेषु यः स मामेति पाण्डव   He who does all work for Me (mat karm krit), who considers Me the Supreme (mat paramah), who is devoted to Me (mad bhakt), who is free from attachment (sang vivrajit), who bears malice towards no being (nirvairah sarv bhuteshu); he comes to Me.

This verse is virtually the complete teaching of the Gita. Those who follow this teaching attain divine bliss and merge with the Supreme. Krishna told Arjuna to fix his mind on him and be devoted to him. Later, Krishna revealed further secrets about himself. Here he again emphasizes devotion. Saibaba also says, "Whoever wants to get rid of the cycle of births and deaths, should 1. lead a righteous life with a calm, composed, and fearless mind; 2. do good deeds; 3. do his duties; 4. surrender himself to God faithfully, and 5. do Naam smaran (chanting, singing God's glories, reading scriptures and books written by realized saints)."

12.12 श्रेयो हि ज्ञानमभ्यासाज्ज्ञानाद्ध्यानं विशिष्यते ध्यानात्कर्मफलत्यागस्त्यागाच्छान्तिरनन्तरम्   Knowledge (wisdom born of yoga practice) is superior to yoga practice, meditation is better than the possession of knowledge, and renouncing fruits of actions (karma yoga) is better than meditation because peace immediately follows the renunciation of the result of your work.

Karma yoga and bhakti yoga bestow lasting peace instantaneously.

13.13 ज्ञेयं यत्तत्प्रवक्ष्यामि यज्ज्ञात्वामृतमश्नुते अनादिमत्परं ब्रह्म न सत्तन्नासदुच्यते

I shall tell you that which you must know to attain immortality. It is the Brahm, which lies beyond existence and non-existence, and has no beginning or end.

Brahm is formless and is the object of worship for jnanis (knowledgeable). The mind cannot comprehend Brahm as it is beyond the mind and senses. Brahm or the eternal essence can be attained by ignoring distractions that limit the understanding of the substance. Later, in verse 14.27 (Topic 26), Krishna states: "brahmaṇo hi pratiṣṭhāham" meaning, I am the basis of the formless Brahm. Krishna declares that he is Brahm himself.

13.24 य एवं वेत्ति पुरुषं प्रकृतिं च गुणैः सह सर्वथा वर्तमानोऽपि न स भूयोऽभिजायते   Those who know the truth about the following entities will not be reborn and will be liberated no matter what their present condition is. 1. Supreme Soul (Paramatma) 2.

The individual soul (Atma); 3. Material nature (Prakriti or Maya); 4. Interaction of the three modes of nature.

Knowledge of the relationship between the changing Prakriti or Maya, unchangeable soul, and God liberates the soul. The soul forgets it is part of God and is attracted to worldly enjoyments because it falls into Maya consciousness due to the influence of the three Gunas. When the soul regains understanding of its position with Paramatma and Maya, it is relieved from the bondage. Scriptures and a realized Guru can help in freeing the soul (jivatma) from bondage with Maya.

13.25 and 13.26 ध्यानेनात्मनि पश्यन्ति केचिदात्मानमात्मना अन्ये साङ् ख्येन योगेन कर्मयोगेन चापरे अन्ये त्वेवमजानन्त: श्रुत्वान्येभ्य उपासते तेऽपि चातितरन्त्येव मृत्युं श्रुतिपरायणा:   Some try to visualize God within their hearts through meditation; others by cultivating knowledge (Jnana Yoga); others strive to attain realization by the path of action. Some are unaware of these paths, but they hear it from others (saints) and begin worshipping. They, too, can gradually cross over the cycles of birth and death.

The various options Krishna offers for liberation are the mind control and meditation, the knowledge route (Jnana Yoga), and Karma Yoga. Those who do not know these paths learn about them from scriptures and qualified saints. Krishna says all paths can free the soul from the bondage of Maya.

13.28 समं सर्वेषु भूतेषु तिष्ठन्तं परमेश्वरम् विनश्यत्स्वविनश्यन्तं य: पश्यति स पश्यति
Whoever sees the supreme Lord present equally in all beings has a clear vision. He sees the imperishable amidst the perishing.

Jnanis see God and the soul residing in the perishable body. The Supreme Soul accompanies the individual soul as it moves from body to body in the cycle of life and death. Elsewhere in Gita also Krishna has disclosed that God is in everyone's heart directing wanderings of the bonded soul attached to Maya.

13.29 समं पश्यन्हि सर्वत्र समवस्थितमीश्वरम् न हिनस्त्यात्मनात्मानं ततो याति परां गतिम्   Because he who sees the same Lord dwelling equally in everyone and everywhere does not degrade himself by his mind, he goes to the highest goal.

Acting with the real knowledge you accept God's presence in everyone. You respect others, not cheat and insult them. Thus, you elevate your mind by seeing God in everyone, and free yourself from the rebirths, gradually, to reach the supreme goal.

13.31 यदा भूतपृथग्भावमेकस्थमनुपश्यति तत एव च विस्तारं ब्रह्म सम्पद्यते तदा   When he realizes that all beings are established in the One; and that everything and everyone has evolved from that one; he then attains Brahm.

Like all waves in water come from the ocean, everyone originates from the infinite and all-pervading Brahm.

13.35 क्षेत्रक्षेत्रज्ञयोरेवमन्तरं ज्ञानचक्षुषा भूतप्रकृतिमोक्षं च ये विदुर्यान्ति ते परम्   Those who perceive with the eyes of knowledge 1. the difference between the body (kshetra) and the knower of the body (kshetrajna), and 2. the process of release from Prakriti or Maya or material nature (moksha), attain the supreme destination.

Those who know that the body (the kshetra) is the doer, insentient and finite; and the knower of the field (the soul or kshetrajna) is consciousness, the non-doer, unchanging and infinite, attain the supreme. Knowing the difference between the material body and the spiritual soul is real knowledge. Such knowledge comes from Guru's teachings, the study of scriptures, and meditation.

14.1 & 14.2 श्रीभगवानुवाच परं भूय: प्रवक्ष्यामि ज्ञानानां ज्ञानमुत्तमम् यज्ज्ञात्वा मुनय: सर्वे परां सिद्धिमितो गता: इदं ज्ञानमुपाश्रित्य मम साधर्म्यमागता: सर्गेऽपि नोपजायन्ते प्रलये न व्यथन्ति च   I will explain to you again the supreme knowledge, the greatest knowledge of all. Knowing which the great saints achieve perfection. Those who take refuge in this knowledge will be united with Me. They will not be reborn at the time of creation or destroyed at the time of dissolution.

The knowledge about the relationship between Brahm, Prakriti (Maya), three gunas, and the soul, leads great saints to perfection. The three Gunas are the cause of the bondage. The knowledge about the three Gunas will show the way out of the bondage.

14.3 & 14.4 मम योनिर्महद् ब्रह्म तस्मिन्गर्भं दधाम्यहम् सम्भव: सर्वभूतानां ततो भवति भारत सर्वयोनिषु कौन्तेय मूर्तय: सम्भवन्ति या: तासां ब्रह्म महद्योनिरहं बीजप्रद: पिता   Nature or Prakriti is the womb that I impregnate with the souls; as a result, the beings are born. The material nature or Prakriti or Maya is the womb, and I am the seed-giving father for all beings that are produced.

Life forms are created based on the karmas. The souls and Prakriti (Maya) remain with God in the unmanifest mode, after dissolution. At creation, various life forms, panch Mahabhuta, panch Tanamatras, and ego come into existence. The souls are cast into appropriate bodies according to their karmas. The wise clearly see that all action is the result of the gunas. Knowing "that" (tat) which is above the gunas, they attain God.

14.19 नान्यं गुणेभ्य: कर्तारं यदा द्रष्टानुपश्यति गुणेभ्यश्च परं वेत्ति मद्भावं सोऽधिगच्छति
When the wise understand clearly that all actions are triggered by the (three) gunas, and know Me (the eternal essence) who is above the gunas, they unite with Me (attain Me).

No other entity but the three Gunas are responsible for and the drivers of actions. Diverting the mind to God loosens the grip of the gunas. God is beyond the three Gunas (trigunatit).

14.20 गुणानेतानतीत्य त्रीन्देही देहसमुद्भवान् जन्ममृत्युजराद:खैर्विमुक्तोऽमृतमश्नुते
Going above the three Gunas that create the body, the soul becomes free from birth, disease, old age, and death (the bondage), consequently becoming immortal.

Prakriti or Maya comprises three Gunas and creates the universe and the bodies. As long as the soul thinks it is the body, it remains in the sorrowful state. When the soul rises above the three Gunas and realizes it is not the body, it is set free from the bondage.

15.5 निर्मानमोहा जितसङ्गदोषा अध्यात्मनित्या विनिवृत्तकामाः द्वन्द्वैर्विमुक्ताः सुखदुःखसंज्ञै-र्गच्छन्त्यमूढाः पदमव्ययं तत्   Free from false pride and delusion, without the evil of attachment, constantly dwelling in the Self, free from the desire to enjoy the senses, and beyond the dualities of pleasure and pain; such undeluded people reach the eternal goal.

Krishna says that the absence of the 'I' or 'Mine' notion makes the heart pure, then, the attachment diminishes. Giving up attachment is very hard to do without the control of the mind and dispassion.

15.20 इति गुह्यतमं शास्त्रमिदमुक्तं मयानघ एतद्बुद्ध्वा बुद्धिमान्स्यात्कृतकृत्यश्च भारत   Thus, I have taught you this foremost secret of scriptures. Knowing this, one achieves the wisdom fulfilling all that is to be attained.

The "foremost secret" is comparing life with the Ashvatth tree, explaining God's powers, revealing qualifications for liberation, indicating God's superiority over everything, and disclosure that Krishna is Brahm. The correct understanding of the secret paves the way to perfect wisdom.

18.50 सिद्धिं प्राप्तो यथा ब्रह्म तथाप्नोति निबोध मे समासेनैव कौन्तेय निष्ठा ज्ञानस्य या परा   Briefly learn from Me how the one who has attained perfection reaches Brahm, the supreme state of knowledge. One who has attained perfection attains Brahm.

After attaining perfection, while working with a detached attitude, you gain knowledge - jnana. With that knowledge, a karma yogi realizes God. In the next verses, Krishna explains how.

18.51, 18.52 and 18.53: बुद्ध्या विशुद्धया युक्तो धृत्यात्मानं नियम्य च शब्दादीन्विषयांस्त्यक्त्वा रागद्वेषौ व्युदस्य च विविक्तसेवी लघ्वाशी यतवाक्कायमानसः ध्यानयोगपरो नित्यं वैराग्यं समुपाश्रितः अहङ्कारं बलं दर्पं कामं क्रोधं परिग्रहम् विमुच्य निर्ममः शान्तो ब्रह्मभूयाय कल्पते   The following are the qualities one must have to unite with Brahm: 1. having a pure intellect, firmly controlling the Self, 2. abandoning hatred and attraction, 3. living in solitude, eating little, 4. having subdued speech, body, and mind, 5. concentrating and meditating, 6. being dispassionate, 7. remaining free of egoism, arrogance, anger, desire, and covetousness, 8. dropping the notion of "mine" and being peaceful.

Qualities or attributes necessary to attain unity with Brahm, in an arrow chart:

Karma yoga >> the attributes listed in these verses >> Union with Brahm

18.54 ब्रह्मभूत: प्रसन्नात्मा न शोचति न काङ् क्षति सम: सर्वेषु भूतेषु मद्भक्तिं लभते परराम्   United with Brahm and serene in the Self, he neither grieves nor desires; he is the same to all beings. Such a yogi or a jnani attains supreme devotion unto Me.

Here is a remarkable endorsement of the path of devotion indicated in a quote from Shankaracharya, the perfect jnani of Kaliyug, "Those who perform righteous actions for the attainment of celestial abodes may do so. Those who desire liberation via the path of jñāna or Aṣhṭāṅg Yoga may pursue that goal. As for me, I want nothing of these two paths. I wish only to engross myself in the nectar of Shree Krishna's lotus feet. I do not desire either worldly or heavenly pleasures, nor do I desire liberation." Other examples of jnanis who turned to the path of devotion are Sanatkumars, Sukdev, King Janak, etc.

TOPIC 11

Adhering to Inherent Duties

Parts of Gita's message are simple and easy to understand and practice. Krishna reiterates the preaching about selfless work (nishkam karma) multiple times – do your work diligently and enthusiastically as a prescribed duty and an offering to God without being preoccupied and attached to the results. The work done this way, called Karma Yoga, will have no karmic reactions; it will not bind the soul. The task done selfishly for personal pleasures, whether good or bad, will have the karmic effect and will further bind the soul and result in rebirths. This message is not complex and is possible to follow by sincere and humble devotees. Karma yoga will lead the soul to peace and liberation. The following verses where extracted from Gita. They relate to performing one's duties selflessly.

❦ *Krishna says:*

2.31 स्वधर्ममपि चावेक्ष्य न विकम्पितुमर्हसि धर्म्याद्धि युद्धाच्छ्रेयोऽन्यत्क्षत्रियस्य न विद्यते
Do not waiver in your duty as a warrior. There is no better opportunity for a warrior than to fight for righteousness.

Krishna now points out to Arjuna the benefits of doing his duty as a warrior.

2.32 यदृच्छया चोपपन्नं स्वर्गद्वारमपावृतम् सुखिनः क्षत्रियाः पार्थ लभन्ते युद्धमीदृशम्
A warrior should be happy when opportunities to defend righteousness come unsolicited. Such opportunities open the door to celestial abodes or heaven.

Gita inspires action and preaches against inaction and abandoning responsibilities. Gita does not encourage people to renounce samsara or active life. Fulfilling duty qualifies one for heaven.

2.33 अथ चेत्त्वमिमं धर्म्यं संग्रामं न करिष्यसि ततः स्वधर्मं कीर्तिं च हित्वा पापमवाप्स्यसि
If you decline to fight the righteous battle, ignoring your responsibility and reputation, there is no doubt that you will reap sin.

A Kshatriya's refusal to fight in a righteous war brings permanent infamy as a coward. Not performing the duty incurs shame and sin.

2.35 भयाद्रणादुपरतं मंस्यन्ते त्वां महारथाः येषां च त्वं बहुमतो भूत्वा यास्यसि
लाघवम्   Great generals who have high respect for you will think you ran away due to fear. Thus, you will lose respect in their eyes.

The consequence of not fighting (not doing assigned duties) is infamy.

2.36 अवाच्यवादांश्च बहून्वदिष्यन्ति तवाहिताः निन्दन्तस्तव सामर्थ्यं ततो दुःखतरं नु
किम्   Enemies will insult and belittle you, and defame you with unpleasant words. What can be more painful than that?

The consequence of not fighting is insult and humiliation by the enemy.

2.38 सुखदुःखे समे कृत्वा लाभालाभौ जयाजयौ ततो युद्धाय युज्यस्व नैवं पापमवाप्स्यसि
Fight to fulfill your duty with equal poise in happiness and misery, gain and loss, and winning and losing. By doing your duty this way, sin will never touch you.

Be resolute and do your work/duty selflessly (nishkam karma - working without attachment).

4.15 एवं ज्ञात्वा कृतं कर्म पूर्वैरपि मुमुक्षुभिः कुरु कर्मैव तस्मात्त्वं पूर्वैः पूर्वतरं कृतम्   Knowing this truth (that selfless action does not bind the soul), even sages seeking liberation in ancient times performed their work (selflessly). You should follow those sages and do your duty.

Selfless (nishwarth) karma does not accumulate karma. The sages come to elevate spirituality in society, selflessly, and as a service to God. Therefore, their work is free from the karmic reaction. God bestows his grace on those working in devotion. So, Krishna is asking Arjuna to follow the example of sages.

18.10 न द्वेष्ट्यकुशलं कर्म कुशले नानुषज्जते त्यागी सत्त्वसमाविष्टो मेधावी छिन्नसंशयः
The true and pure renunciants (a sannyasi) do not hate a disagreeable work, nor are they attached to an agreeable one. They are predominantly in the mode of goodness and have no attachment with the nature of work facing them.

Selfless renunciants are willing to do any work as a prescribed duty without the like and dislike. They do their work without feeling elated or dejected. Krishna suggests to Arjuna that he too should do his work in the spirit of karma yoga.

18.59 यदहङ्कारमाश्रित्य न योत्स्य इति मन्यसे मिथ्यैष व्यवसायस्ते प्रकृतिस्त्वां
नियोक्ष्यति   If you think you will not fight out of vanity, your decision will be in vain. Your (Kshatriya) nature will compel you to fight.

The mind and soul are not independent of God. One is not free to waive their prescribed duties. The three Gunas compel us to act according to our nature.

18.60 स्वभावजेन कौन्तेय निबद्ध: स्वेन कर्मणा कर्तुं नेच्छसि यन्मोहात्करिष्यस्यवशोऽपि तत्   That work which you do not want to do, out of misguided thinking, you will be driven to do it by your inclination, born of your nature.

Again, the three Gunas compel one to take certain actions whether he wishes or not. Krishna points out that due to Arjuna's impressions and inclinations from past lives, he is born with a Kshatriya nature comprising heroism. His nature will compel him to fight against his own will.

18.61 ईश्वर: सर्वभूतानां हृद्देशेऽर्जुन तिष्ठति भ्रामयन्सर्वभूतानि यन्त्रारूढानि मायया   The Supreme Lord dwells in the hearts of all people. According to their karmas, he directs the wanderings of their souls, who are seated on the body (Krishna calls it a machine, yantra) made by Maya. Dwelling in the hearts of everyone, Lord directs the wandering of the souls.

Krishna emphasizes the soul depends upon God, whether it obeys or not. Past karmas decide the type of body everyone gets, and no one has the freedom to choose their body and the environment upon rebirth. God is directing our activities, therefore, the soul must surrender and do the prescribed duty to obtain true freedom (from desires).

TOPIC 12

Vedic Rituals

In ancient times, Vedic rituals were believed to be the paths to attain wealth, prosperity, righteousness, and liberation. People performed fire rituals and offered sacrificial materials to please the heavenly gods. Over time, the focus moved from worldly life to spiritual life. However, the ceremonies were continued by desire-seeking householders. They also practiced breath control, austerities, yoga, and meditation to stabilize their mind in the contemplation of God.

Krishna says he is the one who grants powers to celestial gods to bless people with tangible benefits, and that the worship of the supreme God fulfills both objectives – eternal bliss and liberation. Just worshipping heavenly gods will only bring temporary material enjoyment to people. When their merits are depleted, they will return to this world again. The following verses from Gita include Krishna's thinking regarding the Vedic rituals.

❦ Krishna Says:

2.42 & 2.43 यामिमां पुष्पितां वाचं प्रवदन्त्यविपश्चित: वेदवादरता: पार्थ नान्यदस्तीति वादिन: कामात्मान: स्वर्गपरा जन्मकर्मफलप्रदाम् क्रियाविशेषबहुलां भोगैश्वर्यगतिं प्रति   Those with shallow views are attracted to the flowery words and rituals of Vedas; they do not comprehend the larger purpose of Vedas. They glorify only the portions of Vedas that please their senses and perform elaborate rituals for attaining higher birth, opulence, sensual enjoyment, and elevation to heavenly planets. These are their only goals.

The Rig Veda, the oldest of the four Vedas, guides people to shift their focus from nature to Brahm. The Yajur Veda and Sama Veda have been derived from the Rig Veda. The Yajur Veda consists of rituals for the performance of ceremonial rites. The Sama Veda contains chants and is musical; it explains correct melodic intonation relating to the Vedic rituals. The Atharva Veda came later and is mainly incantations and magical formulas used to calm negative forces and gain ordinary favors. The Atharva Veda also is the foundation for the science of Ayurveda (medical science of India). The Vedas have three sections - 1. Karma kand; 2. Jnan Kand; 3. Upasana Kand. The higher purpose of Vedas is to help the soul reach God, but those motivated by desires do not understand this and focus their energy in Karma kand.

2.44 भोगैश्वर्यप्रसक्तानां तयापहृतचेतसाम् व्यवसायात्मिका बुद्धि: समाधौ न विधीयते
Their minds are attracted to worldly pleasures, and their intelligence is bewildered by such things as Vedic rituals. Hence, they lack firm determination for success on the path to God.

Once the mind goes to objects of pleasure, it becomes unsteady and wavering. It cannot decide right from wrong.

2.45 त्रैगुण्यविषया वेदा निस्त्रैगुण्यो भवार्जुन निर्द्वन्द्वो नित्यसत्वस्थो निर्योगक्षेम आत्मवान्
Vedas describe the three Gunas. 1. Be free from the action of Gunas. 2. Rise above these to a state of spiritual consciousness. 3. Be self-controlled, in the self, free of dualities, set in truth, and without the desire to acquire and hoard.

Maya, by its three constituent modes, makes the soul think it is the body. One must transcend the three gunas to make spiritual progress.

2.46 यावानर्थ उदपाने सर्वत: सम्प्लुतोदके तावान्सर्वेषु वेदेषु ब्राह्मणस्य विजानत:
Realizing that absolute truth also fulfills the purpose of Vedas, like a small lake serves the use of a large lake, the real purpose of Veda is to unite the soul with God.

There are 100,000 mantras in Vedas for various rituals, practices, prayers, ceremonies, and knowledge. The study and practice of these scriptures will liberate the soul and unite it with God.

3.9 यज्ञार्थात्कर्मणोऽन्यत्र लोकोऽयं कर्मबन्धन: तदर्थं कर्म कौन्तेय मुक्तसङ्ग: समाचर   This world is bound by selfish actions. Perform activities selflessly without anticipation of any personal again.

Selfish actions done without the spirit of offering to God will bind the soul. A note of clarification. The word Yajna is often translated as "sacrifice" in English. Most authors translate Yajna as "sacrifice". Yajna often refers to the Vedic fire rituals. The broader meaning of Yajna is any rite, ceremony, devotion, and charity actions done as a duty without expectation of gratification.

3.11 देवान्भावयतानेन ते देवा भावयन्तु व: परस्परं भावयन्त: श्रेय: परमवाप्स्यथ   Respect and appreciate the celestial deities as they do the same to you. Through this mutual feeling of love and honor, both will attain the ultimate good.

The celestial gods are like administrators of different functions in the universe. They are appointed by God. They are souls like us but at a much higher level of spirituality and live much longer than us in the higher planes of the mortal world called heaven (swarg). There are several gods for different functions of the universe. For example, Agni Dev is the god of fire, Varun Dev is the god of oceans, and Indra Dev is the king of all gods in the heavens. The Vedas contain specific rituals done to please each God of heaven who will bless the Yajna performer with prosperity and a spot in heaven after death. The Supreme God says the Vedic rituals should be done without expectation of rewards to avoid further accumulation of karma. Yajna done with selfish motive may get you the heaven for some time but not liberation. After your virtues are depleted, you will be reborn and return to the cycle of birth and death.

3.15 कर्म ब्रह्मोद्भवं विद्धि ब्रह्माक्षरसमुद्भवम् तस्मात्सर्वगतं ब्रह्म नित्यं यज्ञे प्रतिष्ठितम्   Action or duties originate from the Vedas. The Vedas originate from Brahm, the Imperishable Supreme. Therefore, the all-pervading God is always present in acts of sacrifice.

The ultimate recipient of Yajna is God. Brahm is Supreme God, the eternal essence of the universe, the ultimate divine reality, according to the Vedas. See Topic 26, which contains detailed attributes and powers of Brahm.

4.12 काङ् क्षन्तः कर्मणां सिद्धिं यजन्त इह देवताः क्षिप्रं हि मानुषे लोके सिद्धिर्भवति कर्मजा   Those people in this world who desire wealth and prosperity worship celestial gods because you can please gods and attain the material rewards quickly.

The celestial gods respond quickly to Yajna conducted faithfully by granting your desires.

4.33 श्रेयान्द्रव्यमयाद्यज्ञाज्ज्ञानयज्ञः परन्तप सर्वं कर्माखिलं पार्थ ज्ञाने परिसमाप्यते   Knowledge-sacrifice or jnana Yajna is superior to material sacrifice done mechanically (without knowledge). Ultimately, all sacrificial actions in total culminate in knowledge.

If sacrifices as these are done with blind faith and without the real knowledge, they amount to mere mechanical drills. Although such exercises are better than not doing anything at all, they do not entirely purify the mind or result in liberation.

9.20 त्रैविद्या मां सोमपाः पूतपापा यज्ञैरिष्ट्वा स्वर्गतिं प्रार्थयन्ते ते पुण्यमासाद्य सुरेन्द्रलोकमश्नन्ति दिव्यान्दिवि देवभोगान्   Knowers of the three Vedas worship Me by Yajna (fire sacrifice) and drink soma juice to redeem from sins, and then, pray for obtaining access to heaven. They reach the abodes in paradise and enjoy the divine pleasures of the celestial gods.

The performers of Karma Kand (rituals) are rewarded by joyful life in heaven. The Karma Kandis (the doers of ritualistic ceremonies) go to the higher planes known as heaven, where they enjoy pleasures more than anything on the earth.

9.21 ते तं भुक्त्वा स्वर्गलोकं विशालं क्षीणे पुण्ये मर्त्यलोकं विशन्ति एवं त्रयीधर्ममनुप्रपन्नागतागतं कामकामा लभन्ते   They return to the mortal world after the experience in heaven ends, when the balance of their merits is exhausted.

Again, those who follow Vedic rituals to enjoy a life of pleasures are reborn and back again to the cycles of birth and death. The fate of a desire-oriented devotee is never liberation but continued birth and death.

11.48 न वेदयज्ञाध्ययनैर्न दानै-र्न च क्रियाभिर्न तपोभिरुग्रैः एवंरूपः शक्य अहं नृलोके द्रष्टुं त्वदन्येन कुरुप्रवीर   No mortal has ever seen my cosmic form that you have seen, even by performing sacrifice (Vedic Yagna), charities, rituals, or severe austerities (tapashcharya).

Only Arjuna has seen the complete cosmic form, not possible for anyone to see even by performing Vedic rituals. Others have seen this form, but not as magnificent as the one Arjuna saw. Krishna says it is not feasible to see the infinite form by the human eyes unless God graces you with divine eyes.

TOPIC 13

Yoga Kriya

This topic on Yoga Kriya brings together all the verses on Yoga Kriya processes mentioned in different chapters of Gita. The final goal of Yoga Kriya is to reach the state of Samadhi, the state of total and absolute bliss. The yoga processes involve the eight-fold Yoga system known as Ashtang Yoga. The commentary under 5.27 and 5.28 below explains the eight Yoga steps.

Krishna suggests single-pointed focus, sitting in a comfortable posture and environment as a basic technique of meditation. He tells Arjuna the meditator should hold the body, head, and neck in a straight line to allow a free flow of energy that some call Kundalini Shakti. He recommends moderation in food and sleep and other physical activities for success in meditation. Krishna says regular practice with detachment can tame and control the adamant mind, necessary to reach the blissful state.

Samadhi is the ultimate state reached by meditation when the practitioner experiences a complete bliss; the breathing slows down and becomes steady and even, while the mind gets away from the senses and their objects. You lose awareness of your body. Once the deep state of concentration occurs, the aspirant experiences bliss and freedom from negativity. Yogananda Paramhansa said everyone should rely on their own experience from the outcome because no two persons may have an identical experience. He cautions one should not set an expectation of results from what they hear from others to keep the stray thoughts away, which can distract the mind. The Kriya Yoga process is a disciplined approach, more than physical postures and controlled breathing. It requires dedication and regular practice.

❦ Krishna says:

4.29-4.30 अपाने जुह्वति प्राणं प्राणेऽपानं तथापरे प्राणापानगती रुद्ध्वा प्राणायामपरायणा: अपरे नियताहारा: प्राणान्प्राणेषु जुह्वति सर्वेऽप्येते यज्ञविदो यज्ञक्षपितकल्मषा:   Some regulate the outgoing breath in the incoming breath. Some provide the incoming breath into the outgoing breath. Some practice prāṇāyām and restrain the incoming and outgoing breaths, regulating the life-energy. Others restrict food and offer the breath into the life-energy as a sacrifice. All these knowers of sacrifice are cleansed of their impurities as a result of such performances.

As a sacrifice, some devotees offer the incoming breath of prana in the outgoing breath of apana, and the outgoing breath of apana in the incoming breath of prana, thus rendering breath unnecessary, by diligent practice of pranayama or the life-control technique. Various interpretations of this verse exist. While some are clearer than others, the one by Yogananda Paramhansa is among the most clear.

Prana and Apana are the two main currents in the body. Yogananda says the inhalation and exhalation result from the upward flow of Prana and the downward flow of Apana. He says, "Breath is the cord that ties the soul to the body from the opposite pulls of the prana and apana currents in the spine." Prana extracts life force from the oxygen atoms, faster than from liquid and solid food, and moves it to the body to keep the physiological functions alive. The downward apana current in the spine causes exhalation and pushes out the impurities of the lungs. The longevity is directly related to the rate of respiration. What makes the breathing necessary is the toxins in the cells. The absence of toxins makes breathing unnecessary, which explains the prolonged survival of advanced yogis without breathing. This discussion is probably the basis of Krishna's suggestion for pranayama as a yogic method to release the soul from the bondage. The science of breathing, as it relates to physiology and the bondage of soul, is a deep (and somewhat controversial among those who do not understand it) subject, certainly way beyond the scope of this book. The pranayama (control of life force or Jeev Shakti) process as emphasized in the Upanishads is perhaps best explained by Yogananda Paramhansa as part of the Kriya Yoga program taught by his followers at the Self Realization Fellowship (SRF).

A word of caution - one should learn Pranayama from a qualified yoga teacher, and there are many in India and elsewhere. Don't practice pranayama learned from books and videos without expert supervision to avoid serious adverse effects that can occur with wrong methods.

5.27-5.28 स्पर्शान्कृत्वा बहिर्बाह्यांश्चक्षुश्चैवान्तरे भ्रुवो: प्राणापानौ समौ कृत्वा नासाभ्यन्तरचारिणौ यतेन्द्रियमनोबुद्धिर्मुनिर्मोक्षपरायण: विगतेच्छाभयक्रोधो य: सदा मुक्त एव स: Leaving aside distracting thoughts of enjoyment, fixing the gaze between the eyebrows, balancing the incoming and outgoing breath in the nose, and thus controlling the senses, mind, and intellect, the sage becomes free from desire and fear, and always lives in freedom.

This verse describes pranayama and meditation techniques, which are part of the eight-fold yoga (Ashtang yoga) system. The latter includes eight sequential steps briefly explained below. For more detailed information on Ashtang Yoga, refer to the book titled Patanjali Sutra or the SRF program on Kriya Yoga, or equivalent programs offered by other yoga institutes.

1. *Yama (abstinence): Creates harmony and peace. Emphasizes Satya (truthfulness), Ahimsa (non-violence, not hurting other beings physically or mentally), asteya (non-stealing), aparigraha (not accumulating beyond one's needs), and brahmacharya (a balanced sexual life).*
2. *Niyama (observances): Five Niyamas that promote proper conduct are - Saucha (personal hygiene and mental purity), Santosa (contentment), Tapas (self-discipline), Swadhaya (self-study), and Iswara Pranidhana (facing all situations with poise and surrender to the will of God).*
3. *Asana (yoga postures): Includes yoga postures for steadiness, strength, balance, and specific health and spiritual benefits. Examples of poses are Padmasana, Sukhasana, Siddhasana, etc.*
4. *Pranayama (breath control): Regulates breath and life force. Breath, mind, body, and soul are closely linked. One can control the mind by controlling the breath. Pranayama gives steadiness, calmness, removes impurities, clarity of the mind, and the sense of well-being. There are several types of Pranayama.*
5. *Pratyahara (withdrawal of the senses): The withdrawal of senses from their objects leads the mind inwards and prepares it for meditation in quest of inner reality.*
6. *Dharana (concentration): Means concentration of the mind on a fixed object.*
7. *Dhyana: Prolonged Dharana leads to Dhyana, commonly known as meditation. It is the engagement of the mind on one point for a long time, undistracted and uninterrupted.*
8. *Samadhi: Samadhi is the last stage of Ashtang yoga. It results in total bliss and phenomenal individual experiences.*

6.2 यं संन्यासमिति प्राहुर्योगं तं विद्धि पाण्डव न ह्यसंन्यस्तसङ्कल्पो योगी भवति कश्चन Sannyasa (renunciation) is the same as yoga. One cannot become a yogi without renouncing desires.

A sannyasi renounces the pleasures of the mind and senses. More importantly, the sannyasi strives for God-realization, the ultimate goal of a spiritual endeavor.

6.4 यदा हि नेन्द्रियार्थेषु न कर्मस्वनुषज्जते सर्वसङ्कल्पसंन्यासी योगारूढस्तदोच्यते When one is not attached to sense objects or actions and has abandoned desires for the results of efforts, he is considered as an advanced yogi.

This verse states the criteria to identify an advanced yogi. A detached yogi no longer craves for or pursues sense objects. Eventually, he drops thoughts of pleasure from the sense objects. The traits of advanced Yogi are like the one with mental equanimity discussed under Topic 27 on Sthitprajn in verses 6.8, 6.9, and 6.10.

6.7 जितात्मन: प्रशान्तस्य परमात्मा समाहित: शीतोष्णसुखदु:खेषु तथा मानापमानयो:
The yogis who have complete control of the mind are not affected by the dualities such as cold/hot, joy/sorrow, honor/dishonor. Such yogis remain peaceful and steady.

The senses and their objects produce the perception of hot/cold and joy/sorrow. Yogis, with the controlled mind, are not moved by these. The mind lives in either Maya or God. Deep meditation absorbs the mind in God.

6.10 योगी युञ्जीत सततमात्मानं रहसि स्थित: एकाकी यतचित्तात्मा निराशीरपरिग्रह: A Yogi should keep the mind steady on the Self, remain in solitude, control the mind and the body, and give up expectations and the sense of ownership.

To prepare for mastery in Yoga, one must practice the yoga disciplines consistently. Krishna emphasizes that a Yogi should dedicate some time regularly in meditation in a secluded place. Yoga kriya in seclusion is also recommended in verse 18.52 under Topic 10.

6.11 शुचौ देशे प्रतिष्ठाप्य स्थिरमासनमात्मन: नात्युच्छ्रितं नातिनीचं चैलाजिनकुशोत्तरम् रिपुरात्मन: Krishna recommends that the practicing Yogi should sit in a soft asana (seat) in a sanctified place, and the position should not be too high or too low.

Sit comfortably to avoid physical aggravation. Books on yoga suggest several asanas (postures) for meditation. Some teachers insist one must sit in a padmasan position (with crossed legs) when practicing Yoga. However, be informed that such rigidity may be unnecessary. Swami Yogananda Paramahansa, a realized yogi, says in the Autobiography of a Yogi that meditation can be practiced in any comfortable position, including sitting relaxed with the spine erect on the edge of a chair. If you have weak knees, you certainly don't want to break them by sitting in a padmasan. Patañjali Yoga Sūtra (the Bible of Ashtang Yoga) says, "To practice meditation, sit motionless in any posture that you are comfortable in."

6.12 and 6.13 तत्रैकाग्रं मन: कृत्वा यतचित्तेन्द्रियक्रिय: उपविश्यासने युञ्ज्याद्योगमात्मविशुद्धये समं कायशिरोग्रीवं धारयन्नचलं स्थिर: सम्प्रेक्ष्य नासिकाग्रं स्वं दिशश्चानवलोकयन् Sitting firmly, the Yogi should try to purify and concentrate the mind, and focus it in meditation by controlling all thoughts and activities. He must hold the body, neck, and head firmly in a straight line (don't force it but stay relaxed), and gaze at the tip of the nose (the spot between the eyebrows), without looking around.

Again, Patanjali Yoga sutra says, "Sit motionless in any posture that you are comfortable in." In the beginning, it is not easy at all to sit steady in one position with the spine erect. However, with diligent practice over time, one can remain steady and concentrate. You will begin to enjoy the experience and look forward to daily practice. Let the meditation experience happen naturally, without anticipation for quick results, and avoid showmanship.

6.14 प्रशान्तात्मा विगतभीर्ब्रह्मचारिव्रते स्थित: मन: संयम्य मच्चित्तो युक्त आसीत मत्पर: Thus, with a serene, fearless, and steady mind, and firm in the vow of celibacy, the Yogi should meditate on "Me" as the supreme goal.

TOPIC 13 - Yoga Kriya

The ultimate object of meditation is God. Celibacy here means preserving the vital force. The meditation masters teach different techniques of meditation, such as watching the incoming and outgoing breath, chanting Soham mantra, chanting guru mantra, staring at the candle flame, looking at natural entities like mountains and trees, or looking at the void in silence. Only follow the instructions you receive from a realized spiritual teacher who will guide you the right way.

6.15 युञ्जन्नेवं सदात्मानं योगी नियतमानस: शान्तिं निर्वाणपरमां मत्संस्थामधिगच्छति
Constantly keeping the mind absorbed in Me, the Yogi of a disciplined mind attains perfect peace and liberation (nirvana).

This verse repeats that the goal of meditation is God. There are numerous techniques of meditation, like are Zen techniques, Buddhist techniques, Vipassana techniques, Tantric techniques, Taoist techniques, and Vedic techniques. A sincere practitioner should be able to attain success via any of these methods. The aim is to focus and purify the mind and liberate it from the hold of Maya.

Knowledge and truth are realized from regular practice and experience, not from scriptures and theories.

6.16 नात्यश्नतस्तु योगोऽस्ति न चैकान्तमनश्नत: न चाति स्वप्नशीलस्य जाग्रतो नैव चार्जुन
Yoga is not possible for those who overeat or not eat and sleep too much or too little.

Physical health, sensible diet, and rest are essential for success in yoga. Maintaining a healthy body is necessary. Charak Samhita says, "The body is the vehicle for engaging in spiritual activity." Hence, asanas, pranayam, and the science of proper diet are an essential part of Vedic knowledge.

6.17 युक्ताहारविहारस्य युक्तचेष्टस्य कर्मसु युक्तस्वप्नावबोधस्य योगो भवति दु:खहा   Those who are moderate in eating and recreation (like walking) and balanced in exertion in work and reasonable in sleep and wakefulness can alleviate pain and sorrow by practicing Yoga.

Yoga leads you to peace and self-realization. Sensual pleasure and excessive food can inhibit spiritual progress. Buddha also preaches the golden middle path between severe asceticism and sensual indulgence.

6.18 यदा विनियतं चित्तमात्मन्येवावतिष्ठते नि:स्पृह: सर्वकामेभ्यो युक्त इत्युच्यते तदा
When the mind is controlled, it remains fixed in the Self alone (another meaning - in God); and when one is free of physical cravings, then he is considered "united" with the Self.

All three conditions in verse 6.18 are hard to abide by, but again, dedicated and regular practice can take you higher, slowly but surely. With dedication, you can climb the mountain by small steps. That is how those who progress reach the top, not by one giant step.

6.19 यथा दीपो निवातस्थो नेङ्गते सोपमा स्मृता योगिनो यतचित्तस्य युञ्जतो योगमात्मन:

Similar to a lamp that does not glimmer in a calm place, the Yogi with a controlled mind stays steady during meditation on the Self.

The mind is fickle and almost impossible to control. Nevertheless, with practice and detachment, the mind gets steady with the focus on God. Then the yogi's posture becomes steady and he experiences divine bliss.

6.20 यत्रोपरमते चित्तं निरुद्धं योगसेवया यत्र चैवात्मनात्मानं पश्यन्नात्मनि तुष्यति

When the mind is restrained from desires and becomes quiet by the practice of Yoga, then the Yogi can see the soul through the clear mind and gets immersed in the inner bliss (atmanand).

You cannot see through the turbulent and muddy water until you remove the mud and make the water calm. Similarly, you cannot know the Self – atma until the mind is clean and steady. Krishna reassures the doubtful Arjuna that he can still the mind with practice and detachment. The blissful state cannot be explained; one must experience it himself.

6.21 सुखमात्यन्तिकं यत्तद्बुद्धिग्राह्यमतीन्द्रियम् वेत्ति यत्र न चैवायं स्थितश्चलति तत्वत:

In the highest state of Yoga (Samadhi), one experiences limitless bliss, and after this, one never moves from eternal truth (God).

When the mind is in union with God, the soul experiences the divine bliss. In Samadhi, the soul in its desireless state unites with the eternal essence (God) without deviating.

6.22 यं लब्ध्वा चापरं लाभं मन्यते नाधिकं तत: यस्मिन्स्थितो न दु:खेन गुरुणापि विचाल्यते   Once in the Samadhi state, nothing would seem more significant. Afterward, one is never disturbed by anything, not even by the extreme calamity.

In the mundane world, one is never satisfied with any gain and wants more, even though the gain is temporary. In the spiritual world, at the highest state of bliss, one is contented and looks for nothing more. The state of Samadhi cannot be snatched from the Yogi, who remains steady and undisturbed by calamities.

6.23 तं विद्याद् दु:खसंयोगवियोगं योगसञ्ज्ञितम् स निश्चयेन योक्तव्यो योगोऽनिर्विण्णचेतसा   What ends misery is Yoga. Yogi should practice Yoga with determination and optimism.

The physical world is temporary and full of grief. Everyone has some problem or the other from birth through death. The divine bliss loosens and eventually dispels the hold of Maya. The solution is to practice Yoga and meditate resolutely. Verses 6.19 through 6.23 emphasize deep meditation. Yogananda Paramhansa says, "Every yogi should joyfully try to make his daily meditation deeper than the previous day's meditation; his yoga practice of tomorrow should always be deeper than the one of today."

TOPIC 13 - Yoga Kriya

6.24 and 6.25 सङ्कल्पप्रभवान्कामांस्त्यक्त्वा सर्वानशेषत: मनसैवेन्द्रियग्रामं विनियम्य समन्तत: शनै: शनैरुपरमेद्बुद्ध्या धृतिगृहीतया आत्मसंस्थं मन: कृत्वा न किञ्चिदपि चिन्तयेत् Abandon desires for material objects and control the senses with the mind. Slowly, with practice and concentration, and with intellect, the mind will become engrossed in the Self (God) alone, and will not think of anything else.

Meditate by moving the mind away from the worldly thoughts and making it steady on God. The determined practice is necessary to attain a blissful state depicted by the arrow chart below.

DETERMINED PRACTICE ---- Conviction of Intellect >> Firmness of the Mind >> Restrain Senses With the Mind >> Attention Away From the Sense Objects >> Control of Desires >> Steady Mind >> Blissful State

6.26 यतो यतो निश्चरति मनश्चञ्चलमस्थिरम् ततस्ततो नियम्यैतदात्मन्येव वशं नयेत् Whenever and wherever the unsteady mind goes off the tangent, try to bring it back and continuously focus on God.

This verse explains pratyahara, one of the eight yoga steps discussed in comments under verses 5.27 and 5.28. Pratyahara is the process of withdrawing the mind from the senses. The following are steps for pratyahara:

Step 1. Use the intelligence to decide that the world is not our goal.

Step 2. Decide that God is the goal and keep the mind away from the world.

Step 3. Steps 1 and 2 require resolute effort because the mind will tend to wander off.

Step 4. When the mind wanders off, go back to Step 1 and try to refocus.

Beginning the meditation is hard, just like any noble endeavor, but gets easier after you stick with it firmly.

6.27 प्रशान्तमनसं ह्येनं योगिनं सुखमुत्तमम् उपैति शान्तरजसं ब्रह्मभूतमकल्मषम् (As a result of constant practice of meditation) The highest level of bliss comes to the Yogi, whose passions are subdued, who is sinless, and who sees everything concerning Brahm.

The supreme bliss results from control of passions and with Brahm in focus constantly. This means the Yogi identifies everything with God - always sees him, hears him, speaks of him, and thinks of him.

The constant practice of meditation >> passions subdued >> sinlessness >> everything identified with Brahm (God) >> supreme bliss

6.28 युञ्जन्नेवं सदात्मानं योगी विगतकल्मष: सुखेन ब्रह्मसंस्पर्शमत्यन्तं सुखमश्नुते Thus, with the mind connected with God through Yoga, free of sin, and remaining in focus on the Supreme, the Yogi easily enjoys the infinite bliss by contact with supreme Brahm.

Brahm is the source of bliss, the best kind of happiness. What are the different types of happiness?

1. Nirguna - the divine bliss of God; 2. Sattvik - happiness from compassion, Seva, knowledge cultivation, yoga kriya, etc.; 3. Rajasik - joy from the sense gratification; 4. Tamasic - pleasure from alcohol, narcotics, cigarettes, meat, violence, laziness.

6.29 सर्वभूतस्थमात्मानं सर्वभूतानि चात्मनि ईक्षते योगयुक्तात्मा सर्वत्र समदर्शन: With consciousness merged with God, the yogis see all living beings in God and God in all living beings (equality of vision).

This verse identifies another characteristic of a perfect Yogi. The realized Yogi sees everything in its connection with God.

6.30 यो मां पश्यति सर्वत्र सर्वं च मयि पश्यति तस्याहं न प्रणश्यामि स च मे न प्रणश्यति
The yogi who perceives Me everywhere and sees everything in Me, never loses sight of Me, nor do I lose sight of him.

Yogi's oneness with God keeps his mind tied to God. The focus on God comes from seeing God in everything and everyone.

6.31 सर्वभूतस्थितं यो मां भजत्येकत्वमास्थित: सर्वथा वर्तमानोऽपि स योगी मयि वर्तते   The Yogi who is one with Me and worships Me as present in everyone, he dwells only in Me although he may be engaged in all kinds of activities.

God is in the heart of everyone. Thus, dwelling inside everyone's body is two divine entities - the soul and God. An average person sees everyone as the body, but a realized saint sees everyone as the soul. Verse 5.18 (Topic 27) says, "The learned, with the eyes of divine knowledge, see with equal vision a Brahmin, a cow, an elephant, a dog, and a dog-eater."

6.32 आत्मौपम्येन सर्वत्र समं पश्यति योऽर्जुन सुखं वा यदि वा दु:खं स योगी परमो मत: I regard them as perfect Yogis who see everyone as equal and respond to their joys and sorrows as their own.

Perfect yogis see the Atma (the soul) in others and can feel their pain. The one and same God who dwells in the heart of everyone connects the perfect Yogi with the souls in others; this is how they receive the "signals" of pain and other feelings from the others. The reality, according to Krishna, is all individual souls are connected, but only advanced yogis realize this truth.

6.46 तपस्विभ्योऽधिकोयोगी   ज्ञानिभ्योऽपिमतोऽधिक: कर्मिभ्यश्चाधिकोयोगी तस्माद्योगीभवार्जुन| Strive to be a Yogi because a Yogi is superior to a tapasvi (ascetic), jnani (a learned person), and karmi (a ritualistic performer).

Krishna here praises the royal path of yoga as the highest of all spiritual paths, and the scientific yogi as greater than a follower of asceticism, Jnana Marga, and rituals.

TOPIC 13 - Yoga Kriya

91

8.9 and 8.10 अभ्यासयोगयुक्तेन चेतसा नान्यगामिना परमं पुरुषं दिव्यं याति पार्थानुचिन्तयन् कविं पुराणमनुशासितार मणोरणीयांसमनुस्मरेद्य: सर्वस्य धातारमचिन्त्यरूप   God is omniscient and most ancient. He is the controller and subtler than the subtlest. He is the support of all, inconceivable, brighter than the sun, beyond the darkness of ignorance. Those when dying 1. steadily set the mind on God, 2. fix the prana (life airs) between the eyebrows; and 3. continuously remember the divine Lord with great devotion, certainly attain him.

In pure devotion, the mind is focused on God's forms. Krishna preaches the path of devotion combined with yoga practices. Krishna says all roads lead to the same goal, and he helps set your faith in whatever way you choose. Some like bhakti, some like Yoga, and some like service. Krishna frequently points out in Gita that devotion or bhakti is the common factor in these paths.

In Aṣhṭāṅg Yoga, done under expert guidance, the life force is conserved and channeled to the brain via the spine to activate more significant parts of the brain to acquire broader powers. The brain is like a million-watt amplifier, requiring immense input power for it to function at its maximum capacity. Ashtang Yoga and bhakti generate very high levels of input power. Ordinary people not engaging in Yoga utilize most of their God-given power (Jeev Shakti) in tasks to sustain the body and perform pleasure activities. Very little of their Jeev Shakti reaches the brain, and it only activates a small portion of their brain. That is like trying to run a million-watt amplifier with a nine-volt battery. Therefore, their brain transmitters work at low efficiency and can only sustain essential body functions like breathing, digesting, recreation, circulation, and excretion. Human brain, when fully activated, produces an incredible power resulting in many acquired siddhis (extraordinary spiritual powers). These acquired siddhis that manifest from extended yoga practice are different than the powers of the avatars or ansh of God. Avatars are born with those powers due to the Yoga Maya Shakti. Swami Yogananda Paramhansa says the subject of spiritual science and extraordinary powers has a scientific base, something one must discover via their spiritual journey and kriyas he came to teach.

TOPIC 14

Fate of Unsuccessful Yogi

During Krishna's discourse on the yoga process, Arjuna asks abruptly about the fate of an aspirant who abandons the yoga process for some reason before he reaches the goal. Would his efforts go to waste? Krishna assures Arjuna that no spiritual effort will ever be wasted as he will be reborn in an environment and family suitable for the resumption of the progress he made in his last life.

❧ *Krishna says:*

4.40 अज्ञश्चाश्रद्दधानश्च संशयात्मा विनश्यति नायं लोकोऽस्ति न परो न सुखं संशयात्मन:
But those who lack knowledge and faith, and have the doubting nature, they will ultimately perish. The doubtful souls are never happy in this world or the next.

The ignorant (ajnas) and faithless steadily decline in spiritual growth.

6.36 असंयतात्मना योगो दुष्प्राप इति मे मति: वश्यात्मना तु यतता शक्योऽवासुमुपायत:
Yoga is hard to attain with an uncontrolled mind. However, those who have learned to control the mind and try diligently by the right means can achieve perfection. Krishna says this is his opinion.

Topic 13 on Yoga Kriya describes the correct yoga process that can bring perfect peace. However, those with doubting and uncontrolled mind will not attain peace by any method.

❧ *Here Arjuna asks:*

6.37 अर्जुन उवाच अयति: श्रद्धयोपेतो योगाञ्चलितमानस: अप्राप्य योगसंसिद्धिं कां गतिं कृष्ण गच्छति   What is the end of a Yogi, who is unable to control himself? Even though such a yogi has faith, but does not try enough due to an unstable mind. As a result, he does not attain perfection in Yoga.

The spiritual quest begins with shraddha – faith, which comes from the result of past samskaras or the company of saints or adversities in life. However, the practicing yogis do not exert enough effort and get distracted. Such yogis cannot complete their spiritual journey successfully in their current life.

6.38 कच्चिन्नोभयविभ्रष्टश्छिन्नाभ्रमिव नश्यति अप्रतिष्ठो महाबाहो विमूढो ब्रह्मण: पथि
Does not such a person who deviates from Yoga get deprived of both material and spiritual success and perish like a broken cloud with no position in either sphere?

Arjuna asks Krishna if the unsuccessful Yogi perishes.

6.39 एतन्मेसंशयंकृष्णछेत्तुमर्हस्यशेषत:त्वदन्य:संशयस्यास्यछेत्तानह्युपपद्यते   (Arjuna pleading) Please dispel my doubt completely, who else can dispel my doubt but you?

Ignorance raises doubt, but knowledge destroys it. Arjuna surrenders and turns to Krishna to dispel his doubt.

❦ *Krishna explains to Arjuna:*

6.40 श्रीभगवानुवाच पार्थ नैवेह नामुत्र विनाशस्तस्य विद्यते न हि कल्याणकृत्कश्चिद्दुर्गतिं तात गच्छति   The one who engages on the spiritual path and strives for God-realization does not meet with destruction here or in the other world. Evil does not overcome him.

Krishna reassures Arjuna in this verse that the one pursuing God-realization "never" falls off from the spiritual path. The doer of good acts never comes to grief.

6.41 and 6.42 प्राप्य पुण्यकृतां लोकानुषित्वा शाश्वती: समा: शुचीनां श्रीमतां गेहे योगभ्रष्टोऽभिजायते अथवा योगिनामेव कुले भवति धीमताम् एतद्धि दुर्लभतरं लोके जन्म यदीदृशम्   Those who fall from Yoga go to abodes of virtuous after death. And after many years, they are again reborn in the house of pure and wealthy. Advanced yogis who failed in their endeavor are reborn in the family of pious Yogis; it is difficult to attain such a birth.

The failed efforts of a yogi are not wasted. He will continue the quest for perfection after rebirth.

6.43 तत्र तं बुद्धिसंयोगं लभते पौर्वदेहिकम् यतते च ततो भूय: संसिद्धौ कुरुनन्दन   After birth in a pious family, they continue the efforts from previous lives and try harder than before for self-realization (perfection in Yoga).

The yogi's situation can be compared to a traveler taking a break in the journey at night and continuing the tour the next day.

6.44 पूर्वाभ्यासेन तेनैव ह्रियते ह्यवशोऽपि स: जिज्ञासुरपि योगस्य शब्दब्रह्मातिवर्तते   They are attracted to God under the power of past discipline, against their own will; such aspirants rise above those who only perform rituals.

The soul with past sanskaras (tendencies) is inspired to go on the path to God. They feel drawn due to some unknown force, often referred to as "the call of God." The people who receive the call of God reject everything in the world to pursue spirituality.

6.45 प्रयत्नाद्यतमानस्तु   योगी   संशुद्धकिल्बिष: अनेकजन्मसंसिद्धस्ततो   याति   परां गतिम्   With the constant efforts and merits over many lifetimes, they become free from selfish desires and attain the supreme goal of life.

Perfection comes from the accumulated practice of many past lives. The yogi with an incomplete mission in the last life tries harder in this life than ever before.

TOPIC 15

God's Powers – Shakti

Gita mentions three unique powers by which God creates and sustains the universe and all beings- 1. Yoga Maya Shakti, 2. Jeev Shakti, and 3. Maya. By Yoga Maya Shakti, He comes among us as a human, though He is unmanifest and eternal, doing activities not visible to us. We see His human form but cannot recognize the divinity in Him. Jeev Sakti is soul energy or spiritual energy, superior to Maya. Jeev Shakti upholds the universe, activates it, and causes its existence and ultimate dissolution. Maya Shakti creates the body from the five elements. Jeev Shakti powers the body and makes it conscious and alive. Maya creates the physical objects and the inert material, and Jeev Shakti creates the subjects or conscious beings.

Since the objects Maya creates are not permanent, they are there, but then they are not, Maya is illusive. Maya causes the infinite oneness to appear divided and limited. The three Gunas (Sattva, Rajas, and Tamas) attached to Maya make the soul forget that it is one with God; this delusion can only be removed by the grace of God. The aim of the spiritual path (for any religion) is to free us from the effect of Maya.

❧ Krishna says:

4.6 स एवायं मया तेऽद्य योग: प्रोक्त: पुरातन: भक्तोऽसि मे सखा चेति रहस्यं ह्योतदुत्तमम्
Though I am unborn, the Lord of all living entities, and imperishable, I appear in this world under my Yoga Shakti, the divine power.

Yoga Maya Shakti or divine power by which God comes in His human form, except that God's human body is made of sacred elements free of all defects. God's Maya Shakti or the material energy creates the universe and all beings. However, these have material defects. The world and the beings age and disintegrate.

According to the Bṛihadāraṇyak Upaniṣhad, "God incarnates in both ways—as the formless (Brahman) and as a human with a form." To say God never takes birth is in conflict with what Gita says. Does He have the power to take any form He wishes? The readers can draw their conclusion.

7.3 मनुष्याणां सहस्रेषु कश्चिद्यतति सिद्धये यततामपि सिद्धानां कश्चिन्मां वेत्ति तत्वत: Out of thousands of people, only one strives for perfection or Siddhi. Only one out of those who achieve perfection knows me in truth, in essence.

Attaining perfection and various siddhis are significant progress but not enough to know God; without devotion, love, and surrender. Verses 8.22/11.54/18.55 (Topic 1) also convey this message that dedication is necessary to know God for the followers of all paths. Various siddhis (spiritual powers) are described in scriptures and include the acquisition of supernatural power, success, healing energy, beatitude, unusual skill, etc. Briefly, three basic classes of siddhis are:

1. *EXCEPTIONAL, mind-body control; six (6) different siddhis fall in this class.*
2. *CLAIRVOYANCE, the ability to gain knowledge of remote events or people; this class includes precognition and telepathy, and 15 different siddhis are stated to be in this class.*
3. *PSYCHOKINESIS or mind-matter interaction, the ability of the mind to directly influence matter; several siddhis are listed in this class. Here are a few examples of siddhis:*

    1. *Knowledge of the sounds produced by all beings,*
    2. *Knowledge of previous and future births,*
    3. *The disappearance of the body,*
    4. *Foreknowledge of birth, harm, or death,*
    5. *Extraordinary strength,*
    6. *Knowledge of the outer universe,*
    7. *Understanding of the inner world,*
    8. *Survival without food and water,*
    9. *Ability to influence others,*
    10. *Levitation,*
    11. *Ability to create and change material elements.*

Most people who acquire such powers do not display them. Scriptures do not recommend applying these Siddhis for personal gain as the selfish use will inhibit spiritual achievement.

7.4 भूमिरापोऽनलो वायु: खं मनो बुद्धिरेव च अहङ्कार इतीयं मे भिन्ना प्रकृतिरष्टधा   Earth, water, fire, air, ether, mind, intellect, and egoism. These are eight elements of my Maya or Prakriti.

TOPIC 15 - God's Powers – Shakti

Maya Shakti creates the matter (universe) and beings. Its roots are mā (not) and yā (what is). Thus, Maya means, "it is not what it appears to be." An object may seem like material with shape and weight, but it is manifested and can be seen by human eyes because of the energy of God that binds it into a physical shape. If the energy is removed from the matter, nothing remains; hence the phrase, "it is not what you see." The following arrow chart explains the steps of creation by God:

Maya Shakti >> intellect, mind, and ego >> Panch Tanmatras or five perceptions - taste, touch, smell, sight, and sound >> Panch Mahabhoot or five gross elements - space, air, fire, water, and earth >> universe

7.5 अपरेयमितस्त्वन्यां प्रकृतिं विद्धि मे पराम् जीवभूतां महाबाहो ययेदं धार्यते जगत्
Besides the Prakriti or Maya (which is God's lower nature), God has superior power called Jeev Shakti (it is the soul energy, which is superior). Jeev Shakti supports the whole universe and puts life in everyone.

The three entities in existence are Maya, the soul, and the super soul or God. The basis of life in the world is the souls within the bodies. God's lower embodiment - Maya- creates the objects or the inert material, and His higher embodiment creates the subjects or conscious beings. The universe consists of lower and higher embodiments. The lower embodiment or Prakriti is the universe that our eyes can see; it is inert. The higher embodiment is Atma, the experiencer, the conscious principle within the beings.

7.6 एतद्योनीनि भूतानि सर्वाणीत्युपधारय अहं कृत्स्रस्य जगतः प्रभवः प्रलयस्तथा   All living beings are manifested by these two energies of mine – Maya (material energy) and Jeev Shakti (spiritual power). I am the source and dissolution of the entire universe.

The whole universe is manifested by the material and spiritual energy (Maya and Jeev Shakti). The body consists of physical elements and is inert on its own. It is powered by the Jeev Shakti that makes the body conscious.

7.7 मत्तः परतरं नान्यत्किञ्चिदस्ति धनञ्जय मयि सर्वमिदं प्रोतं सूत्रे मणिगणा इव   There is nothing equal to or higher than myself. Like the beads are strung around a string, all this is in me.

Krishna is the Supreme. For those who have faith in scriptures, this verse clears the controversy if Krishna is the Absolute Truth or there is some other formless entity higher than him. This verse states that Krishna is the ultimate Supreme Truth.

7.13 त्रिभिर्गुणमयैर्भावैरेभिः सर्वमिदं जगत् मोहितं नाभिजानाति मामेभ्यः परमव्ययम्
People in this world are deluded by the three Gunas or the material modes. As a result, they do not know me as imperishable and eternal.

With all the brilliant qualities of God, why do people not know him? Because the three modes (Gunas) veil their intellect or power to know.

7.14 दैवी ह्येषा गुणमयी मम माया दुरत्यया मामेव ये प्रपद्यन्ते मायामेतां तरन्ति ते   My divine energy Maya, consisting of three Gunas, is hard to overcome. Those who take refuge in Me alone cross over it easily. Maya, made of the three modes, can be overcome by complete surrender to God.

Surrendering to God assures his grace by which one can overcome Maya. However, only some people surrender, not all. Surrender is not possible in presence of ego.

7.24 अव्यक्तं व्यक्तिमापन्नं मन्यन्ते मामबुद्धयः परं भावमजानन्तो ममाव्ययमनुत्तमम्
Those lacking intelligence think I (Krishna) was formless earlier and have now assumed this form. They do not understand my true nature which transcends birth and death.

God is formless but can also assume human form. God is perfect and complete, and therefore, He is both formless and with a form, as mentioned in verses 4.6 in Topic 15 and 4.7 in Topic 7.

7.25 नाहं प्रकाशः सर्वस्य योगमायासमावृतः मूढोऽयं नाभिजानाति लोको मामजमव्ययम्
I am not manifest to everyone as I truly am because my Yoga Maya blocks the ability of people to see me when they are under delusion. Such people do not know Me as the unborn and imperishable.

Deluded people think of God as an ordinary human. By Yoga Maya power, God comes in the world and does His work; however, He hides His real self from us by the same power. Although God is seated in our hearts, we are not aware of His presence. Hence, even if we see the Lord in His personal form, we think He is human. We cannot recognize His divinity until He grants us the vision. Some people who only view such divinity as an ordinary person even criticize and insult the divine forms such as Jesus, Buddha, Rama, Krishna, Nanak etc.

8.20 परस्तस्मात्तु भावोऽन्योऽव्यक्तोऽव्यक्तात्सनातनः यः स सर्वेषु भूतेषु नश्यत्सु न विनश्यति   Beyond this manifest and unmanifest creation, there is yet another unmanifest realm. The latter does not cease to exist even when all other abodes do; it is the spiritual realm or world (created by God's Yoga Maya Shakti).

Krishna now discloses the mystery about the spiritual realm, which is beyond the influence of Maya. God's Yoga Maya Shakti creates the spiritual abode, which continues to exist when other worlds under Maya disappear.

9.4 मया ततमिदं सर्वं जगदव्यक्तमूर्तिना मत्स्थानि सर्वभूतानि न चाहं तेष्ववस्थितः
I pervade the entire universe in my unmanifested form. All beings exist in Me but I am not limited by them.

God's unmanifested form pervades the universe. The individual souls are created from God's superior energy called Jeev Shakti. God is far more in power and immensity than the total of Maya Shakti and Jeev Shakti. Krishna says, "My unmanifest cosmic form (avyaktha murthy) occupies the whole world, and I sustain everyone (sarva bhuthaani).

But My cosmic form does not dwell in them." This line means people cannot sustain the cosmic and unmanifest God. No visible or manifest entity is capable of visualizing and sustaining Brahm and his powers. The souls and Maya exist within the unmanifest cosmic personality of God, yet He is more than them. Just the way the waves are part of the ocean, but the sea is more than the sum of all waves.

9.5 न च मत्स्थानि भूतानि पश्य मे योगमैश्वरम् भूतभृन्न च भूतस्थो ममात्मा भूतभावन:

Nor do beings exist in Me (in reality): behold My divine Yoga (Yoga Maya Shakti), I am supporting all beings but not dwelling in them. That is My Self, the efficient cause of beings.

See comments under verse 9.6 to clarify the apparent contradiction of verses 9.4, 9.5, and 9.6.

9.6 यथाकाशस्थितो नित्यं वायु: सर्वत्रगो महान् तथा सर्वाणि भूतानि मत्स्थानीत्युपधारय

As the mighty wind blowing everywhere always rests in the sky, similarly, all beings rest always in Me.

The secret knowledge revealed here is that God is present in everyone, and all beings are based on God. The beings cannot contain unmanifest God of infinite magnitude beyond imagination. Krishna used the term mat sthāni three times in verses 9.4, 9.5, and 9.6, meaning "all living beings rest in Him." "All the living creatures though appear to be individually existing, and they are all in reality tied to or embedded in Me, although they have an individual identity." In other words, the souls do not exist independent of the super soul.

9.9 न च मां तानि कर्माणि निबध्नन्ति धनञ्जय उदासीनवदासीनमसक्तं तेषु कर्मसु   None of these (any) actions can bind Me. I remain a neutral witness and always detached from these actions.

God is a non-doer and a witness. God delegates the operations of the universe to the laws of Prakriti (Maya Shakti), which is subservient to God. God remains unaffected by the work of material energy.

9.10 मयाध्यक्षेण प्रकृति: सूयते सचराचरम् हेतुनानेन कौन्तेय जगद्विपरिवर्तते   Working under My orders, this material energy brings into being all animate (sentient) and inanimate (insentient) forms. For this reason, the world experiences the changes from creation, maintenance, and dissolution.

God is a non-doer and supervisor. Refer to related comments under verses 9.7 and 9.8 in Topic 16 on the creation.

10.1 श्रीभगवानुवाच भूय एव महाबाहो शृणु मे परमं वच: यत्तेऽहं प्रीयमाणाय वक्ष्यामि हितकाम्यया   Listen again to My divine teachings. I desire your welfare because you are My beloved friend so I will reveal them to you.

TOPIC 15 - God's Powers – Shakti

To draw Arjun's fascination, the merciful Krishna promises to explain his divine glories and unmatched attributes. Krishna explains his glories without being asked to affirm Arjun's faith in him.

10.2 न मे विदु: सुरगणा: प्रभवं न महर्षय: अहमादिर्हि देवानां महर्षीणां च सर्वश: No one knows My origin, neither the celestial gods nor the great sages. I am the source from which the great sages and the gods (celestial devatas) come.

God's origin is not known to anyone. He revealed earlier that he is beginning-less and endless. The Īshopaniṣhad states: "God cannot be known by the celestial devatās, as he existed before them." Krishna gives such mysterious knowledge to nurture the devotion of his dear friend.

10.4 and 10.5 बुद्धिर्ज्ञानमसम्मोह: क्षमा सत्यं दम: शम: सुखं दु:खं भवोऽभावो भयं चाभयमेव च अहिंसा समता तुष्टिस्तपो दानं यशोऽयश: भवन्ति भावा भूतानां मत्त एव पृथग्विधा:   Various traits in people have come from me, such as intellect, knowledge, clarity of thought, forgiveness, truthfulness, control over the senses and mind, joy, sorrow, birth, death, fear, courage, non-violence, equanimity, contentment, austerity, charity, fame, and infamy.

God is the source of all our attributes. The subtle expressions of God manifest in us positively or negatively, according to our karmas. Electricity can produce light and heat, or it can kill us depending on how we apply it.

10.7 एतां विभूतिं योगं च मम यो वेत्ति तत्वत: सोऽविकम्पेन योगेन युज्यते नात्र संशय: He who knows in truth my diverse manifestations, and Yoga Maya Shakti (divine powers) in its essence, practice unwavering yoga. Of this, there is no doubt.

Vibhuti, in this verse, is the great powers of God manifesting in the universe. The knowledge of God's glory increases our devotion and love for Him. God's splendors are revealed in the fantastic workings of infinite cosmos; Krishna says that those who have this knowledge reach Him through yoga.

🌸 *After listening to Krishna, Arjun says:*

10.12 and 10.13 अर्जुन उवाच परं ब्रह्म परं धाम पवित्रं परमं भवान् पुरुषं शाश्वतं दिव्यमादिदेवमजं विभुम् आहुस्त्वामृषय: सर्वे देवर्षिर्नारदस्तथा असितो देवलो व्यास: स्वयं चैव ब्रवीषि मे   You are the supreme God, the supreme abode, the supreme purifier, the eternal God, the primal being, the unborn, and the greatest. The great sages like Narad, Asit, Deval, and Vyas proclaimed this in the past. Now, you, too, are telling me this.

Several eminent sages say Krishna is the original creator of all beings, including Brahma and all celestial gods. Krishna is himself reconfirming what the sages said by declaring that He is the supreme cause of all creation.

10.14 सर्वमेतदृतं मन्ये यन्मां वदसि केशव न हि ते भगवन्व्यक्तिं विदुर्देवा न दानवा:   I accept everything you have told me as the truth. Neither Gods nor the demons understand your real personality.

Arjun acknowledges that what Krishna says is factual. He addresses Krishna as Bhagawan or the Supreme Lord. The superior and unique qualities of Bhagawan are strength, knowledge, beauty, fame, opulence, and detachment. No one can comprehend the full identity of Bhagawan without His grace. Not even the devatās (celestial gods) or the dānavas (demons), or the mānavas (human beings); because the finite cannot grasp the infinite.

10.15 स्वयमेवात्मनात्मानं वेत्थ त्वं पुरुषोत्तम भूतभावन भूतेश देवदेव जगत्पते   Indeed, you alone know yourself by your incredible energy (Yoga Maya Shakti). You are the Creator and Lord of all beings, the God of gods, the Lord of the universe, and God of all celestial gods.

A human possesses finite intellects, while God is infinite, and hence He is beyond the reach of their intelligence. So, no one can know God in his entirety except He Himself. Only God can reveal his glories.

❦ Krishna Says:

11.47 श्रीभगवानुवाच मया प्रसन्नेन तवार्जुनेदं रूपं परं दर्शितमात्मयोगात् तेजोमयं विश्वमनन्तमाद्यं यन्मे त्वदन्येन न दृष्टपूर्वम्   I showed you my supreme, cosmic form with my Yoga Maya power because I am pleased with you. My form is opulent, cosmic, limitless, and ancient. No one before you has seen it.

Krishna reassures Arjun it was by his grace only how Arjun was able to see the universal form. Krishna exhibited the cosmic form by the power of his Yoga Maya Shakti. Krishna also says in verse 7.25 under the current topic that he is not visible to all. Arjun was the first one to witness the universal form in the immense depth and magnitude, though few others like Jashoda (Krishna's caretaker mother who raised him from birth) also saw the limited version. By the mystery of the Yoga Maya Shakti, God can do the possible, the impossible, and the contradictory, all at the same time.

TOPIC 16

The Creation

The ancient Indian philosophy is pro-evolution, although a superficial study of a few recent Puranas may mislead one into thinking ancient Indians believed in Creation; i.e., the sudden appearance of matter and beings out of nowhere. Everything (seeds, human embryo, etc.) born follows a process and takes time to grow. The Indian religious literature explains how the universe and life comes into being, survives, and disappears. The Indian thought is not rigid but open to and welcomes any novel ideas about the source of the universe and how it grew to its present stage.

The following verses were compiled out of various chapters of Gita relating to when and how the physical universe and the beings came into existence, how it all grew, and its ultimate fate. Gita describes details about the beginning, the end, and the future of the beings in this universe. Gita also identifies the driving forces that transition the universe through different stages. The commentary is confined to the subjects outlined in Gita only, consistent with the object of this book, so we avoid discussion (and criticism) of other beliefs, individual opinions, and speculations.

❧ Krishna says:

3.10 सहयज्ञाः प्रजाः सृष्ट्वा पुरोवाच प्रजापतिः अनेन प्रसविष्यध्वमेष वोऽस्त्विष्टकामधुक्

At the beginning of the universe, Prajapati Brahma created humankind with specific duties assigned to them. He said: "you will prosper by doing Yajnas (sacrifices), which will reward you with all you wish to achieve."

For the definition of the word, Yajna, please refer to comments under verse 3.9 in Topic 3 on Karma Yoga. Briefly, Yajna, in this verse, means performing specific duties. All integral parts of nature work in harmony with the energy. For example, the sun provides light, the earth grows food, and it contains minerals. The air moves the pranas (Jeev Shakti or life force) in our body and transmits sound energy. The light, air, water, food, and minerals are God's gifts to humans. In return, the humans, being parts of the system, have duties to perform. Krishna says we must attend to and finish the prescribed assignments; that is what Yajna means relative to the implied intent of this verse.

Brahma is the most ancient progenitor appointed by God, according to Indian scriptures. He did not create the humankind with a magic wand but through the systematic growth of population resulting from the righteous union of men and women. So, "creation" here does not mean the sudden appearance of everything. This explains the apparent contradiction and misinterpretation of whether the Sanatan Dharma believes in creation or evolution. Interested readers can refer to abundant literature already available on creation vs. evolution to get more insight into diverse views.

8.17 सहस्रयुगपर्यन्तमहर्यद्ब्रह्मणो विदु: रात्रिं युगसहस्रान्तां तेऽहोरात्रविदो जना:
Brahma's one day (called Kalp) lasts a thousand cycles of Maha Yugas (the time to cover the four Yugas). His night extends for the same period. If you know this, you understand the reality of day and night.

Note the source of information on the number of years in the four Yuga combined (4,320,000 years) used here is the ancient scriptures. Few modern saints calculated from astronomical assumptions and logic a much different number; they think the four Yugas equate to 25,920 years. This book follows the figures mentioned in traditional scriptures.

Based on the ancient scriptures –

- *One Maha Yuga = Kali Yuga + Dwapar Yuga + Treta Yuga + Satya Yuga.*
- *Kali Yuga = 432,000 years, Dwāpar Yuga = 864,000 years, Tretā Yuga = 1,296,000 years. Satya Yuga = 1,728,000 years.*
- *One Mahā Yug = The four Yugas = 4,320,000 years.*
- *Brahma's day (a Kalp) = One thousand Mahā Yugas = 4.32 billion years.*
- *One Kalp = 4.32 billion years* is commonly regarded *as the life of the finite physical universe. According to Indian scriptures, there are also infinite spiritual universes. However, this book does not go into additional details.*
- *Brahma's night = 4.32 billion years.*
- *Brahma's day + night = 8.64 billion years.*
- *Brahma's life = 100 (cosmic) years, according to his time scale.*
- *Brahma's 100 years = 8.64 X 360 X 100 = 311 trillion, 40 billion human years*
- *Brahma dies after that period and God appoints another Brahma.*

8.18 अव्यक्ताद्व्यक्तय: सर्वा: प्रभवन्त्यहरागमे रात्र्यागमे प्रलीयन्ते तत्रैवाव्यक्तसञ्ज्ञके　　　At the beginning of Brahma's day, life (all beings) starts from the unmanifested source (God and his powers). At the end of the day, all beings again merge (life, as we know, ends) into their unmanifest source.

The unmanifest source referred to in this verse is Brahm or God. The universe goes through cycles of Creation, preservation, and dissolution, called sṛiṣhṭi, sthiti, and pralaya in Sanskrit.

8.19 भूतग्रामः स एवायं भूत्वा भूत्वा प्रलीयते रात्र्यागमेऽवशः पार्थ प्रभवत्यहरागमे The multitudes of beings repeatedly take birth during Brahma's day and are reabsorbed at His night. They are manifested again on Brahma's next day (cosmic day).

No beings in the physical universe are manifested during Brahma's night (i.e., 4.32 billion years), only darkness, until the dawn of the next day.

The Vedas mention four types of pralayas (dissolution):

1. *Nitya Pralaya or daily dissolution of our consciousness during sleep.*
2. *Naimmitic pralaya means the extinction of life at the end of Brahma's day.*
3. *Mahā Pralaya means the annihilation of the total universe at the end of Brahma's life when all the souls go back to God. Their gross and subtle bodies disappear, but the causal body remains. They take birth again according to their Karmas stored in their causal body.*
4. *Atyantik Pralaya - when the soul is released from cycles of birth and death after liberation.*

8.20 परस्तस्मात्तु भावोऽन्योऽव्यक्तोऽव्यक्तात्सनातनः यः स सर्वेषु भूतेषु नश्यत्सु न विनश्यति Beyond this unmanifest (and manifest) creation, there is yet another unmanifest eternal state or abode, which does not cease even when all others are destroyed.

The unmanifest universe of Brahm remains and is not destroyed when the other universe (the matter) and beings created by Maya and Jeev Shakti are destroyed. It is higher than the unmanifest portion of the universe created by Maya; that portion is not eternal.

9.7 and 9.8 सर्वभूतानि कौन्तेय प्रकृतिं यान्ति मामिकाम् कल्पक्षये पुनस्तानि कल्पादौ विसृजाम्यहम् प्रकृतिं स्वामवष्टभ्य विसृजामि पुनः पुनः भूतग्राममिमं कृत्स्नमवशं प्रकृतेर्वशात् All beings enter into My Prakriti or nature at the end of a Kalp; I send them forth or project them again at the beginning of the next Kalp. Presiding over My material energy, I, again and again, send forth this multitude of beings, helpless by the force of their nature.

This verse explains the transmigration of beings. At the end of one Kalp, all beings merge into God and become manifested again in the next Kalp. Following is the summary of how God, Prakriti, and individual souls are related.

Prakriti (or Maya) is the system that God devised to track everyone's karmas; it functions as an orchestrator of Creation and dissolution. Prakriti is inert, and under the command of God, it cannot do anything outside the rules set forth by God. God stands by as a witness and is not involved in the day-to-day "micro-management". Prakriti comprises the three

Gunas (sattva, rajas, and tamas), each of which delivers results to each individual based on their balance of karma. Each individual is under the control of Prakriti and submits to the cycles of birth and death subject to his karmas and Gunas. This "system" explains why each person ends up with a different fate. God witnesses everything "remaining behind the scene" under this "automatic operation" of Prakriti or Maya.

Regarding the transmigration process, Verse 2.28 under Topic 8 on Soul indicates the soul goes back to the source (God). The gross and subtle bodies merge back into the Maya, and the causal body remains. Upon the next appearance of the universe and beings, the causal bodies receive their subtle and gross bodies. The panch mahabhuta, the panch tanmatra, and ahankār combine with prakriti, which rests within the Supreme Lord.

10.6 महर्षय: सप्त पूर्वे चत्वारो मनवस्तथा मद्भावा मानसा जाता येषां लोक इमा: प्रजा:
The (ancient) seven sages, the four great saints before them, and the fourteen Manus, are all born from my mind. All the people in the world have descended from them.

- *God is the source of everyone and everything. Twenty-five elevated personalities originated from Brahma, who was born out of God's Yoga Maya Shakti - spiritual power. These 25 sages are known as patriarchs of living entities all over the universe.*
- *The four great saints who never got married are Sanak, Sanandan, Sanat, and Sanatan.*
- *The seven sages who were married are Angira, Atri, Pulastya, Pulaha, Kratu, and Vasishtha.*
- *The fourteen Manus were also born by Brahma. All human race is a descendent of fourteen Manus: Svayambhuva, Swarochisha, Uttam, Tamas, Raivat, Chakshusha, Vaivasvat, Savarni, Dakshasavarni, Brahmasavarni, Dharmasavarni, Rudra-Putra, Rochya, and Bhautyaka.*
- *According to scriptures, each Kalp consists of fourteen Manvantaras, and a different Manu heads each Manvantara, the period of a Manu. One Manvantara = 4.32 billion years divided by 14 = 308,571, 430 years. We are presently in the era of Vivasvat Manu, the seventh Manu, according to scriptures.*

Note, different scriptures in India may not have the identical description of Yugas and the great Rishis. The information in this book is based on scriptures prevalent in the Northern states of India.

10.8 अहं सर्वस्य प्रभवो मत्त: सर्वं प्रवर्तते इति मत्वा भजन्ते मां बुधा भावसमन्विता:   I am the source of everything; all creation emerges from Me. Realizing this, the wise is impressed and adores Me.

The devotees understand that Brahm or God is the origin, the supreme truth, and the ultimate goal. Refer to verses 7.7 under Topic 15 on God's Powers, and verse 15.15 under Topic 26 on Brahm.

TOPIC 17

Worship of Celestial Gods – Devatas

Some people worship the celestial gods (Devatas) to fulfill their worldly desires. Celestial gods are in charge of different aspects of the universe. For example, Varun is the god of water, Agni is the god of fire, and Marut is the god of winds, etc. Krishna says he is the one who gives Devatas the power to bestow the benefits to the performers of Yajna. However, such benefits are temporary, including life in heaven. When the beneficiary's pious actions are depleted, the worshipper of heavenly gods returns to the cycle of life and death. However, offering Yajna to God brings liberation and eternal life.

🌿 *Krishna says:*

7.20 कामैस्तैस्तैर्हृतज्ञाना: प्रपद्यन्तेऽन्यदेवता: तं तं नियममास्थाय प्रकृत्या नियता: स्वया
Those without wisdom surrender to other celestial gods (Devatas) swayed by a variety of desires. According to their nature, they pray those Devatas by rituals, which the Devatas like.

The people with desires for material gain follow celestial gods. The Devatas (the heavenly gods) can fulfill desires but cannot liberate them from the bondage. Devatas attained their higher spiritual level due to their pious deeds, but only have limited powers. Devatas themselves are not liberated, and they work under the jurisdiction of the supreme God. An important point Krishna reiterates often is that God can fulfill any desires the Devatas can. And, only God can liberate eligible people.

7.21 यो यो यां यां तनुं भक्त: श्रद्धयार्चितुमिच्छति तस्य तस्याचलां श्रद्धां तामेव
विदधाम्यहम्   Whichever form a faithful devotee wishes to worship, I am the one who fixes his faith in that form.

Krishna says that he is the one who imparts faith in a particular deity of the desire-driven worshippers. Only God can free the eligible. The devotees worshipping the Devatas will also evolve slowly and will eventually surrender to God.

7.22 स तया श्रद्धया युक्तस्तस्याराधनमीहते लभते च तत: कामान्मयैव विहितान्हि तान्
He who worships a particular celestial god faithfully gains the objects of his desire, but I alone arrange these benefits.

Krishna repeats the critical point he made earlier in verse 7.20. The Devatas can grant material benefits only when God sanctions it.

7.23 अन्तवत्तु फलं तेषां तद्भवत्यल्पमेधसाम् देवान्देवयजो यान्ति मद्भक्ता यान्ति मामपि   Verily, the benefits the men of low intellect receive from the Devatas are limited and perishable. The worshippers of the Devatas (the celestial gods) go to them, but My devotees come to Me.

Krishna says that one receives what he desires; worshippers of the devatas go to their abodes after death. Those who worship me come to me. However, the rewards offered by Devatas are temporary and "expire" after a certain period because the Devatas themselves are not eternal. Only God (Brahm) is timeless without the beginning and the end. Why go for a branch instead of the tree?

9.23 येऽप्यन्यदेवता भक्ता यजन्ते श्रद्धयान्विता: तेऽपि मामेव कौन्तेय यजन्त्यविधिपूर्वकम्
Even those devotees who faithfully worship other Gods also worship me, but they worship by the wrong approach.

Faith in Devatas is an indirect route to God. God is the root and should be the object of worship directly. Srimad Bhagawat says, "When we water the root of a tree, its trunk, branches, twigs, leaves, and flowers all become nourished. By worshipping the Supreme, all His parts, including the devatas, receive the prayers."

9.24 अहं हि सर्वयज्ञानां भोक्ता च प्रभुरेव च न तु मामभिजानन्ति तत्वेनातश्च्यवन्ति ते   I am the enjoyer and the only Lord who presides over all sacrifices (Yajna). Those who fail to realize My divine nature must be reborn.

God is the ultimate enjoyer of all sacrifices; those who do not know or accept this fall off the spiritual ladder and return to the mortal world. The point of this verse is repeated several times.

9.25 यान्ति देवव्रता देवान्पितॄन् यान्ति पितृव्रता: भूतानि यान्ति भूतेज्या यान्ति मद्याजिनोऽपि माम्   The worshippers of the celestial Gods take birth amongst them. The followers of the ancestors (Pitru Devata) go to the world of ancestors, and those who worship the spirits take birth among the spirits. My devotees come to Me alone.

The destination of your soul is the abode of the deity you worship, and the result is rebirth. If you worship God, the result is liberation and no rebirth. Your mind takes you where it always dwells.

TOPIC 18

Types of Worship and Offerings

Offering to God with love and devotion is a purifying act and a noble way to express our gratefulness to God for all He has provided us with to support our life. Like other faiths, Sanatan Dharm has the tradition of saying prayers to God before meals. Examples of dinner time prayers are in verses 3.13/4.24/9.27/15.14 in Topic 7. The other offerings to God besides food are Yoga Kriyas like pranayama, austerities, study of scriptures, charities, service to humanity, and wealth used for social service projects. The following verses are about the significance or prayers and offering to God as compiled from different chapters of Gita.

🌿 Krishna explains to Arjun:

3.12 इष्टान्भोगान्हि वो देवा दास्यन्ते यज्ञभाविता: तैर्दत्तानप्रदायैभ्यो यो भुङ्क्ते स्तेन एव स: The heavenly gods are pleased by the Yajna (sacrifice) and will fulfill all your desires, but the ones who only enjoy the rewards granted to them without offering them are thieves.

Offering the results of sacrifice to God brings prosperity; consuming material for our own pleasure and not offering it to God incurs sin. The word offering is frequently used in Gita. It means work done with the real mental feeling (bhavana) of offering in the spirit of devotion. For example, Prasaad is offered to God before you eat your meals, accompanied by faithfully chanting certain mantras. The divine does not come to eat the offering, nor requires anything from you in return. God owns the universe and has no needs. The spirit of offering creates devotion, purifies you, and makes you feel grateful.

3.13 यज्ञशिष्टाशिन: सन्तो मुच्यन्ते सर्वकिल्बिषै: भुञ्जते ते त्वघं पापा ये पचन्त्यात्मकारणात्
The devotees who eat food only after it is offered in sacrifice are released from sin. Those who prepare food only for their consumption and enjoyment, verily incur sin.

Be sure and offer food (Prasaad) to God before you eat to avoid sin. Similar to the practice in the Sanatan Dharm (the universal faith), the faithful followers of Christ also say their prayers to thank God and ask for blessings before meals.

Incidentally, the Sanatan Dharma has come to be known as Hinduism over the last thousand years of foreign domination of India. The word Hinduism is not mentioned in any Indian scriptures.

3.16 एवं प्रवर्तितं चक्रं नानुवर्तयतीह य: अघायुरिन्द्रियारामो मोघं पार्थ स जीवति   Some people do not own up to their share of responsibility in "the eternal cycle of sacrifices" established by Vedas. They only live for enjoying the sense objects; therefore, their lives are in vain.

Not fulfilling the responsibility of studying scriptures and performing prescribed sacrifices, and only living to enjoy sensual pleasures is a waste of precious human life.

4.25 दैवमेवापरे यज्ञं योगिन: पर्युपासते ब्रह्माग्रावपरे यज्ञं यज्ञेनैवोपजुह्वति   Some yogis worship the celestial gods with material offerings. Others offer self as a sacrifice (Atmahuti or Atmasamarpan).

Self-sacrifice or Atma Samarpan is performed by surrendering to God.

4.26 श्रोत्रादीनीन्द्रियाण्यन्ये संयमाग्निषु जुह्वति शब्दादीन्विषयानन्य इन्द्रियाग्निषु जुह्वति
Others offer hearing and other senses in sacrifice (would mean not hearing anything other than God's name). Some offer sound and other objects of the senses in the sacrifice fire (would mean maintaining silence.)

Gita suggests two diverse approaches to achieve sense control: 1. Withdrawal of the mind from the senses by will power, as in the Ashtang Yoga (the eightfold practice of Yoga), 2. Redirecting the mind away from the sensual enjoyment and material pleasures, as in Bhakti Yoga.

4.27 सर्वाणीन्द्रियकर्माणि प्राणकर्माणि चापरे आत्मसंयमयोगाग्नौ जुह्वति ज्ञानदीपिते
Others (like Jnan Yogis) enlightened by knowledge offer the sense functions and the life energy in the fire of the controlled mind.

The mind control involves advanced technique, like restraining the senses and the (five) pranas (pran, apan, udan, vayan, and saman) by the Pranayam technique. Pranayam conserves Jeev Shakti (life force) and directs it upward through the spine as part of advanced Yoga kriya. It is redirected to advance spirituality and achieve specific physical functions. Verse 2.28 in Topic 8 explains the services of each of the five pranas (life forces) in the subtle body.

TOPIC 18 - Types of Worship and Offerings

4.28 द्रव्ययज्ञास्तपोयज्ञा योगयज्ञास्तथापरे स्वाध्यायज्ञानयज्ञाश्च यतय: संशितव्रता:
Others provide the sacrifice of wealth (dravya) or severe austerities or the Ashtang Yoga practice (the eight-fold path of yogic practices), they study the scriptures or cultivating knowledge while observing strict vows.

There are numerous different sacrifices that purify the senses and mind and elevate the Soul when done faithfully as service to God.

4.29 - 4.30 अपाने जुह्वति प्राणं प्राणेऽपानं तथापरे प्राणापानगती रुद्ध्वा प्राणायामपरायणा: अपरे नियताहारा: प्राणान्प्राणेषु जुह्वति सर्वेऽप्येते यज्ञविदो यज्ञक्षपितकल्मषा:   Others offer as sacrifice the outgoing breath in the incoming breath, while some offer the incoming breath into the outgoing breath. Some strenuously practice pranayama and confine the incoming and outgoing breaths to regulate the life-energy. Yet others restrict food and offer the breath into the life-energy as a sacrifice. All these sacrifices clean the impurities.

Summary of sacrifices suggested in above verses 4.25 through 4.29:

1. Worship of the celestial gods, 2. The offering of the self (Atmahuti or Atmasamarpan), 3. The offering of hearing and other senses 4. The offering of sound and other objects of senses, 5. The offering of the functions of the senses and pran (life energy), 6. The offering of wealth (dravya yagna), 7. The offering of severe austerities, 8. The Offering the practice of the eight-fold path (Ashtang Yoga), 9. The study of scriptures and cultivation of knowledge, 10. Performance of Pranayam (outgoing and incoming breath control) to regulate the pran (life energy), 13. Restricting food intake.

Pranayam technique calls for steps, such as the Purak (breathe in), Rechak (breathe out), Antar Kumbhak (hold the breath in), and Bahya Kumbhak (hold the breath out). Some devotees offer as sacrifice the incoming breath of prana in the outgoing breath of apana, and the outgoing breath of apana in the incoming breath of prana, thus rendering breath unnecessary, by diligent practice of pranayama. Various interpretations of this verse exist, some are clearer than others. The explanation of Yogananda Paramhansa is among the best, as covered in Topic 13.

4.31 यज्ञशिष्टामृतभुजो यान्ति ब्रह्म सनातनम् नायं लोकोऽस्त्ययज्ञस्य कुतोऽन्य: कुरुसत्तम
Those who eat the remnants (prasaad) of the sacrifice, which are like nectar, go to the eternal Brahm. This world is not for those who do not perform the sacrifice, nor can they be happy in the other world.

Not performing one or more of the listed sacrifices keep the Soul bound in Maya for infinite lifetimes. The main point is we should first do Yajna and take only the remnants. The meaning of yajna is broader than the fire sacrifice; the word is used to describe other spiritual processes: "worship," "devotion," "prayer," "offering," "oblation," "sacrifice."

TOPIC 18 - Types of Worship and Offerings

For example, the sacrifice of food is a simple discipline of offering food with a prayer as in Verse 4.24, and then, sharing the remnants - prasaad.

Uddhav, a great devotee, says to Krishna in Srimad Bhagavat, "I will only eat, smell, wear, live in, and talk about objects that have first been offered to you. By taking the remnants as your blessing, I will easily conquer Maya."

4.32 एवं बहुविधा यज्ञा वितता ब्रह्मणो मुखे कर्मजान्विद्धि तान्सर्वानेवं ज्ञात्वा विमोक्ष्यसे
The Vedas describe different kinds of sacrifices, originating from different types of work; this understanding severs the bondage.

Everyone should do sacrifice as suitable to their nature and qualifications.

7.15 न मां दुष्कृतिनो मूढाः प्रपद्यन्ते नराधमाः माययापहृतज्ञाना आसुरं भावमाश्रिताः: Four kinds of people do not surrender unto God: 1. the ignorant, 2. The lazy who follow their lower nature, 3. Deluded and/or confused, 4. Those with demoniac quality (duṣhkṛitinaḥ or the evildoers).

Who does not surrender to God? Those who: 1. lack knowledge, 2. are too lazy to strive for spirituality, 3. are opposed to the idea of surrendering to anyone, and 4. hate God and His devotees. Scriptures say, "Laziness is a big enemy, and it resides in our body itself. Work is a good friend of humans, which never leads to downfall."

7.16 चतुर्विधा भजन्ते मां जनाः सुकृतिनोऽर्जुन आर्तो जिज्ञासुरर्थार्थी ज्ञानी च भरतर्षभ Four types of virtuous people worship Me: 1. the distressed (aarta) - suffering from miseries, 2. the seekers of knowledge (Jignashu - curiosity drives them to God), 3. seekers of wealth. Artharthi also means desirous of achieving life's purpose. 4. those situated in knowledge (Jnani).

"Aarta" or the distressed may suffer from a health condition, monetary problems, anxiety, or rejection by society. "Jignyaasu" or the curious seek knowledge in various ways. "Arthaarthee" is attracted to worldly possessions and goals. "Jnani" or self-realized always thinks and sees God without any motives.

7.17 तेषां ज्ञानी नित्ययुक्त एकभक्तिर्विशिष्यते प्रियो हि ज्ञानिनोऽत्यर्थमहं स च मम प्रियः: Among the four categories, I consider them to be the highest, who worship God with knowledge (Jnani) and those exclusively devoted to God. I am dear to them, and they are precious to Me.

God likes the Jnani, who is devoted, as the best among the four types of followers. This verse emphasizes devotion to reach God based on knowledge. The Jnani pursues Karma Yoga for purification of the mind and meditation for the focus of the mind.

7.18 उदारा: सर्व एवैते ज्ञानी त्वात्मैव मे मतम् आस्थित: स हि युक्तात्मा मामेवानुत्तमां गतिम्

All these who are devoted to Me are indeed noble, but I regard the man of knowledge (Jnani) as Myself. With a steadfast mind, he is established in Me alone as the ultimate goal.

God praises Jnani with His mind and intellect merged with God as the ultimate goal.

TOPIC 19

Remembering God at Death

This topic discusses several destinations for the soul after death upon leaving the body. The right path and the state of mind at the end decide the destiny for the soul: liberation or continued cycle of birth and death. Unless liberated, the soul keeps taking birth in a new body, in a unique environment, as driven by the accrued karma. The memory gets erased, so the soul does not remember the number of rebirths and the misery it suffered. No wonder we continue to seek pleasures like business as usual, even after knowing the risk and danger of not turning the mind to God. The general tendency is to wait until the old age knocks at the door before we follow Krishna's messages repeated again and again. His instruction for single-pointed devotion to God is not just for Arjun but for everyone.

8.5 अन्तकाले च मामेव स्मरन्मुक्त्वा कलेवरम् य: प्रयाति स मद्भावं याति नास्त्यत्र संशय: Whoever remembers Me at the end will come to me, no doubt.

The state of consciousness determines the next birth at the time of death. If one is absorbed in God at the end, one attains Him and becomes God-like. The pure-hearted one, blessed with the grace of God, thinks of God always, including at the time of death.

8.6 यं यं वापि स्मरन्भावं त्यजत्यन्ते कलेवरम् तं तमेवैति कौन्तेय सदा तद्भावभावित:
Whatever one remembers at the time of passing away, one reaches that state, being always engrossed in such thoughts.

It is quite likely the thoughts at the time of death will be the same or similar to whatever the mind contemplated during the lifetime. To be able to think of God in those final moments, God must be made the priority throughout life.

8.12 सर्वद्वाराणि संयम्य मनो हृदि निरुध्य च मूर्ध्न्याधायात्मन: प्राणमास्थितो योगधारणाम्
One should be steady in yogic concentration by 1. restraining all gates of the body, 2. fixing the mind on the heart, 3. fixing the life-breath in the head.

114

The senses are the mind's conduit to the worldly thoughts. So, the stream of thoughts should be blocked by restraining the sense organs (the nine gates). The senses dwell on the objects of pleasure and create attachment, thus, the thoughts arise in the mind. Again, it is not easy to stop the senses from being attracted to pleasures without the rigorous practice of diverting the mind to God. The nine gates mentioned in this verse are two ears, two nostrils, two eyes, mouth, anus, and genital.

8.13 ओमित्येकाक्षरं ब्रह्म व्याहरन्मामनुस्मरन् य: प्रयाति त्यजन्देहं स याति परमां गतिम्
He who thus engages in the yoga practice (as described in verse 8.12), remembers Me at death, and chants the syllable Om; he will attain the supreme goal.

Om chanting synchronized with the breathing process is one of the paths to God. The chanting of Om produces vibrations, makes the body steady, and focuses the mind. Om is also known as 1. the word of God, 2. Anahat Nad - the sound of the universe which pervades creation, 3. the original sound, 4. The maha vakya (the significant sound vibration), 5. the Beej Mantra (attached to the beginning of many Vedic mantras), 6. the Pranav sound (the object of meditation).

8.23, 8.24, 8.25 & 8.26 यत्र काले त्वनावृत्तिमावृत्तिं चैव योगिन: प्रयाता यान्ति तं कालं वक्ष्यामि भरतर्षभ अग्निर्ज्योतिरह: शुक्ल: षण्मासा उत्तरायणम् तत्र प्रयाता गच्छन्ति ब्रह्म ब्रह्मविदो जना: धूमो रात्रिस्तथा कृष्ण: षण्मासा दक्षिणायनम् तत्र चान्द्रमसं ज्योतिर्योगी प्राप्य निवर्तते शुक्लकृष्णे गती ह्येते जगत: शाश्वते मते एकया यात्यनावृत्तिमन्ययावर्तते पुन: नैते सृती पार्थ जानन्योगी मुह्यति कश्चन तस्मात्सर्वेषु कालेषु योगयुक्तो भवार्जुन I will now explain to you the various paths the Soul takes after passing away from the body. One of the routes liberates the Soul, while the other leads to rebirth. When yogis die during the six months of the sun's northern travel, the bright half of the month, and the bright half of the day, they attain Brahm or the highest abode. When the Yogis die during the six months of the sun's southern course, the dark half of the month and in the night, they go to the lunar space (what we call heaven), and they are reborn as humans after many years of pleasure in heaven.

The paths the Soul takes upon the death of the body leads the Soul to either liberation or rebirth. To summarize, when the Soul of a God-focused yogi takes the path of light after death, it attains liberation. If it takes the way of darkness after the end, the Soul goes to heaven, but after some time, it will be reborn. The light equates to "knowledge" and "Brahm consciousness". Darkness relates to ignorance, worldly awareness, and body consciousness. There are many different interpretations of this verse by various spiritual personalities; again, the one by Yogananda Paramhansa makes the most sense.

According to Yogananda, these verses suggest deeply symbolic references to the discipline of yoga. The upward or northern way of light means the opening of the third eye, the activation of the chakras, and the rise of life force (Jeev Shakti) through the chakras to the highest chakra (Sahasra chakra on the center of the head). The Sahasra chakra is the abode of the "sun" of absolute consciousness and a gate to the liberation of the yogi. The verses also describe the opposite descension (southward) of life force to body consciousness or rebirth. According to Verse 24, the yogi must follow the path of fire or light or life energy (some call it the kundalini shakti) to attain liberation. The devotee must control the life force (prana) as the first step to liberation. For most people, the course of prana is downward from the brains. "Light" in verse 24 refers to the spiritual eye in the forehead and the "six months" are the six chakras or spinal centers.

8.27 नैते सृती पार्थ जानन्योगी मुह्यति कश्चन तस्मात्सर्वेषु कालेषु योगयुक्तो भवार्जुन   With the knowledge (jnana) of these two paths, a Yogi is not deluded. Therefore, be situated in yoga at all times.

Knowing the two tracks, the real yogis do not get attracted to desires and diversions. Yogis choose devotion to God and not to sense pleasures, so they strive to get on the bright path. Those deluded by the Maya go for material desires, thus charting the path of darkness. Krishna tells Arjun to know the two ways and "be yogi at all times" (sarveshu kaleshu yoga yukto bhav). What this implies for ordinary people is that it is OK to enjoy life, BUT do not become a slave to pleasure-focused activities. See related comments under verse 6.6 in Topic 6 on Senses, Desires, and Lust.

8.28 वेदेषु यज्ञेषु तप:सु चैव दानेषु यत्पुण्यफलं प्रदिष्टम् अत्येति तत्सर्वमिदं विदित्वा योगी परं स्थानमुपैति चाद्यम्   The yogis who know this secret (about the bright and dark paths) gain merits more than the study of Vedas, and the performance of sacrifices (yajna), austerities (tapa), and charities (daan). Such yogis attain the supreme abode of God.

The jnanis who have a deep understanding of the path of light and the path of dark, reach their goal faster than by doing austerities (tapascharyas). Because of this understanding, Krishna says the jnanis receive the benefits beyond those resulting from other processes.

14.14 यदा सत्वे प्रवृद्धे तु प्रलयं याति देहभृत् तदोत्तमविदां लोकानमलान्प्रतिपद्यते   When the death occurs during the Satva Guna (the righteous mode), then, the self goes to the pure abodes of the learned.

Atma or the Soul goes to higher abodes (swarg) when death occurs during the predominance of the Sattva Guna. When the subtle body develops sattvic (sacred or pure) thoughts, it goes to higher and purer abodes after death.

14.15 रजसि प्रलयं गत्वा कर्मसङ्गिषु जायते तथा प्रलीनस्तमसि मूढयोनिषु जायते   When one dies during the Rajas mode (mode of passion), his Soul is born among those who are attached to work and pleasures. When the death occurs during the Tamas mode (darkness), the self is born in Mudh Yoni (lower birth in uneducated or violent families).

The result of a death in Rajo Guna is the soul is reborn among those attached to work aimed to fulfill materialistic and sensual desires.

When one dies in the predominance of Tamo Guna, the Soul is reborn, as described in this verse, in "mudh yoni" among the ignorant and deluded people.

TOPIC 20

God's Abode

According to Gita, the manifest and unmanifest (visible and invisible) part of the non-eternal universe is one-fourth of the entire creation, containing heavenly abodes, the planet earth, and the regions of hell. All these are temporary; they come and go. The souls that have not reached the state of spiritual perfection, including the celestial gods, live there and undergo birth and death. Beyond this physical universe is the eternal divine abode, brighter than a million suns (Surya Koti Samaprabham); it comprises most of the universe. A Rigveda hymn called the Purush Suktam says the mortal universe is only one part of creation, the other three parts are the eternal Abode of God. Note that it is symbolic to quantify the universe because, in reality, you cannot quantify infinity. The eternal universe contains divine abodes of God. Upon reaching the eternal abode after liberation, one does not return to this material world again unless chosen by God to carry out a specific mission on the earth.

Brahm and its abode are the unmanifested universe, not visible to human eyes or space microscopes. It is the ultimate destination for all souls. It is the abode of all names of Brahm in different faiths and religions. Brahm is 'One'. Those who understand this truth have transcended sectarianism.

The divine abode has no beginning or end; it remains unscathed when other mortal worlds and beings created by Maya and Jeev Shakti are destroyed, including the heavenly abodes (swarg lokas) of the celestial gods and Brahma.

8.16 आब्रह्मभुवनाल्लोकाः पुनरावर्तिनोऽर्जुन मामुपेत्य तु कौन्तेय पुनर्जन्म न विद्यते   In all different material worlds (where the celestial gods or Devatas live), including and up to Brahma's abode (what are known as Swarg or heavens), everyone including all Devatas is subject to rebirth. However, attaining the supreme home (of God), there is no rebirth.

Again, the celestial gods and Brahma encounter death and rebirth, like humans. However, there are no more births after attaining God. Some saints and great prophets do come back to our world, after liberation, for the spiritual welfare of humankind, call it individual assignments from God. The latter explains how some elevated saints are born with the siddhis that are different than the siddhis acquired by perfecting the yoga processes.

Vedic literature describes seven planes (called Narak) that are lower than the earth, where serpents and demons live - tal, atal, vital, sutal, talātal, rasātal, and pātāl. Seven planes that are higher than earth are called Swarg: bhūh, bhuvah, swah, mahah, janah, tapah, and satyah.

8.20 परस्तस्मात्तु भावोऽन्योऽव्यक्तोऽव्यक्तात्सनातन: य: स सर्वेषु भूतेषु नश्यत्सु न विनश्यति
Beyond this unmanifest (and manifest) creation, there is yet another unmanifest eternal (state or abode), which does not cease even when all others are destroyed.

Krishna repeats his message here. Brahm remains when other worlds consisting of the created matter and beings are destroyed, including the swarg lokas. The other unmanifested eternal is different than the unmanifested portion of the non-eternal universe, the home of the Devatas and Siddhas, etc.

8.21 अव्यक्तोऽक्षर इत्युक्तस्तमाहु: परमां गतिम् यं प्राप्य न निवर्तन्ते तद्धाम परमं मम   That unmanifest dimension is My supreme abode (dhama) and is the goal. Upon reaching it, one never returns to this mortal world.

As previously discussed, the unmanifested universe is the abode of Brahm. It is the ultimate destination for all souls. God is known and worshipped by many names in different faiths and religions. However, He is 'One', and the spiritual kingdom is His abode.

☙ Here, Arjun acknowledges to Krishna:

11.38 त्वमादिदेव: पुरुष: पुराण-स्त्वमस्य विश्वस्य परं निधानम् वेत्तासि वेद्यं च परं च धाम त्वया ततं विश्वमनन्तरूप   You are the oldest person, and the universe is your abode. You are the knower, the knowable, and the supreme abode. O' One with Infinite forms (Viswam Anant Rupam), you pervade the entire universe.

Arjun's prayer includes the divine attributes of Krishna. Arjun acknowledges that he now understands the origin and mission of Krishna. God occupies the entire universe. Refer to related verses 9.6 in Topic 15 on God's Powers, 11.12/11.24 in Topic 22 on Universal Form regarding the immensity and opulence of the spiritual world and God.

☙ Krishna says:

15.6 न तद्भासयते सूर्यो न शशाङ्को न पावक: यद्गत्वा न निवर्तन्ते तद्धाम परमं मम
Neither the sun nor the moon, nor the fire can illumine the (naturally self-luminous) Supreme Abode of mine.

Divine Abode is 1. made from spiritual energy, Yoga Maya Shakti, 2. transcendental to the dualities and defects of Maya (material nature), 3. perfect in every way, 4. Sat-Chit-Anand – full of eternality, knowledge, and bliss, 5. consists of a spiritual sky called Paravyom.

Material World is made up of Maya Shakti, the material energy. It is temporary and perishable.

TOPIC 21

Caste System and Inherent Duties

Krishna says society was classified originally in four groups based on their roles, merits, and aptitudes: Brahmin (priests), Kshatriya (warriors), Vaishya (business), and Shudra (labor). Over the years, the structure of society and the intent of the classifications changed drastically. The higher castes, the ones with power to decide, forced the caste system to degenerate into a hereditary-based system, so the descendants of Brahmins were called Brahmins, and so forth. As an unfortunate result, immense social injustice prevailed as the lower class lost the opportunity to rise to a higher status because their descendants were categorized as lower caste. For those born to "lower caste" parents, there was no way for them to get out of this designation. The government is intervening to ensure justice prevails among all classes by enforcing equal rights to all. Presented below are all the Gita verses relating to the caste system.

❦ Krishna says:

4.13 चातुर्वर्ण्यं मया सृष्टं गुणकर्मविभागशः तस्य कर्तारमपि मां विद्ध्यकर्तारमव्ययम्

I created the four castes "according to people's activities and merits". I am the impartial creator of these categories.

Note Krishna makes it abundantly clear the castes were determined by activities and merits, he does not say the castes were designated hereditarily.

Four classifications of society are based on the aptitudes and activities of people. 1. Brahmins teach and worship, and they are predominantly in the mode of goodness (Sattva), 2. Kshatriyas protect and defend citizens from the enemy attacks, and they are mostly in the way of passion (Rajas) mixed with some good, 3. Vaishyas doing commerce, trade, and agriculture are primarily in the mode of passion with some ignorance, 4. Shudras do manual work and are generally in the mode of ignorance.

18.41 ब्राह्मणक्षत्रियविशां शूद्राणां च परन्तप कर्माणि प्रविभक्तानि स्वभावप्रभवैर्गुणै:   The duties of the Brahmins, Kshatriyas, Vaishyas, and Shudras—are distributed according to their nature and merits (the Gunas).

The four classes were NOT intended to be by birth. Varna is the right word for the classes, the word "caste" was introduced by the British.

Originally, the society was organized by four castes according to their role, nature, and merits. No one was considered low or high. Over time, the basis of Varnas changed from consideration to one's nature and then to one's birth. Brahmin's decedents started calling themselves brahmins, no matter whether they had the right qualities. The same situation transpired with the kshatriya, vaishya, and shudra classes. The higher rank had the power to rule, and the lower caste lived as subservient. For example, the famous Dr. Ambedkar was born in a Shudra family, so he was treated as a lower caste all his life, although he had the qualities and knowledge of a Brahmin. On the other extreme, there are Brahmins who live undisciplined life but are still treated as Brahmins because their parents belong to this caste.

18.42 शमो दमस्तप: शौचं क्षान्तिरार्जवमेव च ज्ञानं विज्ञानमास्तिक्यं ब्रह्मकर्म स्वभावजम्
Tranquility, restraint, austerity, purity, patience, integrity, knowledge, wisdom, and faith; these are the intrinsic qualities of work done by the Brahmins.

Brahmins are believed to be predominantly sattvic (in the mode of goodness). However, this is no longer always true as some brahmins have rajasic and tamasic tendencies. According to Krishna's definition, such brahmins would not be considered Sattvic.

18.43 शौर्यं तेजो धृतिर्दाक्ष्यं युद्धे चाप्यपलायनम् दानमीश्वरभावश्च क्षात्रं कर्म स्वभावजम्
Valor, strength, courage, skill in weaponry, resolve never to retreat from battle, large-heartedness in charity, and leadership abilities; these are the natural qualities of Kshatriyas (warriors).

Kshatriyas are believed to be predominantly rajasic (in the mode of passion). They are skilled in the use of defensive and offensive weapons. to

18.44 कृषिगौरक्ष्यवाणिज्यं वैश्यकर्म स्वभावजम् परिचर्यात्मकं कर्म शूद्रस्यापि स्वभावजम्
Agriculture, farming, and trading are the original works for those with the qualities of Vaishyas (businessmen); whereas, the job done with their hands as service to higher castes is the essential duty for those with the traits of Shudras (labor workers).

Vaishyas are of the rajasic nature predominantly, mixed with some tamo guna (the mode of darkness). Shudras are tamasik with some rajasic tendencies; again, as defined originally.

18.45 स्वे स्वे कर्मण्यभिरत: संसिद्धिं लभते नर: कर्मनिरत: सिद्धिं यथा विन्दति तच्छृणु
Each man, devoted to his duty, attains perfection. Hear now how he attains perfection while doing his duty.

When a person does his duties righteously according to his innate qualities (Swadharma), that purifies his heart, and he goes to heaven.

18.46 यत: प्रवृत्तिर्भूतानां येन सर्वमिदं ततम् स्वकर्मणा तमभ्यर्च्य सिद्धिं विन्दति मानव:
He from whom all the beings have evolved and who pervades the entire space in the universe is worthy of worship of everyone. When one worships God as his duty, the human attains perfection.

If we discharge our natural duty (swadharma) based on competence with no expectation of gain, we will purify ourselves.

18.47 श्रेयान्स्वधर्मो विगुण: परधर्मात्स्वनुष्ठितात् भावनियतं कर्म कुर्वन्नाप्नोति किल्बिषम्
It is better to do one's dharma, although it may be lacking merits than to do another's dharma, even though perfectly.

Here in this verse, the intended meaning of the word dharma is the prescribed duty or inherent duty. By performing one's ordained duties, a person does not incur sin. Doing the allotted work within the limits of your natural skills will make you comfortable, happy, and sinless. A carpenter is happy with his work and will not enjoy plumbing. Srimad Bhagavat says, "We must keep doing our prescribed occupational duties". A compelling Mahabharat story will make the message of this verse succinct. A sannyasi who had acquired spiritual powers from years of austerity and meditation was sitting under a tree, and a crow's droppings fell on him. He glared at the crow, and the crow died instantly. Suddenly, the sannyasi became aware of his newly acquired siddhi (power) and became egotistical. Once, he stopped to beg for food at a house. The lady of the house asked him to wait as she was in the middle of tending her ill husband. The monk looked at the woman angrily. The woman told him not to look at her with anger and said she was not a crow he could burn quickly. The monk was amazed and asked her how she knew about the incident. The woman said she had not done any severe austerity; all she does is her work with dedication. Perhaps that is how she could read his mind. She recommended him to see a butcher who would teach him dharma. The sannyasi was initially hesitant to see the lowest caste butcher but decided to go ahead out of cynical curiosity. The butcher explained to Sannyasi that we all have our respective swadharma, based upon our past karmas and skills. Nevertheless, if we perform our essential duty selflessly, whether it is viewed as good or bad, that will remove the layers of dirt from our mind and inspire devotion to God. Thus, no work is low, and doing our work as worship, the soul will gradually rise from gross to divine consciousness. This story is known as the Vyadha Gita of the Mahabharat.

18.48 सहजंकर्मकौन्तेयसदोषमपिनत्यजेत्सर्वारम्भाहिदोषेणधूमेनाग्निरिवावृता: One should not abandon duties inherent in one's nature, even if one sees defects in them. All types of work have some evil or negative aspect to it just as all types of fire is covered with smoke.

Perform your essential duties even though they may be viewed lowly. The practical aspect of this verse is you are more likely to be successful in doing work that suits your skills and aptitude.

TOPIC 21 - Caste System and Inherent Duties

TOPIC 22

Cosmic Form – Universal Darshan

Arjun asks Krishna to show him his original form. Krishna grants Arjun's wish and shows him a full cosmic form as the almighty God. The cosmic form dazzled Arjun with the splendor of a thousand suns, and everything and everyone seemed to disappear in God. He sees Krishna as Vishnu with his weapons, the mace and the discus, and wearing a crown. As the vision becomes more intense, Arjun feels afraid of the immensity of the form and its terrifying features. He sees the light of God become a fire that burns and consumes everything as if it is the end of time. Arjun sees the future and watches all the warriors on the battlefield rush into the mouth of the cosmic God. This was an indirect message from Krishna that he had already done Arjun's work and all Arjun has to do is act as Krishna's instrument (Nimita matra) without fear, ego, and a false sense of ownership.

Arjun is horrified and frightened as the exceptional form of God bears no resemblance to Krishna. He fearfully inquires, "Who are you?" Krishna's reply to this question is in verse 11.32, "I am Kaal (kaalasmi ahm)." Kaal is time but here it means death as the time consumes everything. The atom bomb blast, world wars, and natural calamities, pandemics such as plague, flu and Corona Virus – these are examples of the Kaal as Krishna meant. Arjun praises Krishna and requests him to restore his original form as he could not stand the fearful cosmic vision any longer. Krishna returns to his human form and tells Arjun that no one before has seen the complete universal form which one can see only by pure devotion.

❦ Arjun says:

11.1 अर्जुन उवाच मदनुग्रहाय परमं गुह्यमध्यात्मसञ्ज्ञितम् यत्वयोक्तं वचस्तेन मोहोऽयं विगतो मम   I heard the supreme confidential spiritual knowledge which you revealed out of compassion for me. Now my illusion is gone.

Arjun's illusion has disappeared, and he surrenders. Arjun is now accepting Krishna as the Supreme Being. He begins by thanking Krishna for his mercy for teaching him the precious knowledge.

11.2 भवाप्ययौ हि भूतानां श्रुतौ विस्तरशो मया त्वत्त: कमलपत्राक्ष माहात्म्यमपि चाव्ययम्
You described to me in detail the beginning and dissolution of beings. You also told me about your eternal majesty.

Arjun acknowledges what he heard so far.

11.3 एवमेतद्यथात्थ त्वमात्मानं परमेश्वर द्रष्टुमिच्छामि ते रूपमैश्वरं पुरुषोत्तम   Now, I wish to see your Divine form, as you have described yourself.

11.4 मन्यसे यदि तच्छक्यं मया द्रष्टुमिति प्रभो योगेश्वर ततो मे त्वं दर्शयात्मानमव्ययम्
Kindly show me that imperishable form, if you think I will be able to see it.

Arjun expresses complete faith in Krishna's personal form, and yet, he wants to see the cosmic form. Arjun knows that the universal form is too bright for human eyes and that he needs Krishna's grace to be able to withstand the splendor.

🌸 Krishna says:

11.5 श्रीभगवानुवाच पश्य मे पार्थ रूपाणि शतशोऽथ सहस्रश: नानाविधानि दिव्यानि नानावर्णाकृतीनि च   Behold my hundreds and thousands of beautiful forms of various shapes, sizes, and colors.

Krishna displays the indescribable and immense cosmic form.

11.6 पश्यादित्यान्वसून् रुद्रानश्विनौ मरुतस्तथा बहून्यदृष्टपूर्वाणि पश्याश्चर्याणि भारत
Behold in me the Adityas, the Vasus, the Rudras, the two Asvins, and the Maruts. See many wonderful forms never seen before.

Krishna shows Arjun the marvelous universal form containing heavenly deities as follows:

Twelve Adityas - Aditi, the wife of Kashyap Rishi, had twelve sons known as Adityas or sun gods

Eight Vasus – The eight vasus are wealth givers and represent the elements of nature

Eleven Rudras – These are gods of roaring form

Two Asvini Kumars – These are twin brothers and physicians of gods

The forty-nine Maruts – Maruts are wind Gods

Srimad Bhagavatam includes the names of all Aditya, Vasus, Rudras and Maruts.

11.7 इहैकस्थं जगत्कृत्स्नं पश्याद्य सचराचरम् मम देहे गुडाकेश यच्चान्यद्द्रष्टुमिच्छसि   See the entire universe with movable and immovable objects united here in My body, and anything else you like to see.

Every entity of the universe is present in the mind-boggling universal form. Also, past and future events.

TOPIC 22 – Cosmic Form – Universal Darshan

11.8 न तु मां शक्यसे द्रष्टमनेनैव स्वचक्षुषा दिव्यं ददामि ते चक्षु: पश्य मे योगमैश्वरम् You cannot see the divine vision with the physical eyes. Therefore, I grant you divine vision. Now see my Majestic opulence.

God grants the divine vision to Arjun so he can withstand the brightness of the form. The light emanating from the divinities who descend for a mission from God is so intense it can blind the human eye. God's opulence is described in the Vedic mantras as exceeding the light from a million suns.

Sanjay says to Dhritrashtra, the blind king and father of the Kauravas:

11.9 सञ्जय उवाच एवमुक्त्वा ततो राजन्महायोगेश्वरो हरि: दर्शयामास पार्थाय परमं रूपमैश्वरम् O' King, then, the great Lord of Yoga, Hari, displayed his divine and opulent form to Arjun.

Verse 11.4 refers to Krishna as Yogeshwar; this verse describes Krishna as a Maha Yogeshwar. Sanjay was blessed with the divine eyes by Vyas so he could see remotely, from where he was, everything "live" as happening in the Mahabharata battlefield, including the Universal form of Krishna. According to scriptures, a few other people like Jashoda, Krishna's mother, also saw the divine form. However, no one saw it in its entirety, as Arjun did.

11.10 and 11.11 अनेकवक्त्रनयनमनेकाद्भुतदर्शनम् अनेकदिव्याभरणं दिव्यानेकोद्यतायुधम् दिव्यमाल्याम्बरधरं दिव्यगन्धानुलेपनम् सर्वाश्चर्यमयं देवमनन्तं विश्वतोमुखम् The cosmic form has many faces and eyes, wearing many heavenly ornaments and displaying many weapons. The form is wearing beautiful garlands and clothing, fragrant with heavenly perfumes, showing wonders, luminous, infinite, and having faces in all directions.

Sanjay describes the phenomenal details of the Universal Form as it was being displayed to Arjun on the battlefield. To Sanjay, the entire creation seemed like the body of the cosmic form containing countless faces, eyes, mouths, shapes, colors, and styles.

11.12 दिवि सूर्यसहस्रस्य भवेद्युगपदुत्थिता यदि भा: सदृशी सा स्याद्भासस्तस्य महात्मन: A thousand suns shining together in the sky would not match the intensity of light from the marvelous cosmic form.

God's light is unlimited and impossible to quantify, compared to any bright stars. God's splendor has been described in a Sanskrit prayer as suryakoti samaprabh - like a million suns, in human terms, as it is impossible to imagine and relate God's eternal effulgence called akhand jyoti in Sanskrit.

11.13 तत्रैकस्थं जगत्कृत्स्नं प्रविभक्तमनेकधा अपश्यद्देवदेवस्य शरीरे पाण्डवस्तदा There, Arjun can see the totality of the entire universe established in one place, in the body of the God of gods (Devdevasya).

Amazingly, Arjun saw the entire creation of infinite universes with the galaxies and planets in a mere fraction of the body of Krishna. The Cosmic vision is one example of the power of Krishna's Yoga Maya Shakti or divine power.

11.14 तत: स विस्मयाविष्टो हृष्टरोमा धनञ्जय: प्रणम्य शिरसा देवं कृताञ्जलिरभाषत   Then, Arjun, shocked by the glorious form, with his hair rising straight up, lowers his head with hands folded before the Lord and expresses his reaction (as detailed in Verse 17 and after). He is baffled with wonder.

Arjun developed a deep sense of devotion by seeing the cosmic form. The sincere devotion (bhakti) is characterized by eight physical symptoms - becoming stupefied, perspiring, hair raised, voice choking, shaking, ashen complexion, tears, and fainting.

🦋 *Arjun says:*

11.15 अर्जुन उवाच पश्यामि देवांस्तव देव देहे सर्वांस्तथा भूतविशेषसङ्घान् ब्रह्माणमीशं कमलासनस्थ- मृषींश्च सर्वानुरगांश्च दिव्यान्   I see in your body all the gods and different beings; Lord Brahma resting on the lotus flower. I see Lord Shiva, all saints, and the divine serpents.

Arjun saw many deities, sages, and divine serpents in the universal form.

11.16 अनेकबाहूदरवक्त्रनेत्रं पश्यामि त्वां सर्वतोऽनन्तरूपम् नान्तं न मध्यं न पुनस्तवादिं पश्यामि विश्वेश्वर विश्वरूप   I see many hands, bellies, mouths, and eyes, and infinite forms in every direction. Your shape is the entire universe itself. I am unable to identify your end or the middle or the beginning.

Arjun saw the universal form of God spread wide to occupy the whole universe. What Arjun saw implies that the world is nothing but God's manifestation and subservient to God. Arjun could not identify the beginning and the end, due to the infinite size of the cosmic form.

11.17 किरीटिनं गदिनं चक्रिणं च तेजोराशिं सर्वतो दीप्तिमन्तम् पश्यामि त्वां दुर्निरीक्ष्यं समन्ताद् दीप्तानलार्कद्युतिमप्रमेयम्   I see you decorated with a crown and armed with the club and disc, with your splendor shining everywhere in the whole universe. It is hard to see you in the middle of a massive fire of your effulgence blazing everywhere.

What Arjun saw matches the description of Lord Vishnu, whose effulgence overwhelms Arjun. Human eyes can go blind by the unimaginably intense bright light.

11.18 त्वमक्षरं परमं वेदितव्यं त्वमस्य विश्वस्य परं निधानम् त्वमव्यय: शाश्वतधर्मगोप्ता सनातनस्त्वं पुरुषो मतो मे   I see you as the Supreme Being, the ultimate truth, and the support of the whole universe. You are the sole protector of the sanātan dharma (the eternal religion); and the everlasting Supreme God.

Arjun acknowledges Krishna's position as the Supreme Lord. Kathopanishad, a major Upanishad, says: "All the Vedic mantras aim to guide us in the direction of God. He is the object of the study of the Vedas."

11.19 अनादिमध्यान्तमनन्तवीर्य- मनन्तबाहुं शशिसूर्यनेत्रम् पश्यामि त्वां दीप्तहुताशवक्त्रं- स्वतेजसा विश्वमिदं तपन्तम्   You have no beginning, middle, or end; you have infinite powers, infinite arms, the eyes like the sun and moon, and the mouths full of blazing fire. You are scorching this universe with your powerful light and heat.

Arjun continues to be dazzled by the splendor of the supreme Lord. Verse 11.16 also says the form of the Lord is without the beginning, middle, or end.

11.20 द्यावापृथिव्योरिदमन्तरं हि व्याप्तं त्वयैकेन दिशश्च सर्वा: दृष्ट्वाद्भुतं रूपमुग्रं तवेदं लोकत्रयं प्रव्यथितं महात्मन्   The space between the heavens and the earth, and all the directions, is occupied by you alone. I can see all worlds are trembling in fear by seeing your wondrous and terrifying form.

Arjun describes God occupying all space in the universe.

11.21 अमी हि त्वां सुरसङ्घा विशन्ति केचिद्भीता: प्राञ्जलयो गृणन्ति स्वस्तीत्युक्त्वा महर्षिसिद्धसङ्घा: स्तुवन्ति त्वां स्तुतिभि: पुष्कलाभि:   All the gods are taking refuge by entering into You; some are frightened and admiring You with folded palms. The great sages and the perfect ones (Siddhas) are praising You with sacred hymns and prayers.

Arjun sees in the universal form, which frightened the celestial gods. He sees the great sages chanting auspicious hymns.

11.22 रुद्रादित्या वसवो ये च साध्या विश्वेऽश्विनौ मरुतश्चोष्मपाश्च गन्धर्वयक्षासुरसिद्धसङ्घा वीक्षन्ते त्वां विस्मिताश्चैव सर्वे   The Rudras, Adityas, Vasus, Sadhyas, Visvadevas, Ashwini Kumars, Maruts, ancestors, Gandharvas, Yakshas, Asuras, and Siddhas, - are amazed by observing You.

All the deities Arjun saw, receive the power and positions to discharge their duties from God. Scriptures provide the description of various heavenly gods and their roles. This book does not, due to space limitation.

11.23 रूपं महत्ते बहुवक्त्रनेत्रं महाबाहो बहुबाहूरुपादम् बहूदरं बहुदंष्ट्राकरालं दृष्ट्वा लोका: प्रव्यथितास्तथाहम्   The worlds are utterly terrified, and so am I by seeing Your frightening form comprising many mouths and eyes, many arms, thighs and feet, and many bellies, and horrifying teeth.

All worlds are terrified by seeing Krishna's scary universal form. Arjun's wonder turned into fear.

11.24 नभ:स्पृशं दीप्तमनेकवर्णं व्यात्ताननं दीप्तविशालनेत्रम् दृष्ट्वा हि त्वां प्रव्यथितान्तरात्मा धृतिं न विन्दामि शमं च विष्णो   My heart is shaking with fear; I have lost all mettle and peace of mind. I no longer have the courage or serenity by seeing Your form touching the sky.

Arjun is terrified, looking at God's fearful form. Earlier, Arjun looked at Krishna as a close friend, but now, seeing the terrifying form, the friendship is replaced by fear.

11.25 दंष्ट्राकरालानि च ते मुखानि दृष्ट्वैव कालानलसन्निभानि दिशो न जाने न लभे च शर्म प्रसीद देवेश जगन्निवास   I forget where I am and don't know where to go after seeing your terrible teeth and mouths blazing like fires of annihilation. Lord, you are the shelter of the universe. Please have mercy on me.

Arjun is afraid and begs for mercy. He seems feeble in front of the Supreme power and realizes he has come face-to-face with the point of no return. His ego vanishes, and he surrenders, asking for mercy.

11.26 and 11.27 अमी च त्वां धृतराष्ट्रस्य पुत्रा: सर्वे सहैवावनिपालसङ्घै: भीष्मो द्रोण: सूतपुत्रस्तथासौ सहास्मदीयैरपि योधमुख्यै: वक्त्राणि ते त्वरमाणा विशन्ति दंष्ट्राकरालानि भयानकानि केचिद्विलग्रा दशनान्तरेषु सन्दृश्यन्ते चूर्णितैरुत्तमाङ्गै:   I see the sons of Dhritrashtra along with allied kings and their generals, including the great warriors Bhishma, Drona, Karna, and also the generals on our side. I see they are all rushing into your mouths, some with their heads cracked between your teeth.

Arjun saw in the Vishwarup Darshan (Universal vision) all great warriors and his cousins dying. Arjun received great surprise now - witnessing the future of his enemies all dying.

Bhishma was the grandsire of Pandavas and Kauravas. Drona was the teacher who taught the Pandavas and their cousins, the martial art of archery. Karna was Pandavas' stepbrother, known as the son of Suta, which means someone with a brahmin mother and a kshatriya father. Deep down within themselves, all three knew already they would die because Krishna will not allow the evil element to defeat the righteous.

11.28 and 11.29 यथा नदीनां बहवोऽम्बुवेगा: समुद्रमेवाभिमुखा द्रवन्ति तथा तवामी नरलोकवीरा विशन्ति वक्त्राण्यभिविज्वलन्ति यथा प्रदीसं ज्वलनं पतङ्गा विशन्ति नाशाय समृद्धवेगा: तथैव नाशाय विशन्ति लोका-स्तवापि वक्त्राणि समृद्धवेगा:   These great warriors are entering rapidly in your blazing mouths, just the way rivers flow into the ocean and moths rush with high speed into the fire to perish.

Arjun witnesses the great warriors marching rapidly towards death. The gruesome scene projected in verse 11.27 is a reminder of the uncertainty of our lives in this world. God's power can crumble the entire universe in seconds. This verse also points out that God is not killing anyone; the warriors who chose to fight and not comply with the peace proposals are entering his mouth on their own will. The result – they are meeting death in a horrifying manner.

11.30 लेलिह्यसे ग्रसमान: समन्ता-ल्लोकान्समग्रान्वदनैर्ज्वलद्भि: तेजोभिरापूर्य जगत्समग्रं भासस्तवोग्रा: प्रतपन्ति विष्णो   You are devouring the human beings with your blazing mouths, licking up the fiery tongue. You are burning the universe with the fierce rays of your radiance.

Arjun is frightened by the spectacle of the cosmic form devouring people and burning the universe. A frequent question arising in this verse is if the "merciful" God would really destroy people. Death is the ultimate reality of life and inevitable. Think of how the natural calamities like tornados, hurricane, earthquake, tsunami, and pandemics destroy and kill.

TOPIC 22 - Cosmic Form – Universal Darshan

11.31 आख्याहि मे को भवानुग्ररूपो नमोऽस्तु ते देववर प्रसीद विज्ञातुमिच्छामि भवन्तमाद्यं न हि प्रजानामि तव प्रवृत्तिम् Tell me, who you are, so fierce in form. Obeisance to you, O God Supreme. "Have mercy; I desire to know you, the original Being. I do not know indeed your doing."

Arjun is bewildered and agitated. He begs Krishna to tell him, "who are you, and what is your purpose?" Arjun wants to know with humility, and surrender, who Krishna is in the terrible form? As the universal form changed from a pleasant to a scary sight, Arjun is confused and wants to know why God is destroying everything.

❧ Krishna replies to Arjun:

11.32 श्रीभगवानुवाच कालोऽस्मि लोकक्षयकृत्प्रवृद्धो लोकान्समाहर्तुमिह प्रवृत्त: ऋतेऽपि त्वां न भविष्यन्ति सर्वे येऽवस्थिता: प्रत्यनीकेषु योधा: I am the Time (Kaal), a seasoned annihilator of the worlds and the source of destruction that annihilates the worlds, engaged in destroying all these people. Even without your participation, all these warriors will cease to exist.

The natural calamities, wars, epidemics, and accidents may be viewed as God's Kaal Swarup (destructive form).

Krishna shows Arjun his Kaal Swaroop - the destroyer of the worlds. God, as Kaal swaroop demonstrated a tiny display of his power when the

> ## Official Scenic Historic Marker
> ## TRINITY SITE
>
> The nuclear age began with the detonation of the world's first atomic bomb at the Trinity Site on July 16, 1945. The site may have been named Trinity by J. Robert Oppenheimer, director of the Los Alamos Nuclear Physics Laboratory, who said at the blast, "Now, I have become Death, the destroyer of worlds", quoting from the *Bhagavad Gita*. The detonation of the bomb marked the culmination of the Manhattan Project.

experimental atom bomb was detonated at the Trinity site in New Mexico, the USA, in 1945. The inventor and maker of these bombs, Robert Oppenheimer, was reminded of Verse 11.32, after seeing the phenomenal and horrific result of the blast. A permanent sign as above was posted on the New Mexico Highway 380 near the entrance to the site, which is open to visitors on certain days.

The US government designated this sign as the Official Scenic Historical Marker. Soon after the experiment, two bombs were dropped by the US Air force on Hiroshima and Nagasaki in Japan which ended World War 2. The two cities were almost 100% destroyed instantly, a sad reminder of human history.

11.33 तस्मात्त्वमुत्तिष्ठ यशो लभस्वजित्वा शत्रून्भुङ्क्ष्व राज्यं समृद्धम् मयैवैते निहता: पूर्वमेव निमित्तमात्रं भव सव्यसाचिन् Therefore, wake up and be honorable. Defeat your enemies and appreciate the kingdom. These fighters are already killed by Me, and you will only serve as an instrument to execute My plan.

People have to exercise free will to do their work free of ego and with the understanding that the divine is pulling the strings in the background and we are doing what we do as instruments of God.

11.34 द्रोणं च भीष्मं च जयद्रथं च कर्णं तथान्यानपि योधवीरान् मया हतांस्त्वं जहि मा व्यथिष्ठा युध्यस्व जेतासि रणे सपत्नान्   I have already killed Drona, Bhishma, Karna, Jaydratha, and all other brave warriors, and you will simply be an instrument to execute My plan. Arise and attain fame, defeat your enemies, and enjoy the prosperity of your kingdom.

The four warriors mentioned in Verse 11.34 were protected by certain boons awarded to them. Jayadratha had a blessing that whoever cuts his head, the killer's head would instantly burst. Karna received a weapon (Shakti) from Indra, the king of heavens, which could kill anyone. Bhishma could only be killed if he wanted to die. Drona had the power to neutralize any weapons under the training he received from Parsurama, an incarnation of God. However, Krishna's presence on the Pandava side neutralized the powers of the four extraordinary generals on the enemy side. The cosmic form showed these warriors were already dead.

❧ *Sanjay says:*

11.35 सञ्जय उवाच एतच्छ्रुत्वा वचनं केशवस्य कृताञ्जलिर्वेपमान: किरीटी नमस्कृत्वा भूय एवाह कृष्णं सगद्गदं भीतभीत: प्रणम्य   Arjun shook with fear hearing these words of Krishna. With joined hands, he bowed before Krishna and spoke with a shaky voice, overwhelmed with fear.

Arjun, the crowned one, was shocked by the terrifying scenes of warriors on both sides dying. Sanjay gave a hint that Pandavas will win and be crowned as the kings, but Dhritrashtra remained unmoved and did not stop the war.

❧ *Arjun says:*

11.36 अर्जुन उवाच स्थाने हृषीकेश तव प्रकीर्त्या जगत्प्रहृष्यत्यनुरज्यते च रक्षांसि भीतानि दिशो द्रवन्ति सर्वे नमस्यन्ति च सिद्धसङ्घा:   It is natural that the universe is happily praising You, and is full of love for you. Demons are fleeing fearfully from You in all directions, and the perfected beings (the Siddhas) bow down to You.

Arjun is complimentary of Krishna's glories. The Sanskrit word "sthane" means everything that is going on is precisely how it is supposed to be.

11.37 कस्माच्च ते न नमेरन्महात्मन् गरीयसे ब्रह्मणोऽप्यादिकर्त्रे अनन्त देवेश जगन्निवास त्वमक्षरं सदसत्परं यत्   As You are more significant than even the original creator Brahma, so why should they not bow to You? You are the imperishable, the unmanifest, and the manifest. You are also beyond the manifest and unmanifest.

Arjun's description of Krishna's powers confirms that he now understands the origin and mission of Krishna. God is the eternal and original cause of the universe and beyond everything and everyone that are manifest and unmanifest. Brahma came from him. Brahma created the universe, but many Brahmas came from God.

❧ *Sanjay says:*

11.50 सञ्जय उवाच इत्यर्जुनं वासुदेवस्तथोक्त्वास्वकं रूपं दर्शयामास भूय: आश्वासयामास च भीतमेनंभूत्वा पुन: सौम्यवपुर्महात्मा   After speaking to Arjun, Krishna again showed his (four-armed) form to Arjun. Then, again assuming his pleasant (two-armed) form, Krishna calmed down frightened Arjun.

Arjun first saw the four-armed form and then the gentle two-armed manifestation, which he felt more secure with as a friend of the human Krishna.

❧ *Arjun says:*

11.51 अर्जुन उवाच दृष्ट्वेदं मानुषं रूपं तव सौम्यं जनार्दन इदानीमस्मि संवृत्त: सचेता: प्रकृतिं गत: I have regained my composure seeing your human form. My mind has come back to its normal state.

Arjun has now regained his confidence and composure. The beautiful two-armed appearance strengthened Arjun's spirits. He is no longer afraid of the Supreme.

❧ *Krishna says:*

11.52 and 11.53 श्रीभगवानुवाच सुदुर्दर्शमिदं रूपं दृष्टवानसि यन्मम देवा अप्यस्य रूपस्य नित्यं दर्शनकाङ्क्षिण: नाहं वेदैर्न तपसा न दानेन न चेज्यया शक्य एवंविधो द्रष्टुं दृष्टवानसि मां यथा   It is not easy for anyone to see My cosmic form which you have seen (sudurdarsham). Even the gods are ever looking forward to beholding it. Not even by the study of Vedas, austerity, charity, or sacrifice, one can see My cosmic form.

The cosmic form cannot be seen even by gods. It requires Krishna's grace and divine vision to be able to see the rare form. God's grace is not arbitrarily bestowed on anyone. God grants his grace only to those who have pure devotion for him.

TOPIC 23

Arjun's Prayer to the Cosmic Form

Arjun, after seeing the cosmic God, is convinced Krishna is God who has assumed human appearance. He asks Krishna for forgiveness for not realizing his divinity and treating him as a human being. Out of the mixed feeling of fear and abundance of devotion, Arjun offers Krishna prayers in well-articulated Sanskrit verses, included in this topic.

✤ Arjun says:

11.39 वायुर्यमोऽग्निर्वरुण: शशाङ्क: प्रजापतिस्त्वं प्रपितामहश्च नमो नमस्तेऽस्तु सहस्रकृत्व: पुनश्च भूयोऽपि नमो नमस्ते   You are Vayu (the wind god), Yamraj (the God of death), Agni (the God of fire), Varun (the God of water), Chandra (the moon god), and the creator Brahma (the great grandfather of all beings). I offer my salutations to you a thousand times, again and yet again.

Experiencing abundant reverence toward Shree Krishna, Arjun is offering repeated obeisance (sahasra-kritvaḥ - thousands and thousands of times).

11.40 नम: पुरस्तादथ पृष्ठतस्ते नमोऽस्तु ते सर्वत एव सर्व अनन्तवीर्यामितविक्रमस्त्वं सर्वं समाप्नोषि ततोऽसि सर्व: O one with infinite power (anant virya). O one with endless valor (anant vikramah). You pervade all (samapnoshi sarvah). Therefore, you are everything (asi sarvah). Salutations to you from the front and rear, indeed from all sides.

Arjun was regarded as a mighty archer, and he thought it was his power that was enough to defeat the enemy. Now, he knows his power came from God. After beholding the cosmic God, his pride vanished. In Topic 40 on God's vibhutis, he saw God's opulence in everything; in Topic 22 on Cosmic Form, he saw everything in God. In the ecstatic state, he offered his obeisance from all sides.

11.41 and 11.42 सखेति मत्वा प्रसभं यदुक्तं हे कृष्ण हे यादव हे सखेति अजानता महिमानं तवेदं मया प्रमादात्प्रणयेन वापि यच्चावहासार्थमसत्कृतोऽसि विहारशय्यासनभोजनेषु एकोऽथवाप्यच्युत तत्समक्षं तत्क्षामये त्वामहमप्रमेयम्   Thinking you as a friend, I addressed you casually as Krishna or Yadav or my dear mate. I was ignorant of your majesty and showed negligence and inordinate affection for you. Not knowing your greatness, I beg forgiveness, I said it out of carelessness and also out of friendship.

Until now, Arjun did not recognize Krishna's divinity and considered him as a human. Divinity manifests as a human often in different roles and missions, but the human eyes cannot detect God. Scriptures say unless your time has come (meaning you are high enough on the spiritual ladder), you will neither recognize nor accept the truth about divinity descending as a human. For instance, only a handful of people believed Christ was the son of God or God; many did not and thought he was a criminal; actually, they contrived against him and crucified him. Similarly, there were evil people who insulted Lord Rama and Krishna. So, even if God comes in human form, only the spiritually progressed souls are able to recognize Him, that too if He graces those souls with this awareness. The rest remain ignorant.

11.43 पितासि लोकस्य चराचरस्य त्वमस्य पूज्यश्च गुरुर्गरीयान् न त्वत्समोऽस्त्यभ्यधिक: कुतोऽन्यो लोकत्रयेऽप्यप्रतिमप्रभाव   You are the father of the universe, of all moving beings and non-moving objects. You are most deserving to be revered and the supreme master. Who can be higher than you as there is none equal to you in all three worlds?

Arjun describes more of Krishna's divine attributes. Arjun surrenders his ego by announcing that there is nothing else in the universe like God. The Upanishads states, no one is equal to or superior to God.

11.44 तस्मात्प्रणम्य प्रणिधाय कायं प्रसादये त्वामहमीशमीड्यम् पितेव पुत्रस्य सखेव सख्यु: प्रिय: प्रियायार्हसि देव सोढुम्   So, I solicit your grace, prostrating before you. Please forgive my faults as a father forgives his son; a friend, his friend; and a lover, his beloved.

Arjun asks for forgiveness again.

11.45 अदृष्टपूर्वं हृषितोऽस्मि दृष्ट्वा भयेन च प्रव्यथितं मनो मे तदेव मे दर्शय देवरूपं प्रसीद देवेश जगन्निवास   I feel great joy seeing your universal form, which I never saw before. But I am frightened. I beg your mercy on me to again show me your pleasant appearance.

After seeing the terrifying universal form, Arjun prays to Krishna to show him the four-handed form and two-handed human form.

11.46 किरीटिनं गदिनं चक्रहस्त-मिच्छामि त्वां द्रष्टुमहं तथैव तेनैव रूपेण चतुर्भुजेन सहस्रबाहो भव विश्वमूर्ते   Wearing a crown, holding a mace and disc (Sudarshan chakra) in that four-armed form is what I want to see. I was hoping you could show me the four-armed Swarup (manifestation).

The four-armed form of God as Vishnu is the most admired form and the object of meditation of sages.

TOPIC 23 - Arjun's Prayer to the Cosmic Form

TOPIC 24

Worship of Unmanifest

The humans are used to forms and names from many lifetimes, so visualizing God with form (Saguna Brahm) is easier for them. The imperishable Self is difficult to reach for those who are attached to their bodies. Their restless minds will not remain steady on the Self without attributes. It is easier for them to focus the mind on a form. The path to imperishable Brahm is complex for most humans so they cannot grasp or visualize a formless entity and therefore are not attracted to worship an unmanifest entity (Nirguna Brahm). Yogis and Jnanis pursue the unmanifest by yoga and meditation.

◈ Krishna says:

8.11 यदक्षरं वेदविदो वदन्ति विशन्ति यद्यतयो वीतरागा: यदिच्छन्तो ब्रह्मचर्यं चरन्ति तत्ते पदं संग्रहेण प्रवक्ष्ये   Those who know the Vedas describe "that" as imperishable (Akshara), "that" which the detached ascetics who abide by the vow of celibacy enter; I will explain to you briefly the path to reach "that."

The followers of Imperishable (Akshara), for example, do severe austerities, renounce desires, practice celibacy, and do Ashtang Yoga. The path to Imperishable or Akasha Brahm is complex. Verse 8.12 in Topic 19 describes yogic concentration. Verse 8.13 in Topic 19 explains the power of chanting Aum mantra. Verse 8.14 in Topic 1 emphasizes keeping God in mind without deviation as part of bhakti marg.

9.15 ज्ञानयज्ञेन चाप्यन्ये यजन्तो मामुपासते एकत्वेन पृथक्त्वेन बहुधा विश्वतोमुखम्   Others who engage in the Jnana Yajna (the knowledge sacrifice) worship Me by many methods. Some see Me as non-different from them, while others see Me as separate from them. Still, others worship Me in the infinite manifestations of My cosmic form.

This verse describes divergent approaches to worshipping God. Jñāna-yogis see themselves to be non-different from God and glorify His formless all-pervading aspect. Ashtang yogis see themselves as distinct from God. Still, others worship the Vishwarup (cosmic form) of God. Seeing God in everything and everyone is the simplest bhakti (devotion). Gita offers many options to reach God and does not particularly favor one over the other. Gita even acknowledges without criticism, the atheists, and the faiths that do not believe in the existence of God. All Santana Dharma literature is respectful of other faiths and refrain from their criticism.

❦ *Here, Arjun asks:*

12.1 अर्जुन उवाच एवं सततयुक्ता ये भक्तास्त्वां पर्युपासते ये चाप्यक्षरमव्यक्तं तेषां के योगवित्तमा:   Those steadfast devotees who worship You (Krishna's human form) and those who worship the imperishable and the unmanifested (Nirguna Brahm)—which of the two is in a better versed in Yoga?

Arjun is asking a direct question – is the path of Saguna Brahm easier than Nirguna Brahm.

❦ **To this, Krishna replies to Arjun:**

12.2 श्रीभगवानुवाच मय्यावेश्य मनो ये मां नित्ययुक्ता उपासते श्रद्धया परयोपेतास्ते मे युक्ततमा मता:   The one who sets his mind on Me and worships Me steadily with great faith, I consider them to be the best yogis.

Srimad Bhagavatam states there is only one supreme entity that manifests in three ways in the world – Brahm (Nirguna Brahm), Paramatma (Super Soul), and Bhagawan (Saguna Brahm). The 12th chapter of Gita says that Bhakti Yoga is easier than Jnana Yoga (the Yoga of Knowledge).

12.5 क्लेशोऽधिकतरस्तेषामव्यक्तासक्तचेतसाम् अव्यक्ता हि गतिर्दुःखं देहवद्भिरवाप्यते
The path of realization is very challenging for those whose minds are attached to the unmanifest (the formless). Worship of the unmanifest is very difficult for embodied beings.

The humans are used to forms and names from many lifetimes, so focusing on forms is easier for them. Their restless minds will not remain steady on the Self without attributes.

TOPIC 25

Knowledge of Prakriti, Purush, Kshetra, and Kshetrajna

This topic covers one of the most mystical thoughts of Gita. The eternal Soul, with its physical cover called the body, is the central theme of this topic. The supreme Atma or Paramatma, which is known as the supreme reality, is beyond both. The one who knows it is liberated. Krishna says the knowledge of the Field and the Knower of the Field is the true knowledge. This body is the Field (Kshetra); the eternal soul living in the body is the Knower of the Field (Kshetrajna). The soul is an expression of the Supreme Being. Krishna also reveals the mystery of the individual soul within the mortal body.

The panch mahabhuta (five elements), the ego, the mind, intellect and the ten organs, desire, and aversion and such factors make up the Field. Specifically, a total of 24 elements in the field are panch Mahabhuta - earth, water, fire, air, and space; the panch Tanamatras or sense objects – sound, sight, taste, touch, and smell; the five working senses - voice, hands, legs, genitals, and anus; the five knowledge senses - ears, eyes, tongue, skin, and nose; mind; intellect; ego; and Prakriti (the primordial form of material energy).

The supreme soul (Brahm) pervades all and shines in our heart as the witness, the guide, supporter, and experiencer. Krishna says, the one who knows this mystery is free from the bondage.

Once we know the supreme God is in every being, we will develop compassion for everyone and not injure anyone.

❧ *Arjun says:*

13.1 अर्जुन उवाच प्रकृतिं पुरुषं चैव क्षेत्रं क्षेत्रज्ञमेव च एतद्वेदितुमिच्छामि ज्ञानं ज्ञेयं च केशव
I wish to understand: 1. What are Prakriti and Purusha? 2. What are Kshetra and Kshetragna? 3. What is the right knowledge, and 4. What is the goal of this knowledge?

Arjun wants to know what these terms mean: Prakriti, Purusha, Kshetra, and Kshetragna. Please note that in some versions of Gita, this verse has been omitted.

❧ *Krishna explains to Arjun:*

13.2 श्रीभगवानुवाच इदं शरीरं कौन्तेय क्षेत्रमित्यभिधीयते एतद्यो वेत्ति तं प्राहुः क्षेत्रज्ञ इति तद्विदः   Know me to be the Kshetrajna (the perceiver, the witness), meaning the soul and the super soul, dwelling in the Kshetra (the body, the field of activity). The understanding of the Kshetra as "the known" and Kshetrajna as "the knower" is true wisdom.

The realized sages with pure Antahkarana (the inner abstract instrument made up of the mind, ego, and intellect) have a correct understanding of these terms - Kshetra and Kshetragna. The purity of the heart requires the removal of three defects:

1. *Dirt made of selfish desires – Karma Yoga removes this*
2. *Unsteadiness, a tendency to jump from one thought to another – Bhakti Yoga makes the mind steady*
3. *The cover that hides understanding of who we really are – Jnana Yoga or the basic knowledge imparts the understanding of who we are*

13.3 क्षेत्रज्ञं चापि मां विद्धि सर्वक्षेत्रेषु भारत क्षेत्रक्षेत्रज्ञयोर्ज्ञानं यत्तज्ज्ञानं मतं मम   Know that I am the knower (Kshetrajna) of all fields (Kshetra). That knowledge of the field and the knower of the field is the right knowledge, in my opinion.

To grasp the real essence of the Kshetra and Kshetrajna, it takes an understanding of the self (Atma), God (Paramatma, or super soul), the body (Kshetra or matter), and the distinction amongst all these. Krishna calls this understanding as real knowledge.

13.4 तत्क्षेत्रं यच्च यादृक्च यद्विकारि यतश्च यत् स च यो यत्प्रभावश्च तत्समासेन मे शृणु   Now hear from me briefly: 1. What is Kshetra or field, and what it is like or what is its nature? 2. How changes take place in Kshetra, and from what position is it created? 5. Who is the knower of the field of activities (Kshetrajna), and what are his powers?

Krishna is going to explain what Kshetra and Kshetrajna mean in further detail.

13.5 ऋषिभिर्बहुधा गीतं छन्दोभिर्विविधैः पृथक् ब्रह्मसूत्रपदैश्चैव हेतुमद्भिर्विनिश्चितैः
Sages have sung (about the field and the knower of the field) in many ways as in various Vedic hymns, and also in the logical and conclusive texts in Brahmsutra.

This knowledge of Kshetra and Kshetragna was revealed to great Rishis in their meditation; it is also recorded in all four Vedas and three sections of Veda - the Samhita (hymns), Brahmana (theology), and Upnishads (discourse on divine knowledge). The philosophy of Kshetra and Kshetrajna did not originate from any human and is beyond the grasp of senses and the mind. This knowledge can be assimilated only with the use of logic contained in Brahmsutra, which analyzes Vedas in the step-by-step thesis.

What are some of the primary scriptures of Sanatana Dharm (universal philosophy)? They include 1. Four Vedas; 2. 52 Upnishads (the ten principal Upnishads in North India are Isha, Kena, Katha, Prashan, Mundaka, Mandukya, Tattiriya, Aitareya, Chhandogya, and Brihadaranyaka.); 3. Itihas - Ramayan (24,000 verses), Mahabharat (100,000 verses); 18 Puranas of which Srimad Bhagavat is the main, all Puranas comprise of 400,000 verses; 4. Six Darshans - Mimansa, by Sage Jaimini, about rituals, Vedant Darshan: by Sage Ved Vyas, about the nature of the Absolute Truth, Nyaya Darshan, by Sage Gautam, about logic for understanding life and the Absolute Truth, Vaisheshik Darshan by Sage Kanad about cosmology and physical creation, Yoga Darshan Sage Patañjali about Ashtang Yoga (eight-fold Yoga process), Sankhya Darshan: by Sage Kapil, about the evolution of the Universe from Prakriti, the Maya Shakti. NOTE: Overall, there are 108 Upnishads classified as Mukhya, Samanya Vedanta, Sannyāsa, Vaishnava, Shaiva, Shakta, and Yoga. Note also that besides those mentioned above, there are hundreds of other scriptures on many physical, sociological, and spiritual subjects (astronomy, astrology, medicine, surgery, architecture, finance, commerce, agriculture, and what not) in the Sanatan Dharm or universal philosophy. The list does not account for many scriptures that were stolen by the invaders and burnt by the barbarians who invaded India within the last two thousand years. The complexity, diversity, and depth of Sanatan Dharm scriptures are impossible to describe and difficult to comprehend.

Now, a slight diversion from the subject in the interest of clarifying the genesis of the term Hinduism. Sanatan Dharm or Universal Philosophy is an accurate description of the spiritual path the ancient Indians pursued to attain absolute and eternal bliss. In the recent past, following the British invasion of India, a false description of this philosophy by the introduction of a new term "Hinduism" was recorded and widely publicized. It should be noted that none of the scriptures contain the word Hinduism. However, the British made this word world-famous. Worse yet, few prominent and westernized Indians accepted the corrupted description of Sanatan Dharm and called that a religion. Sanatan Dharm is not meant to be a religion, but a meaningful way of life.

13.6 महाभूतान्यङ्ककारो बुद्धिरव्यक्त मेव च इन्द्रियाणि दशैकं च पञ्च चेन्द्रियगोचरा:   The field of activities (Kshetra) is composed of the Panch Mahabhoot (five great elements), the ego, the intellect, the unmanifested primordial matter; and the eleven senses (five knowledge senses, five working senses, and mind), and the five objects of senses.

Again, a total of 24 elements in the field are panch Mahabhut - earth, water, fire, air, and space; the panch Tanamatras or sense objects – sound, sight, taste, touch, and smell, the five working senses - voice, hands, legs, genitals, and anus; the five knowledge senses - ears, eyes, tongue, skin, and nose; mind; intellect; ego; and Prakriti (the primordial form of material energy).

13.7 इच्छा द्वेष: सुखं दु:खं सङ्घातश्चेतना धृति: एतत्क्षेत्रं समासेन सविकारमुदाहृतम्
Desire, aversion, happiness, misery, the body-consciousness, and will - all these are attributes of the field and its modifications.

Krishna just explained the makeup of the world and the individual from the 24 constituent elements. We come to this world with piles of unfulfilled desires that bind us to Maya. We get happy when we get what we desire and angry if we don't. Desires are the state of the mind and intellect. Material desires lead to bondage while spiritual desires lead to liberation. Aversion is also a state of mind and intellect that causes disgust to worldly objects. Happiness is the feeling in the mind. The pleasure of the senses can never be satisfied until the human experiences divine bliss. Misery is pain experienced in the mind due to unfulfilled expectations.

13.8 to 13.12 अमानित्वमदम्भित्वमहिंसा क्षान्तिरार्जवम् आचार्योपासनं शौचं स्थैर्यमात्मविनिग्रहः इन्द्रियार्थेषु वैराग्यमनहङ्कार एव च जन्ममृत्युजराव्याधिदुःखदोषानुदर्शनम् असक्तिरनभिष्वङ्गः पुत्रदारगृहादिषु नित्यं च समचित्तत्वमिष्टानिष्टोपपत्तिषु मयि चानन्ययोगेन भक्तिरव्यभिचारिणी विविक्तदेशसेवित्वमरतिर्जनसंसदि अध्यात्मज्ञाननित्यत्वं तत्त्वज्ञानार्थदर्शनम् एतज्ज्ञानमिति प्रोक्तमज्ञानं यदतोऽन्यथा The following attributes are real knowledge, and what is contrary to it is ignorance. Humbleness, freedom from hypocrisy, non-violence, forgiveness, simplicity, service of the teacher, purity, steadiness, self-control, dispassion toward the objects of the senses, absence of ego, constant perception of sorrow in body transformations (birth, disease, old age, and death), non-attachment, indifference to the family (spouse, children, home), apathy to desired and undesired events in life, single-pointed devotion in Me through unwavering Yoga, liking for solitary locations away from the assembly of people, steadfastness in the knowledge of the self, and pursuit of the Absolute Truth.

This verse lists the virtues and attributes that are said to be knowledge, which lead to the absolute truth. All the virtues, habits, behaviors, and attitudes described above lead to the growth of wisdom and knowledge, which is the goal of human birth (the field of activity). The opposite dispositions are adverse to the attainment of self-knowledge (Atmajnana).

13.20 प्रकृतिं पुरुषं चैव विद्ध्यनादी उभावपि विकारांश्च गुणांश्चैव विद्धि प्रकृतिसम्भवान् Prakriti and Purush have no beginning (and end). All modifications of the body and the three modes (triguna) of nature have come from Prakriti or Maya (material nature).

Purush or the individual soul is a fragment of God's Jeev Shakti or soul energy, which is sentient. Prakriti or Maya manifest the world and beings. The soul is divine and remains unchanged through different lifetimes, and the various stages of each lifetime. God is the super soul or Paramatma.

13.21 कार्यकारणकर्तृत्वे हेतुः प्रकृतिरुच्यते पुरुषः सुखदुःखानां भोक्तृत्वे हेतुरुच्यते The Prakriti is responsible for cause and effect. In the matter of experiencing happiness and distress, Purusha (individual soul) is responsible.

The Maya Shakti creates the elements and forms of life. The "bonded" soul receives a body (the field of activity) according to its past karmas, and it identifies itself with the body, mind, and intellect. Thus, it seeks the pleasure of the bodily senses. When the senses come in contact with the sense objects, the mind experiences a pleasurable sensation. Since the soul identifies with the mind, it indirectly enjoys pleasure. Thus, the soul, in its bonded state, experiences pleasure and pain through the medium of the senses, mind, and intellect.

13.22 पुरुष: प्रकृतिस्थो हि भुङ्क्ते प्रकृतिजान्गुणान् कारणं गुणसङ्गोऽस्य सदसद्योनिजन्मसु

When Purusha (individual soul) seated in Prakriti is tempted to enjoy desires from the three Gunas, the attachment to desires is the result. Then the attachment becomes the cause of its birth in good or evil wombs.

The soul or Purush is responsible for pleasure and pain, as described in the last verse. The soul causes the body to enjoy pleasures born out of desires. The body experiences the nature or Maya made of the three modes (Triguna). Under the influence of the ego, the soul identifies itself as the doer and the enjoyer of the body.

13.23 उपद्रष्टानुमन्ता च भर्ता भोक्ता महेश्वर: परमात्मेति चाप्युक्तो देहेऽस्मिन्पुरुष: पर:

Also, residing within the body is the ultimate controller (Supreme Lord). He is the witness, the permitter, the supporter, transcendental enjoyer, the ultimate controller, and the Paramatma.

Verse 13.2 stated the soul is the knower of the body while the Paramatma is the knower of infinite bodies; he witnesses karmas of everyone, and bestows the results. He accompanies the jivatma (individual soul) to whatever body it receives in each lifetime. Jivatma has free will but is in bondage.

TOPIC 26

Attributes of Brahm

Krishna is beyond not only matter but also the eternal soul (Atma), the knower in everyone. Though he said he is the soul, he is also beyond the soul as he is Brahm, the cosmic God, in his supreme aspect. The freed soul unites with Brahm and lives in his home but does not become God even after liberation. The human language cannot describe God, the Tat in what Upanishad says Om Tat Sat or Tat Twam Asi (you are that). Gita says the divine abode of God is a thousand times brighter than the sun, some mantras say millions of times brighter. Coincidentally, the modern astronomers reported seeing countless stars million times brighter than the sun, millions of light-years away, confirming the vision of ancient Indians as recorded in scriptures. The abode of Brahm is invisible and unmanifest, according to an interpretation of Gita, so the bright stars the astronomers saw are in the physical universe which is manifest and different from the spiritual universe as related in scriptures. The bright light Krishna mentions cannot be seen by human telescopes, no matter how powerful.

Krishna, by his Yoga Maya power, dispatches 'minuscules' of himself as the individual souls in each being that come in the body at birth, live there, and depart at death. Krishna is the prana (vitality) in the body that enables breathing, digesting, and other vital functions. Brahm has no beginning and end, and it is the source and destination of everything. The verses listed in this topic come from several Gita chapters and they all relate to Brahm and its characteristics. In 14.27, Krishna announces he is Brahm. There are many other verses in Gita where Krishna says he is Brahm, the supreme controller. Refer to the topic "Did Krishna Disclose He was Brahm?" for more information from which you can draw your conclusion on this question.

Refer to the Note on page xv regrading the difference in three terms Brahm (ब्रह्म), Brahma (ब्रह्मा), Brahman (ब्राह्मण).

🦋 *Krishna says:*

8.9 कविं पुराणमनुशासितारं मणोरणीयांसमनुस्मरेद्यः सर्वस्य धातारमचिन्त्यरूप मादित्यवर्णं तमसः परस्तात्   God is omniscient, most ancient, the controller, subtler than the subtlest, and the support of all. He has an inconceivable form, is brighter than the sun, and beyond the darkness of ignorance.

13.14 सर्वतः पाणिपादं तत्सर्वतोऽक्षिशिरोमुखम् सर्वतः श्रुतिमल्लोके सर्वमावृत्य तिष्ठति
With hands, feet, eyes, heads, and faces everywhere, it permeates everything in this world (sarvamavruty).

God is all-pervading and sees and hears everything. The Chhāndogya Upanishad states: "Everywhere is Brahman."

13.15 सर्वेन्द्रियगुणाभासं सर्वेन्द्रियविवर्जितम् असक्तं सर्वभृच्चैव निर्गुणं गुणभोक्तृ च
It is manifest in functions of all sense organs, yet devoid of sense organs (sarvandriyvivarjitam). Unattached (asaktam) yet sustaining (sarvbhrit). Without attributes (nirgunam) yet the enjoyer of three modes of material nature.

Attributes of Brahm sound contradictory on the surface. Krishna says his senses are everywhere, then states that he does not have any senses. He is unattached, but he sustains; he is without attributes, but he enjoys the material nature (Maya). The mundane logic by our physical mind will find these examples contradictory. However, he is beyond the reach of the intellect, so the human logic won't prevail. God possesses infinite opposite attributes at the same time. The Brahm Vaivarta Purāṇ states, "The Supreme Lord is the reservoir of innumerable contradictory attributes." Shwetāshvatar Upanishad says: "God does not possess material hands, feet, eyes, and ears. Yet He grasps, walks, sees, and hears. "The contradictions are among the amazing qualities of Brahm, beyond the reasoning ability of the finite human mind.

13.16 बहिरन्तश्च भूतानामचरं चरमेव च सूक्ष्मत्वात्तदविज्ञेयं दूरस्थं चान्तिके च तत्   He is outside and inside all beings. He is moving and not moving. Also, subtle hence incomprehensible (avijneyam). He is very far yet very near.

Consider Ishopanishad mantra 5 - "The Supreme Brahman does not walk, and yet he walks; He is far, but He is also near. He exists inside everything, but He is also outside everything."

Verse 13.3 (Topic 25) says that to know God is the right knowledge, but here in verse 13.16, he says that God is incomprehensible. The last line sounds contradictory, but it is not. It means God is not knowable by the senses, mind, and intellect, which are the products of the field created by Maya; so they cannot decipher Brahm who is Divine, without his grace. The field (the body) itself is a machine and can operate only in the presence of the consciousness or Jeev Shakti. The device is dead without the Jeev Shakti. Brahm is knowable only with the grace of God or a realized guru.

13.17 अविभक्तं च भूतेषु विभक्तमिव च स्थितम् भूतभर्तृ च तज्ज्ञेयं ग्रसिष्णु प्रभविष्णु च
He is undividable (avibhaktam) yet appears divided among the beings. He is

the sustainer (bhutbhartru), annihilator (grasishnu), and creator of all people (prabhavishnu).

Consider an example to illustrate the apparent contradiction. Space is unlimited but looks divided into empty pots, as viewed by our limited senses. It may seem as if space is divided, but it is not. Waves are created, sustained momentarily, and absorbed back in the ocean. Waves are an excellent example of "upadhi" or distraction to our understanding that the sea is the foundation. Similarly, lives are created and sustained. Then, after annihilation, they return to the source, which is the Supreme entity.

13.18 ज्योतिषामपि तज्ज्योतिस्तमस: परमुच्यते ज्ञानं ज्ञेयं ज्ञानगम्यं हृदि सर्वस्य विष्ठितम्

He is the source of light in everything that shines (luminary). He is beyond the darkness of ignorance. He is knowledge (jnana), the object of knowledge (jneyam), and the goal of knowledge (jnangamyam). He dwells within the heart of everyone.

The luminaries include sun, moon, stars, and fire, which cannot illuminate without God's Yogamayapower. Kaṭhopaniṣad says: "God makes all things luminous. It is by His light that all bright objects emit light."

13.32 अनादित्वान्निर्गुणत्वात्परमात्मायमव्यय: शरीरस्थोऽपि कौन्तेय न करोति न लिप्यते

The supreme soul is imperishable (avyayah), without beginning (anadivaat), and has no material qualities (Nirgun). Though situated in the body, it neither acts nor is corrupted by Maya. Imperishable Brahm sits in the body but does not operate or get affected.

God (Paramatma) resides within the heart as a witness. The soul receives its power from Paramatma. Consciousness in the body is due to the soul. God is not subject to the law of karma and the cycle of birth and death. However, the soul is, in its bonded state, due to the body-consciousness and influence of Trigunas.

14.27 ब्रह्मणो हि प्रतिष्ठाहममृतस्याव्ययस्य च शाश्वतस्य च धर्मस्य सुखस्यैकान्तिकस्य च

I am the basis of the formless Brahm, the immortal, the imperishable, the eternal dharma, and of absolute bliss.

This verse clarifies that Krishna is the formless Brahm. See the topic in this book entitled 'Did Krishna pronounce in Gita he was Brahm?'

15.12 यदादित्यगतं तेजो जगद्भासयतेऽखिलम् यच्चन्द्रमसि यच्चाग्नौ तत्तेजो विद्धि मामकम्

I am the light in the sun that illuminates the world. I am the brightness of the moon and the fire.

God is the source of light in all bright entities. The light of the sun, moon, and fire comes from the power of God. The sun itself produces light equivalent to millions of nuclear bombs exploding every second and has existed for billions of years and continues to exist with no sign of degradation in its power. Therefore, the theory that the sun came into existence because of some random colossal bang sounds far-fetched. Scientists have now concluded that there are billions of suns in the universe brighter than our sun. Then imagine the infinite energy content of all atoms in the universe. God is the source of all

TOPIC 26 - Attributes of Brahm

energy and light in the universe. Compare this verse with verse 13.18 in the current topic where Krishna says God is the source of light. In this verse 15.12, Krishna says, "He" is the source of light, suggesting that Krishna and God are the same divine entities.

15.13 गामाविश्य च भूतानि धारयाम्यहमोजसा पुष्णामि चौषधी: सर्वा: सोमो भूत्वा रसात्मक: I nourish all beings by my energy by permeating the earth. Becoming the moon, I feed all plants with the juice of life.

God's energy nourishes all living beings and plants. God's energy is the foundation for all life forms. Krishna states that he is the one behind the nourishing power of the moonlight.

15.15 सर्वस्य चाहं हृदि सन्निविष्टो मत्त: स्मृतिर्ज्ञानमपोहनं च वेदैश्च सर्वैरहमेव वेद्यो वेदान्तकृद्वेदविदेव चाहम् Sitting in the heart of all, I provide the ability to remember and understand. It is I who withdraw that power (capacity). The Vedas and Vedantas come from me; I am the author and the wisdom in the scriptures.

God alone is the source of all knowledge. Know that God is the goal of the Vedas, although they contain many material and spiritual instructions. The Kaṭhopaniṣad states: "All the Vedic mantras are pointing toward God."

15.16 द्वाविमौ पुरुषौ लोके क्षरश्चाक्षर एव च क्षर: सर्वाणि भूतानि कूटस्थोऽक्षर उच्यते There are two types of beings in this world. 1. Kshar (perishable) - all people in the world who are not liberated and take birth again and again, 2. Akshar (imperishable) - the liberated beings (kutasth), those who will not be born again.

15.17 उत्तम:पुरुषस्त्वन्य:परमात्मेत्युदाहृत:यो लोकत्रयमाविश्य बिभर्त्यव्यय ईश्वर: The indestructible Lord is different from these perishable and imperishable beings. He pervades the three worlds and supports them.

This verse suggests that besides the visible and perishable world, and the imperishable soul or Atma, there is another entity – the super soul or Paramatma, who supports everyone and everything. This verse clarifies that Paramatma is distinct from and superior to imperishable Atma and the perishable world. Here, Krishna makes a reference to God as an entity other than him. If that is so, then, who is he? The next verse explains.

15.18 यस्मात्क्षरमतीतोऽहमक्षरादपि चोत्तम: अतोऽस्मि लोके वेदे च प्रथित: पुरुषोत्तम: I transcend the perishable world, and am superior to the imperishable (Atma); hence I am praised in the world and Vedas as the highest purush or supreme God (Purushottam).

This verse makes the same point mentioned earlier in verses 14.27, 15.12, and 15.13 that Krishna is the same as Brahm or the Supreme God.

A summary of Brahm as defined by the Upnishads.

God, the formless Sat Chit Anand (Existence, Consciousness, and Bliss), the Universal Spirit, the Ultimate Reality, the Pure Consciousness; the One existence; the Absolute; 'the Truth of truth'. "Not this, not this" (Neti, Neti); with no name, or form, or action.

TOPIC 26 - Attributes of Brahm

All this is Brahm (Sarvam khalvidam brahm), Para Brahm (Nirguna Brahm), Brahm qualified by limiting conditions (Saguna Brahm), Pure Consciousness (prajñānam brahma), I am Brahm (aham brahmāsmi), that thou art (You are Brahm, Tat Tvam Asi). Brahm is one, without a second (ekam evadvitiyam brahm); all this is Brahm (Sarvam khalvidam brahm); Brahm is unperceived, unrelated, incomprehensible, uninferable, unthinkable, and indescribable.

The Vedas list literally countless descriptions of Brahm (One God) of which a few are given below in English:

One God Omkar, Ultimate Truth, Sustainer of the Universe, Absolutely Fearless, Free of Revenge, Immortal, Unborn, Self Luminous, Attainable by Guru's Grace, Pure, Formless, Everywhere, Most Powerful, All Knowing, the Oldest, Eternal, Ultimate Controller, Smaller than Atom, All Remembering, Universal Support, Unimaginable, Effulgent like Sun, Brighter than Million Suns, Beyond Darkness, Unattached, Free of Material Qualities, Incomprehensible, Cannot be Divided, Creator of All Beings, Imperishable, Beginning-less, Cannot be Destroyed, Capable of Assuming Divine Form.

TOPIC 26 - Attributes of Brahm

TOPIC 27

Signs of Sthitprajna and the One Beyond Triguna (trigunatit)

A devotee may achieve success in many aspects of spirituality but cannot experience the truth until one rises above the dualities of life, such as joy and misery, gain and loss, heat and cold. Gita is not about showing how to live an enjoyable life here and after, nor about gaining power here and after. Gita shows how to attain Atma Jnana (self-realization) by removing ignorance. It teaches one must detach from happiness and unhappiness, as mentioned multiple times under the current topic. Note, Gita does not require reading of the scriptures as a means to gain knowledge, but it recommends everyone should endeavor to get a direct experience. Knowledge (jnana) without practice and experience (vijnana) is virtually the same as the lack of knowledge (ajnana).

Sthitprajna is the one who has transcended the dualities; the one who is free of selfish desires and cravings of the senses. The following verses from Gita all relate to the subject of this topic; they describe the characteristics of such a person.

❧ *Arjun says:*

2.54 अर्जुन उवाच स्थितप्रज्ञस्य का भाषा समाधिस्थस्य केशव स्थितधी: किं प्रभाषेत किमासीत व्रजेत किम्   What is the disposition of one in divine consciousness? How does he talk? Sit? Walk?

After listening about perfect Yoga, Arjun is asking about the visible traits of people in the state of perfect Yoga. NOTE - Altogether Arjun asks sixteen questions in Gita, as listed in Topic N on Arjun's Questions to Krishna.

❧ *Krishna replies:*

2.55 श्रीभगवानुवाच प्रजहाति यदा कामान्सर्वान्पार्थ मनोगतान् आत्मन्येवात्मना तुष्ट: स्थितप्रज्ञस्तदोच्यते Sthitpragna (one with stable disposition always) discards desires and cravings of senses and is satisfied in the realization of the self.

Sthitpragna does not live merely to satisfy the senses (Indriyas). The lack of control over the senses is the reason for the troubles in life, and the cycle of death and rebirths. Various characteristics of Sthitprajna are described in verses 2.55 through 2.58 and are summarized in the commentary under verse 2.58.

2.56 दु:खेष्वनुद्विग्नमना: सुखेषु विगतस्पृह: वीतरागभयक्रोध: स्थितधीर्मुनिरुच्यते
Sthitprajna is one whose mind is not disturbed by gloom, who does not crave for pleasure, and who is without attachment, fear, and anger; is a sage of steady disposition.

2.57 य: सर्वत्रानभिस्नेहस्तत्तत्प्राप्य शुभाशुभम् नाभिनन्दति न द्वेष्टि तस्य प्रज्ञा प्रतिष्ठिता
Sthitapragna has perfect knowledge. He is detached, not delighted by fortune, nor sad due to misery.

2.58 यदा संहरते चायं कूर्मोऽङ्गानीव सर्वश: इन्द्रियाणीन्द्रियार्थेभ्यस्तस्य प्रज्ञा प्रतिष्ठिता
Sthitprajna retrieves senses (Indriyas) from their objects like a tortoise withdraws its limbs. He is always in a state of wisdom.

The characteristics of Sthitprajna are summarized from verses 2.55 through 2.58:

1. *Without desires and cravings of senses,*
2. *Satisfied with the self,*
3. *Undisturbed by misery,*
3. *Devoid of attachment, fear, anger,*
4. *Unattached,*
5. *Not delighted by fortune, nor depressed by suffering,*
6. *With senses pulled away from pleasure,*
7. *In controls of the senses (Indriyas).*

Gita contains other terms synonymous with Sthitprajna, as follows:

1. *In divine consciousness,*
2. *Transcendentally situated,*
3. *With steady wisdom,*
4. *With perfect knowledge,*
5. *Fixed in divine wisdom,*
6. *Established in transcendental wisdom,*
7. *Always in a state of perfect peace, and*
8. *In the state of being in divine knowledge, bliss, and love.*

TOPIC 27 - Signs of Sthitprajna and the One Beyond Triguna (trigunatit)

5.18 विद्याविनयसम्पन्ने ब्राह्मणे गवि हस्तिनि शुनि चैव श्वपाके च पण्डिता:समदर्शिन:　The wise regard everyone as the same. They see the same Atma (Pragna Chakshu) in a spiritual person and an outcaste, in an elephant, a cow, and a dog.

The eyes of knowledge view all beings as the same, regardless of their status. The spiritual experience breeds humility, whereas, the scholarly knowledge breeds pride and ego. The jnani (one with the right knowledge) sees every soul as parts of God. It is false to think the Brahmins (the priests) are higher, and the Shudras (labor) are lower because Krishna does not approve of social injustice. All castes have their roles and responsibilities according to their nature, skills, and merits. Krishna makes it clear that no work is superior or inferior. All humans have souls that are parts of the same one God. See Topic 21 on Caste System and Duties.

5.20 न प्रहृष्येत्प्रियं प्राप्य नोद्विजेत्प्राप्य चाप्रियम् स्थिरबुद्धिरसम्मूढो ब्रह्मविद् ब्रह्मणि स्थित:　The wise people are not elated by good fortune and depressed by bad. With their mind in Brahm, they are not suffering from delusion.

Sthitprajna does not rejoice in pleasure nor lament the unpleasant. The virtue of equanimity follows the attitude of surrender to God in all circumstances. Refer to verse 18.62 Topic 1 on Bhakti Yoga about what surrendering to God means.

6.8 ज्ञानविज्ञानतृप्तात्मा कूटस्थो विजितेन्द्रिय: युक्त इत्युच्यते योगी समलोष्टाश्मकाञ्चन: The self-realized yogis have spiritual wisdom. With their senses under control, the yogis are satisfied with jnana (the acquired knowledge), and Vijnana (realized knowledge), and remain undisturbed in all circumstances. To these yogis, the dirt, stones, and gold are the same.

A realized yogi remains undisturbed and views everything as the same. The advanced yogi sees all objects as modifications of the energy and does not differentiate between objects based on their attractiveness. Energy forms all materials and nothing can exist without the energy from God. Do not be deluded by the dissimilar appearance and function of matters, which are only because of the unique atomic structure of each element. Those Yogis who have the realized knowledge, called Vijnan, understand this. Swami Ramakrishna explained brilliantly the three terms: ajnana, jnana, and vijnana with a simple example. "One who has merely heard of the fire has ajnana, ignorance. One who has seen fire has jnana, but one who has built a fire with his own hands and cooked on it has vijnana." The bookish knowledge is like satisfying curiosity but you don't reach the goal without applying it to gain first-hand experience.

Note that this verse like many others emphasizes the sense control because no progress is possible without it regardless of which path you pursue. In modern terms, all bets are off for those who have no control over senses, who always dwell on thoughts of pleasure activities, who exercise no control over the senses, and who are disturbed when the senses are not satisfied.

6.9 सुहृन्मित्रार्युदासीनमध्यस्थद्वेष्यबन्धुषु साधुष्वपि च पापेषु समबुद्धिर्विशिष्यते The one who has the same disposition towards all men – patrons, friends, enemies,

TOPIC 27 - Signs of Sthitprajna and the One Beyond Triguna (trigunatit)

strangers, the neutral, the hateful, the relatives, the virtuous, ungodly, and the unrighteous, he shines and is considered eminent.

The traits mentioned in this verse are those of a Sthitprajna: Controlled senses, undisturbed, desireless, lives in seclusion, meditates, views everyone the same (enemies, relatives, friends, good, bad, dirt, stone, gold), sees creation in unity with God, believes everyone is a divine soul and form of God.

🌸 *Arjun asks:*

14.21 अर्जुन उवाच कैर्लिङ्गैस्त्रीन्गुणानेतानतीतो भवति प्रभो किमाचार: कथं चैतांस्त्रीन्गुणानतिवर्तते 1. What are the characteristics of those who have gone above and beyond the three Gunas? 2. How do they act? 3. How do they overcome the bondage of the Gunas?

Note the similarity between three types of followers described by different terms, all having common characteristics:

1. *The signs of a Sthitprajna in verse 2.58 above,*
2. *Characteristics of devotees Krishna likes in verse 12.13 through 12.20 in Topic 2, and*
3. *Aspects of those who rise above the three Gunas in verses 14.22 through 14.25 below.*

🌸 *Krishna replies:*

14.22 and 14.23 श्रीभगवानुवाच प्रकाशं च प्रवृत्तिं च मोहमेव च पाण्डव न द्वेष्टि सम्प्रवृत्तानि न निवृत्तानि काङ् क्षति उदासीनवदासीनो गुणैर्यो न विचाल्यते गुणा वर्तन्त इत्येवं योऽवतिष्ठति नेङ्गते The characteristics of yogis, who transcend the Gunas (Trigunatita), are 1. They are unmoved by the light born of sattva, or the activity born of rajas, or the delusion born of tamas; 2. They remain unconcerned when these forces exist, nor do they long for them when these forces are absent. They are not disturbed by the actions of the Gunas, knowing that it is the Gunas that act. They remain firmly situated and unmoved.

Spiritually elevated persons are detached from thoughts, which pass through the mind due to the interaction of the Gunas. They know the mind causes the body to act strictly due to the Gunas only, independent of the soul.

14.24 and 14.25 समदु:खसुख: स्वस्थ: समलोष्टाश्मकाञ्चन: तुल्यप्रियाप्रियो धीरस्तुल्यनिन्दात्मसंस्तुति: मानापमानयोस्तुल्यस्तुल्यो मित्रारिपक्षयो: सर्वारम्भपरित्यागी गुणातीत: स उच्यते Those who have risen above the three Gunas have the following traits: 1. They are alike in happiness and distress; 2. They are established in the self; 3. look at a clod, a stone, and gold as having equal value; 4. remain the same and firm amidst pleasant and unpleasant events; 5. react the same to praise and blame; 6. Apathetic about honor and dishonor; 7. treat a friend and foe alike; 8. have abandoned all enterprises.

Signs of one who rises above the three Gunas (Trigunatit), summarized from verses 14.22 through 14.25: 1. Indifferent to light born of sattva, activity born of rajas, or illusion born of tamas. 2. Unconcerned, indifferent, undisturbed, unmoved by the three Gunas. 3. Alike in happiness and distress; 4. Established in the self; 5. View everything as the same; 6. Same amidst pleasant and unpleasant events; 7. Same to praise and blame; 8. Same in honor and dishonor; 9. Alike with a friend and foe; 10. Have abandoned all enterprises.

14.26 मां च योऽव्यभिचारेण भक्तियोगेन सेवते स गुणान्समतीत्यैतान्ब्रह्मभूयाय कल्पते   He who serves me with steadfast devotion and has risen above the three Gunas becomes fit for attaining Brahm.

Krishna shows an easier way to reach Brahm, by unwavering devotion (avyabhicharen), which means not moving frequently from one path to another in search of pleasures. Detach from the Gunas and attach to something higher, which is God. This passage on devotion is similar to many such verses in Gita singing the glory of the path of devotion. One can transcend the three Gunas by fixing the mind on God.

TOPIC 28

Maya, Three Gunas, and the Soul

Maya is also called Prakriti of God which creates entities that are impermanent such as the matter and the bodies of all beings. However, the source of consciousness is Jeev Shakti (another energy of God); it charges life into the bodies. Three Gunas – Sattva, Rajas, and Tamas - are part of Maya and a result of past karmas. Each person carries the Gunas in a different proportion, and the proportion changes according to the status of the accrued karma. The soul is not affected by Maya or the Gunas, but when in bondage, it is the recipient of pleasures and pain felt by the senses (Indriyas). Gita shows the way to overcome the effect of Maya and the Gunas to liberate the soul. A majority of Gita verses referring to this topic reside in Topics 28 and 34. Topic 34 discusses how the Gunas manifest.

Krishna says:

14.5 सत्वं रजस्तम इति गुणा: प्रकृतिसम्भवा: निबध्नन्ति महाबाहो देहे देहिनमव्ययम् It is the three Gunas born of Maya or Prakriti – Sattva (goodness), Rajas (Passion), and Tamas (ignorance), which bind the soul to the mortal body.

Everyone carries the three Gunas (in the "baggage") in varying proportions. Sometimes Sattva predominates, and at other times Rajas or Tamas predominates. Maya possesses three Guṇas—goodness, passion, and ignorance. The mix and intensity of Gunas is always changing according to karmas. Each Guna individually determines personality traits based on the past sanskaras. Don't be attached to these three Gunas, even to Sattva Guna, only be a witness and transcend the Gunas. The following verses explain the impact of the Gunas upon the person.

14.6 तत्र सत्वं निर्मलत्वात्प्रकाशकमनामयम् सुखसङ्गेन बध्नाति ज्ञानसङ्गेन चानघ Of the three modes, Sattva Guna, or the mode of goodness is purer than the others; it is luminous and free from evil. Sattva binds the soul by creating the attachment for happiness and knowledge.

Sattva (the mode of goodness), though the most desirable among the three, is also within the influence of Maya. It creates serenity and happiness, but one gets attached to joy inadvertently and can succumb to ego. The attachment even to pleasant qualities will also result in the binding of the soul to Maya.

14.7 रजो रागात्मकं विद्धि तृष्णासङ्गसमुद्भवम् तन्निबध्नाति कौन्तेय कर्मसङ्गेन देहिनम्
Rajas is the nature of passion, the source of desire and attachment. It binds the soul by attachment to the results of actions.

Rajas (the mode of passion) manifests as an attachment to sensual enjoyment and pursuit for status, prestige, career, family, etc. Attachment to worldly pleasures binds the soul to Maya.

14.8 तमस्त्वज्ञानजं विद्धि मोहनं सर्वदेहिनाम् प्रमादालस्यनिद्राभिस्तन्निबध्नाति भारत
Tamas, born of ignorance, is the cause of illusion for the souls. It inspires negligence, laziness, and sleep; deludes people and binds them to Maya.

Symptoms of Tamas are sleep, laziness, intoxication, violence, gambling, loss of discrimination, and negligence of duty. The one under the spell of tamas lacks spiritual identity, the goal in life, and the opportunity for progress.

14.9 सत्वं सुखे सञ्जयति रज: कर्मणि भारत ज्ञानमावृत्य तु तम: प्रमादे सञ्जयत्युत Sattva binds one to material happiness; rajas to actions; and tamas clouds wisdom and binds one to delusion.

All three Gunas bind the soul, therefore, Krishna is telling Arjun to rise above the three Gunas to relieve the soul from the bondage to Maya. Further, he suggests to remain detached from the changes and interaction of the Gunas and understand that the thoughts and emotions are merely a play of the Prakriti (Maya).

14.10 रजस्तमश्चाभिभूय सत्वं भवति भारत रज: सत्वं तमश्चैव तम: सत्वं रजस्तथा
Sometimes, goodness (sattva) prevails over passion (rajas) and ignorance (tamas). Sometimes passion (rajas) dominates goodness (sattva) and ignorance (tamas). At other times ignorance (tamas) overcomes goodness (sattva) and passion (rajas).

The implication of this verse is all three Gunas are present in everyone's personality to varying proportion with the predominance of one of the Gunas, as indicated in the commentary under verse 14.5 in the current topic.

14.11 सर्वद्वारेषु देहेऽस्मिन्प्रकाश उपजायते ज्ञानं यदा तदा विद्याद्विवृद्धं सत्वमित्युत When the light of knowledge radiates through all the gates (sense-openings), then, know that Sattva has significantly increased.

The effect of Sattva is the light of knowledge. Clear thinking and calmness in crisis are symptoms of sattva.

14.12 लोभ: प्रवृत्तिरारम्भ: कर्मणामशम: स्पृहा रजस्येतानि जायन्ते विवृद्धे भरतर्षभ

Greed, activities, work plans, restlessness, and desires arise when Rajas is predominant.

The effect of rajas is greed, push for worldly gain, restlessness, and craving. When Rajas is the primary mode, the purpose of work is to satisfy ambition and desire.

14.13 अप्रकाशोऽप्रवृत्तिश्च प्रमादो मोह एव च तमस्येतानि जायन्ते विवृद्धे कुरुनन्दन

Darkness, inactivity, inadvertence, and delusion prevail when Tamas predominates.

The effect of tamas is inertia, negligence, and delusion.

TOPIC 28 - Maya, Three Gunas, and the Soul

TOPIC 29

Transmigration of Soul

The concept of rebirth or reincarnation of the individual soul is supported by the Vedantic scriptures. The Darshan Shastra (scripture) says, "jātasya harshabhayaśhoka sampratipatteh." Meaning - infants change their expressions without any external impulse, happy at times, and unhappy the other times. This happens because the memory of their past life is passing through their minds. They lose memories and impressions of the past as the present memories get etched sharply in their minds. The Darshan Shastra also says, "stanyābhilāṣhāt." Meaning – infants know no language, but based on the memory from many births, they automatically suck in the milk from the mother's breast as soon as born.

Another puzzling aspect is the condition and environment in which an infant is born. The extreme disparity in the physical, mental, and financial states of the humans from birth is quite baffling. It becomes impossible to explain if you reject the reincarnation concept. Examples of diversities from birth - rich or poor, healthy or unhealthy, virtuous, or promiscuous. Why such extreme diversity from birth, and what causes it? Some explain it is due to God's will. It is illogical to rationalize that the fate in the present life is due to God's will because God is just and compassionate, not arbitrary with unsound logic. He is the ultimate witness and impartial chief justice.

As explained in verse 2.28 under Topic 8, the soul goes back to the source (God) upon the death of the body, and gross and subtle bodies merge back into the Maya. After rebirth, the causal bodies receive their subtle and gross bodies, and the soul is reborn in a new body in an environment according to the accrued karma and unfulfilled desires.

🦋 *Krishna says:*

2.11 श्रीभगवानुवाच अशोच्यानन्वशोचस्त्वं प्रज्ञावादांश्च भाषसे गतासूनगतासूंश्च नानुशोचन्ति पण्डिता: You do not need to grieve for the dead. Wise lament for neither living nor dead.

The body is transient, not worthy of grief.

154

2.13 देहिनोऽस्मिन्यथा देहे कौमारं यौवनं जरा तथा देहान्तरप्राप्तिर्धीरस्तत्र न मुह्यति   The soul passes through different states during life (like birth, childhood, youth, old age, and death). Similarly, the soul passes on to another body after death, which does not delude the wise.

The soul changes the bodies which are transient. Note two key words here in this verse - deha and dehi. Deha means the body (mortal, made of Panch Mahabhoot), and dehi means the owner or controller of the body (the soul). Krishna said before that the wise do not lament the death, and happiness and distress are inevitable in our lives. Krishna explains in verse 2.14 (Topic 6) that the reason for the changing perception of joy and grief is the contact between the sense (Indriya) and its object.

2.22 वासांसि जीर्णानि यथा विहाय नवानि गृह्णाति नरोऽपराणि तथा शरीराणि विहाय जीर्णा न्यन्यानि संयाति नवानि देही   Like a person discards worn-out garments to replace them with new ones, upon death, the soul casts off the worn-out body and moves to a new body.

Refer to the commentary in the introduction above on reincarnation. Verse 2.22 is also included in Topic 8 on the Nature of the Soul.

9.7 and 9.8 सर्वभूतानि कौन्तेय प्रकृतिं यान्ति मामिकाम् कल्पक्षये पुनस्तानि कल्पादौ विसृजाम्यहम् प्रकृतिं स्वामवष्टभ्य विसृजामि पुन: पुन: भूतग्राममिमं कृत्स्नमवशं प्रकृतेर्वशात्   All beings enter into my Prakriti (Maya) at the end of a Kalp (one day of Brahma according to the celestial calendar); I send them back again at the beginning of the next Kalp. Presiding over Maya, I, again and again, send forth this variety of beings, helpless by the force of their Karma.

Refer to Verse 8.17 in Topic 16 on Creation for details of one kalp (one day in Brahma's life). At the end of one kalp, all beings merge into God and become manifested again in the next kalp.

Verses 9.9 and 9.10 in Topic 16 explain how God, Prakriti, and individual souls are related. Prakriti (or Maya) is the system that God devised to track everyone's karmas; and how Prakriti functions as an "automatic" system in the cycles of creation and dissolution.

Regarding the transmigration process, Topic 8 indicates that after dissolution the soul goes back to the source (God or whatever name for God your faith uses), and gross and subtle bodies merge back into the Maya. The causal body remains in suspended animation. After returning, the causal bodies receive their subtle and gross bodies.

9.11 अवजानन्ति मां मूढा मानुषीं तनुमाश्रितम् परं भावमजानन्तो मम भूतमहेश्वरम्
Ignorant people ridicule Me when I descend in human form. They do not know the divinity of My personality.

Verse 4.6 (Topic 15) says God takes human form by his Yoga Maya Shakti, "Although I am unborn and imperishable, and the Lord of all living entities, yet I appear in this world by my Yoga Maya power, in My original divine form." Swami Sivananda's interpretation of verse 9.11: "Fools who do not have discrimination despise Me, dwelling

TOPIC 29 - Transmigration of Soul

in human form. I have taken this body to bless My devotees. These fools do not know My higher Being. I am the great Lord, the Supreme." Some people make offensive remarks and use abusive language for high-level divinities who gracefully show up among us from time to time. Such evil minds existed also in the Ram, Krishna, and Jesus eras, not just in the current era.

15.8 शरीरं यदवाप्रोति यच्चाप्युत्क्रामतीश्वर: गृहीत्वैतानि संयाति वायुर्गन्धानिवाशयात्
The soul (upon death) carries the mind and senses from the old body to a new one.

Upon death, the soul discards the old body and carries with it the subtle and causal bodies, which include the mind and senses - refer to the comments under verse 2.28 for details of three kinds of bodies. While the soul gets a new body in every life, the mind continues journeying with it from past lifetimes.

What is the mind, as frequently mentioned in Gita? The mind is called manas in the Vedas, not the same as the mind as defined in modern science. The mind is not the same as the brain, which is an organ. The mind is a subtle element, not an organ. In the Vedic sense, the mind is a receptacle for the senses (Indriyas).

The memories, perceptions, and impressions of many lifetimes are stored in mind. Some define the mind as awareness (sanjna), consciousness, comprehension (ajnanam), understanding (vijnanam), insight (drsti), resolution (dhrtih), reflection (manas), impulse (jut), and will (sankalpa). The Upanishads call the mind the manas, prajna, Sankalpa, and Chita.

The mind is said to be two-fold: pure and impure. The impure mind is driven by desire and volition; the pure mind is devoid of desire. The mind alone is the cause of bondage or liberation for humans. Attached to objects, it leads to bondage; and freed from objects, it leads to liberation. When the mind is freed from contact with objects, then it is in the supreme state. When the five organs of perception become still, the mind ceases to be active.

The nervous system provides the channels through which the mind travels. The pure mind takes an upward course toward liberation. The mind full of desires accumulated over past lives takes a downward path towards the realms where those desires can be satisfied. That leads to the so-called bondage in the Gita lingo. The mind is difficult to stabilize; scriptures say that abandoning desires, chanting, and meditation calms the mind.

TOPIC 29 - Transmigration of Soul

TOPIC 30

Ashvatth Tree, Complex Samsara

Krishna says the supreme Lord is the original source of this visible universe that gave birth to everything, just like an Ashvatth tree with all its parts emerging from the earth. He declares that the Lord is the source of all existence, and the universe is like an upside-down tree with its roots in Brahm, and its branches and twigs are the things and factors in the creation. This is a complex tree, hard to identify its beginning and end, and is a product of Maya. This tree depicts the Samsara (the worldly life), and the one who understands it has transcended Maya. Those who are attached to it are trapped in it inescapably. Krishna tells Arjun the only guaranteed way to get out of the tree (freedom from Maya) is by dispassion and detachment, suggesting Arjun should chop down the tree with these weapons of dispassion and detachment. The one who gets out of the tree and goes beyond it is liberated and will not return to the mortal world of pain.

Krishna declares that a part of him is the individual soul (self) in each body, and he is the super soul (paramatma) seated in the body. He is the splendor in the sun, moon, and fire, and nourishes the earth. He is the inner witness of all beings, and the knower even beyond the Vedas. He is beyond both the perishable creation and the imperishable soul. Therefore, the Vedas and the world know him as the Supreme.

❧ *Krishna says:*

15.1 श्रीभगवानुवाच ऊर्ध्वमूलमध:शाखमश्वत्थं प्राहुरव्ययम् छन्दांसि यस्य पर्णानि यस्तं वेद स वेदवित्   They speak of an eternal ashvatth tree (Banyan tree) with its roots above and branches below. Its leaves are Vedic hymns and rituals. One who knows this tree is the knower of the Vedas.

The Samsara (our life in this universe) is compared to the massive, endless, and eternal Ashvattha tree whose source is Parabrahm. To explain the brilliant allegory, the infinite tree of

Samsara is continuous and changing. The human eyes cannot identify the beginning and the end of this tree. The leaves are Vedic hymns and rituals, meaning desire-prone karma, which supports the worldly existence and perpetuate life and death cycles. One who knows the source, how the tree grows, and how to cut it down, is a true knower and experiencer of the Vedas.

15.2 अधश्चोर्ध्वं प्रसृतास्तस्य शाखा गुणप्रवृद्धा विषयप्रवाला: अधश्च मूलान्यनुसन्ततानि कर्मानुबन्धीनि मनुष्यलोके Its branches are spread above and below, nourished by the (three) Gunas. Its sprouts or shoots or tender buds are the sense objects.

There is a close similarity between the physical world and the massive, endless, and eternal Ashvattha tree. The three Gunas irrigate the tree of worldly existence (Samsara). Sense objects (the buds) sprout into several aerial roots of desires and keep spreading continuously. The roots of the tree are hanging downward, below in the human realm. The roots bind people with desires and actions. The branches are spread far and wide.

One can go "above" to celestial abodes or "below" to the nether regions subject to the past karmas. The three Gunas irrigate the tree of "samsara" or the pleasure-seeking nature of humans. The buds (sense-objects) sprout into many aerial roots of desires for physical pleasures; they multiply uncontrollably. Selfish actions amplify the never-ending and ever-increasing desires; similar to the aerial roots feeding the growth of the giant tree.

The soul attached to the "tree of Samsara" gets trapped inescapably in the vicious cycle of births with no recovery in sight. We all do more of the same thing day in and day out going after sense objects and sink deeper into the "hole" from one life to the next.

15.3 and 15.4 न रूपमस्येह तथोपलभ्यते नान्तो न चादिर्न च सम्प्रतिष्ठा अश्वत्थमेनं सुविरूढमूल मसङ्गशस्त्रेण दृढेन छित्वा तत: पदं तत्परिमार्गितव्यंयस्मिन्गता न निवर्तन्ति भूय: तमेव चाद्यं पुरुषं प्रपद्ये यत: प्रवृत्ति: प्रसृता पुराणी The real form of this tree is not understood in this world (viewing it from the ground level where most people are), nor its beginning nor the end, nor its continuous existence. So, what to do or how to get out of the tree? This deep-rooted tree must be chopped with an ax of detachment. Then, one must find the base of the tree, the Primeval Purusha (Supreme Lord), from whom the ancient energy emerged eons ago. By surrendering to God, the birth/death cycle will end, and one will not return to this world again.

Krishna says the humongous tree cannot be understood from the ground level. He explains you can find your way out of the maze by detachment and taking refuge in God. The base of the tree is the Supreme Lord, as Krishna said in 10.8 in Topic 7: "I am the source of everything. Everything emanates from Me. Realizing this the wise is impressed and adores me.

Krishna reverts to his emphasis on the path of devotion. His message to Arjun is, abandon the ego and surrender to God to relieve yourself from the birth/death cycle. Swami Shivananda says, "Single-minded devotion, which consists of ceaselessly remembering the Supreme Being, is the surest and most potent means of attaining Self-realization."

TOPIC 31

Daivy (Divine) and Asuri (Demoniac) Nature

Krishna identifies the relationship between the virtuous life and spiritual path as it provides practical guidance to the aspirants. He classifies the divine and demoniac qualities, and instructs Arjun to develop divine qualities while eliminating the opposite qualities. Whereas the pure divine qualities are beneficial for peace and liberation, the opposite ones lead to bondage. Truthful conduct is a must for attaining higher levels of spirituality and respectable life here.

Lack of purity, truth, and faith in God degenerates one into an animalistic state, causing harm to others. Desires, cravings for food, and sensual pleasures, one's life degrades the soul. Realized sages and scriptures promote the life of virtues; therefore, one should abide by scriptural injunctions.

❧ Krishna says:

9.11 अवजानन्ति मां मूढा मानुषीं तनुमाश्रितम् परं भावमजानन्तो मम भूतमहेश्वरम्
Ignorant people ridicule Me when I descend in human form. They do not know the divinity of My personality.

Verse 4.6 in Topic 15 says God takes human form by his Yoga Maya Shakti. Swami Shivananada's interpretation of this verse: "Fools who do not have discrimination despise me, dwelling in human form. I have taken this body to bless my devotees. These fools do not know my higher being. I am the great Lord, the Supreme." Some ignorant people are offensive to high-level divinities, not knowing their divine mission. Such an unfortunate attitude also prevailed in the Ram, Krishna, and Jesus eras.

9.12 मोघाशा मोघकर्माणो मोघज्ञाना विचेतस: राक्षसीमासुरीं चैव प्रकृतिं मोहिनीं श्रिता:
"The knowledge of such deluded people is empty; their lives are fraught with disaster and evil, and their work and hopes are in vain."

This verse is translated differently in each book on Gita, some versions are very hard to understand. Above is a simple and concise translation borrowed from Eknath Easwaran's book on The Bhagawad Gita.

Some people argue that God does not take birth as a human or that Krishna was merely a Yogi or a wanderer with loose character or a lower level Divinity due to his contact with Maya. Krishna uses powerful language and says that the knowledge of such evil-minded people is empty and their life is a waste.

16.1, 16.2, and 16.3 श्रीभगवानुवाच अभयं सत्वसंशुद्धिर्ज्ञानयोगव्यवस्थिति: दानं दमश्च यज्ञश्च स्वाध्यायस्तप आर्जवम् अहिंसा सत्यमक्रोधस्त्याग: शान्तिरपैशुनम् दया भूतेष्वलोलुप्त्वं मार्दवं ह्रीरचापलम् तेज: क्षमा धृति: शौचमद्रोहोनातिमानिता भवन्ति सम्पदं दैवीमभिजातस्य भारत   The pious virtues of those who have the divine nature (daivy) are listed as follows: Fearlessness, purity of mind, steadfastness in spiritual knowledge, charity, self-control, sacrifice, the study of scriptures, austerity, and righteousness; non-violence, truthfulness, absence of anger, renunciation, peacefulness, restraint from fault-finding, compassion, non-covetousness, gentleness, modesty, and lack of fickleness; vigor, forgiveness, fortitude, cleanliness, bearing no enmity, and absence of vanity.

This is an overwhelming list of virtues for ordinary people to adopt, perhaps not possible. How can you develop so many virtues? Sant Shiromani Buddhadevji Maharaj offered brilliant advice to his followers, "Just follow one virtue diligently without exception and it will become part of you and draw other virtues automatically." He also said often that complete surrender to God invites many virtues and brings you in contact with devotees (Sangat). Surrender and Sangat, he said persistently, are two traits that will place you on the ladder to God. He lived in India and visited his followers in the USA a few times. He was a true renunciant, a Jnani, and the follower of the path of devotion. Originally from Punjab, he lived in Gujarat and passed away at the age of 103 in 2008 in Bulsar, Gujarat.

16.4 दम्भो दर्पोऽभिमानश्च क्रोध: पारुष्यमेव च अज्ञानं चाभिजातस्य पार्थ सम्पदमासुरीम्
The traits of those with a demoniac nature (Asuri) are as follows: hypocrisy, arrogance, conceit, anger, harshness, and ignorance.

People with demoniac traits are impure internally but behave and act as if they are pure. They will resort to extraordinary means to project themselves as righteous.

16.5 दैवी सम्पद्विमोक्षाय निबन्धायासुरी मता मा शुच: सम्पदं दैवीमभिजातोऽसि पाण्डव
The divine qualities lead to liberation. The demoniac attributes lead to bondage. Grieve not, as you were born with saintly virtues.

Krishna reassures Arjun not to worry as he has divine qualities.

16.6 द्वौ भूतसर्गौ लोकेऽस्मिन्दैव आसुर एव च दैवो विस्तरश: प्रोक्त आसुरं पार्थ मे शृणु
Some have divine attributes, others have demoniac. I have described the divine qualities in detail. Now hear from me about the demoniac.

16.7 प्रवृत्तिं च निवृत्तिं च जना न विदुरासुरा: न शौचं नापि चाचारो न सत्यं तेषु विद्यते
Those with demoniac qualities do things they should avoid and avoid the things they should do. They have neither purity nor ethical conduct nor truthfulness.

Verses 16.7 through verse 16.18 describe the demoniac nature in greater detail. Verses 16.19 and 16.20 explain the destiny of those with sinister ways.

The wicked people reject scriptures. Therefore, they do not know the correct moral standard to tell right from wrong. They believe in far-fetched thinking such as empiricism, communism, existentialism, skepticism, and distorted interpretation of freedom. For them, every thought and opinion is "relative" and individual perception. They would often argue, "Maybe it applies to you but not to me and not for me." As a result, there is no right or wrong action for them. The demoniac people are confused, arguementative and violent.

16.8 असत्यमप्रतिष्ठं ते जगदाहुरनीश्वरम् अपरस्परसम्भूतं किमन्यत्कामहैतुकम्   Those with demoniac traits say: "The world is without absolute truth, without any basis (for moral order), and without a God. It is created from the combination of the two sexes and has no purpose other than sexual gratification.

Those with demoniac nature challenge authority, regulation, and scriptural injunctions. They rationalize sexual indulgence with multiple partners and disrespect of law and order.

16.9 एतां दृष्टिमवष्टभ्य नष्टात्मानोऽल्पबुद्धय: प्रभवन्त्युग्रकर्माण: क्षयाय जगतोऽहिता:
Steadfastly adhering to such views, these misguided souls with small intellect and cruel actions emerge as enemies of the world threatening its destruction.

The demoniac-minded views reject the eternity of the soul and karmic reactions. They are self-serving and do cruel deeds. They violently pursue their ego-centric goals and cause destruction. Examples from recent history - Hitler, Mussolini, Lenin, Stalin, Mao Zedong.

16.10 काममाश्रित्य दुष्पूरं दम्भमानमदान्विता: मोहाद्गृहीत्वासद्ग्राहान्प्रवर्तन्तेऽशुचिव्रता:
The demoniacs hang on to their false beliefs, concealing unquenchable lust, hypocrisy, pride, and arrogance. Thus illusioned, they are attracted to the impermanent and work with impure resolve.

Demoniacs are attracted to pleasures, pretend to be what they are not, believe nobody is more intelligent than them, and do exactly the opposite of what is commonly acceptable to most people.

16.11 चिन्तामपरिमेयां च प्रलयान्तामुपाश्रिता: कामोपभोगपरमा एतावदिति निश्चिता:
They have endless worries and anxieties that end only with death. Still, they remain convinced that the sense gratification is the highest purpose in life.

The demoniacs have unquenchable desire for material objects. They are always scheming to fulfill aspirations and experience momentary pleasure. Then, due to fear of losing the success, they fiercely hold on to the object by any means, right or wrong.

16.12 आशापाशशतैर्बद्धा: कामक्रोधपरायणा: ईहन्ते कामभोगार्थमन्यायेनार्थसञ्चयान्

Slaves of hundreds of desires and driven by lust and anger, they strive to accumulate wealth by unfair means; all for the gratification of their senses.

Earning and hoarding money by whatever means for 'sense gratification' is predominant among the demoniacs.

16.13, 16.14, and 16.15 इदमद्य मया लब्धमिमं प्राप्स्ये मनोरथम् इदमस्तीदमपि मे भविष्यति पुनर्धनम् असौ मया हत: शत्रुर्हनिष्ये चापरानपि ईश्वरोऽहमहं भोगी सिद्धोऽहं बलवान्सुखी आढ्योऽभिजनवानस्मि कोऽन्योऽस्ति सदृशो मया यक्ष्ये दास्यामि मोदिष्य इत्यज्ञानविमोहिता:

These verses list the thought process of persons suffering from ignorance:

1. I have gained enormous wealth,
2. I shall now fulfill my desires,
3. I have a lot,
4. Tomorrow, I shall have more,
5. I destroyed that enemy,
6. I shall ruin others also,
7. I am like God;
8. I am the enjoyer,
9. I am dominant,
10. I am happy,
11. I am wealthy,
12. I have relatives in top status,
13. Who else is equal to me?
14. I shall perform sacrifices (to please celestial gods),
15. I shall give alms,
16. I shall rejoice.

Krishna describes the evil nature of the ego-centric demoniac-natured people. They will remove obstacles in their way and, in the process, will not hesitate to harm or kill others. Ego triggers the biggest lie and makes people believe what they are not.

16.16 द्वाविमौ पुरुषौ लोके क्षरश्चाक्षर एव च क्षर: सर्वाणि भूतानि कूटस्थोऽक्षर उच्यते

Possessed and misled by many imaginations, lost in delusion, and addicted to sense gratification they fall into a foul hell.

Impractical and repetitive thoughts possess egoistic people. They continuously complain and are resentful about many things. Their crooked ways drive them to hell.

16.17 आत्मसम्भाविता: स्तब्धा धनमानमदान्विता: यजन्ते नामयज्ञैस्ते दम्भेनाविधिपूर्वकम्

They are self-conceited, stubborn, full of pride, and arrogant in their wealth. They perform flamboyant sacrifices in name, ignoring the scriptures.

Demoniac people perform sacrifices with an impure intent to show off their wealth and project a look of piety. Their sacrifices do not follow scriptural injunctions. Mahabharat

TOPIC 31 – Daivy (Divine) and Asuri (Demoniac) Nature

says: "If we advertise a good deed we have done, its merit decreases; if we keep it secret, its merit multiplies."

16.18 अहङ्कारं बलं दर्पं कामं क्रोधं च संश्रिता: मामात्मपरदेहेषु प्रद्विषन्तोऽभ्यसूयका:
Given over to ego, power, vanity, desire, and anger, they despise Me in their own bodies and others'.

They sing their own praise and criticize others. If anyone opposes their schemes, they become angry, disrespecting God seated within the heart of everyone.

16.19 and 16.20 तानहं द्विषत: क्रूरान्संसारेषु नराधमान् क्षिपाम्यजस्रमशुभानासुरीष्वेव योनिषु आसुरीं योनिमापन्ना मूढा जन्मनि जन्मनि मामप्राप्यैव कौन्तेय ततो यान्त्यधमां गतिम् Here is the destiny of these cruel, vicious, and vile people. I throw them into the wombs of those with similar nature in the cycle of rebirth. These ignorant souls take birth repeatedly in demoniac wombs. Not reaching Me, they sink to an abominable existence eventually, after many births.

The fate of demoniac personalities includes the following outcomes. Demoniacs gradually sink to hell. In their next lives, they are born in families with similar mentalities, where they get a suitable environment to exercise their free will. The soul is not the one that chooses the next body, abode, and environment, but the accrued Karma determines the body for the soul (still in bondage), with the super soul or Paramatma acting as the witness. For further explanation of how the law of Karma works, see the commentary under 9.7 and 9.8 in Topic 29 on Transmigration.

TOPIC 32

Gates to Hell

Krishna declares that lust, anger, and greed are the three gates to hell. Lust, if not satisfied, causes anger, and when satiated, breeds greed for more. Then, more. It is impossible to quench lust once your mind is absorbed in continued thoughts of the objects you pursue to satisfy lust. These three evils attract many other undesirable traits such as the lack of faith and rejection of the existence of God. The freedom from lust, anger, and greed clears the way to God and liberation for devoted aspirants. Again, the control of the senses is essential to drive away lust.

૪ Krishna says:

3.32 ये त्वेतदभ्यसूयन्तो नानुतिष्ठन्ति मे मतम् सर्वज्ञानविमूढांस्तान्विद्धि नष्टानचेतस: But those who knock and degrade my teachings and those who lack knowledge and discrimination, they ignore the principles of Karma Yoga and invite their ruin (destruction of the path to God).

The lack of respect for the teacher, knowledge, and discrimination causes one also to lose faith. Without faith (Shraddha), one becomes confused and argumentative and is lost in his mental world. Shankaracharya says, "Shraddha is a deep faith in what the Guru and the scriptures say."

16.21 त्रिविधं नरकस्येदं द्वारं नाशनमात्मन: काम: क्रोधस्तथा लोभस्तस्मादेतत्त्रयं त्यजेत्
The three gates that lead to the hell of self-destruction for the soul are lust, anger, and greed. Therefore, everyone should abandon these three.

Verse 16.21 here and 2.62/2.63 in Topic 6 collectively reinforce the danger of these enemies of humanity – lust, anger, and greed. They obstruct spiritual progress. In reply to arjun's question. Krishna's answer – lust compels one to sin. When lust is not satisfied, it turns into anger, which leads one to commit many sinful acts. Passion, when satiated, transforms into greed, as indicated in verse 2.62. Together, lust, anger, and greed form the foundation from which many other evil vices develop, further tightening the grip of Maya on the bondage of the soul.

16.22 एतैर्विमुक्त: कौन्तेय तमोद्वारैस्त्रिभिर्नर: आचरत्यात्मन: श्रेयस्ततो याति परां गतिम्

Release from these vices, which are gates to hell, will clear the path to liberation of the soul and the prospect of reaching the Supreme.

Abandoning lust, greed, and anger would attract one to the company of realized people (satsang) and the spiritual path, thus opening the door to liberation. In the company of sages and other spiritual aspirants, one receives instructions from scriptures for practicing internal purity, yoga, prayer, service of humanity, and meditation.

TOPIC 33

Follow Scriptural Injunctions

Scriptures set the standard for noble behavior. They provide a guide for moral code and teach authentic spiritual processes such as performing Yajna and austerities. Krishna says following scriptures leads to the higher goals. Those pursuing activities on their own whim but against the scriptures are on way to degradation. It is advisable to consult experts to interpret scriptures accurately when you are not sure.

◈ *Krishna says:*

16.23 य: शास्त्रविधिमुत्सृज्य वर्तते कामकारत: न स सिद्धिमवाप्नोति न सुखं न परां गतिम्

Those who act under the influence of desire, neglecting the preaching of the scriptures, accomplish neither perfection, happiness, nor the supreme goal in life.

Scriptures guide us regarding what to do (vidhi) and what not to do (nishedh), leading to enlightenment. By following the scriptures faithfully, one becomes eligible for perfection. However, people of demoniac tendencies do the opposite; they ignore and discard scriptures and engage in impure acts.

16.24 तस्माच्छास्त्रं प्रमाणं ते कार्याकार्यव्यवस्थितौ ज्ञात्वा शास्त्रविधानोक्तं कर्म कर्तुमिहार्हसि

Let scriptures be the authorized standard in deciding what to do and what not.

Vedic scriptures guide the faithful in deciding the right from the wrong. When necessary, check the authentic scriptures or consult those who understand them to determine if you are on the right course. The Manu Smriti states: "bhutam bhavyam bhavishyam cha sarvam vedat prasidhyati," which means, "The authenticity of any spiritual principle of the past, present, or future, must be according to the Vedas."

❦ *Arjun asks:*

17.1 अर्जुन उवाच ये शास्त्रविधिमुत्सृज्य यजन्ते श्रद्धयान्विता: तेषां निष्ठा तु का कृष्ण सत्वमाहो रजस्तम: What is the status of the one who worships with faith but disregards the injunctions of scriptures? Is their faith considered in the mode of goodness (sattvic), passion (rajasic), or ignorance (tamasic)?

Arjun's question is about the standing of those who worship faithfully without following the correct instructions from scriptures.

❦ *Krishna responds as follows:*

17.5 and 17.6 अशास्त्रविहितं घोरं तप्यन्ते ये तपो जना: दम्भाहङ्कारसंयुक्ता: कामरागबलान्विता: कर्षयन्त: शरीरस्थं भूतग्राममचेतस: मां चैवान्त:शरीरस्थं तान्विद्ध्यासुरनिश्चयान्   Some people who are driven by ego and hypocrisy perform severe austerities, not instructed by the scriptures. They are encouraged by desire and attachment. They torment not only the body but also 'I' (Paramatma) who dwell within them. These senseless people (mudhmate) have demoniac resolves.

Austerities against scriptural recommendations are tamasic. Some resort to extreme austerities in the name of spirituality to satisfy their whims and impress people. For example, some lie on beds of thorns or drive spikes through their bodies or keep one hand raised for years or continuously gaze at the sun or undertake long fasts. They are faithful, but their austerities are against scriptures. According to Krishna, their faith is tamasic (in the mode of ignorance).

17.11 अफलाकाङ्क्षिभिर्यज्ञो विधिदृष्टो य इज्यते यष्टव्यमेवेति मन: समाधाय स सात्विक:
Sacrifice performed according to scriptural injunctions, without the expectation of rewards, and as a matter of duty is sattvic (of the nature of goodness).

The sacrifice done in the mode of goodness must meet three criteria as specified. 1. Aphala-ākānkshibhih means the sacrifice done without expectation of personal benefits. 2. Vidhi drishtah means making the sacrifice as defined in scriptures. 3. Yashtavyam evaiti implies that it must be done as the worship of the Supreme God.

TOPIC 33 – Follow Scriptural Injunctions

TOPIC 34

Manifestation of Three Gunas

The three Gunas propel the senses to perform all actions, but out of ignorance and ego, the soul thinks it is the doer. Ignorance causes attachment to the results of actions. The three Gunas are inherent in everyone in varying proportions according to their karma. The Gunas are the cause of the particular type of faith everyone has, the food they like, and the worship they do. The types of sacrifice, austerity, and charity people prefer are also because of the three Gunas. Krishna defines one's inclination in what they do for the three categories of people who are predominantly: sattvic, rajasic, and tamasic, in the following verses selected from Gita chapters. While the mode of goodness (Sattva) is preferable over the modes of passion (Rajas) and ignorance (Tamas), the thrust of Krishna's message is one should rise above all three modes.

🦋 *Krishna says:*

3.27 प्रकृते: क्रियमाणानि गुणै: कर्माणि सर्वश: अहङ्कारविमूढात्मा कर्ताहमिति मन्यते   All activities are carried out principally by the three modes of material nature, but in darkness, ignorance, and illusion, the soul thinks it is the body and regards itself to be the doer.

Under the influence of Maya, the soul thinks it is the body, and falsely considers itself as the doer. This verse says the ahankāra vimūḍhātmā (those who are dazed by their ego and think they are the body) think they are doing everything.

3.28 तत्त्वविन्तु महाबाहो गुणकर्मविभागयो: गुणा गुणेषु वर्तन्त इति मत्वा न सज्जते
Enlightened people undearstand the domain of the Gunas and Karmas, and are not attached. Knowing that the Gunas interact with each other, the wise are not confused and attached.

The wise people (the knowers of the Truth) are not affected by the three modes; they know it is the Gunas that drive the senses to their objects. Just as waves are part of the ocean, the body is a part of Maya, and Maya is the doer of everything according to the three Gunas.

Why then does the soul think it is the doer? Because, it is in the grip of the powerful ego that misleads the soul to believe it is the body; in other words, the soul is under a delusion.

3.29 प्रकृतेर्गुणसम्मूढाः सज्जन्ते गुणकर्मसु तानकृत्स्नविदो मन्दान्कृत्स्नविन्न विचालयेत् The deluded people who are misled by the workings of the Gunas become attached to the results of their actions. The enlightened people who understand these truths should not unsettle the ignorant.

The Gunas cause the attachment. Krishna has a few words for those who have gained wisdom. The wise who understand the role of the Gunas should not bombard the followers with criticism but be considerate to them. Be patient with your audience of sincere spiritual seekers. Motivate and inspire them, teach them what they need to know, and help them rise and receive the right knowledge at their natural pace. Those at the lower level of understanding will welcome such consideration. They will not be confused, offended, and repulsed.

5.14 न कर्तृत्वं न कर्माणि लोकस्य सृजति प्रभुः न कर्मफलसंयोगं स्वभावस्तु प्रवर्तते The notion of 'doership' or the actions or the fruits of efforts does not come from God. These arise from one's nature (based on the Gunas).

The three modes are the doers and the cause, not God or the soul. God does not direct or dictate our actions. He is not the reason for the soul's false notion of doership. Out of ignorance and under the influence of Maya, the soul perceives itself as the doer and the cause. The soul, once it is free, drops the notion of doership and understands that the three Gunas are the doers and the cause.

17.2 श्रीभगवानुवाच त्रिविधा भवति श्रद्धा देहिनां सा स्वभावजा सात्विकी राजसी चैव तामसी चेति तां शृणु Everyone has faith born of innate nature (Svabhavja). There are three kinds of faith: sattvic, rajasic, and tamasic. Hear about this from Me.

Everyone has faith that is either sattvic, rajasic, or tamasic. As Swami Mukundananda explained well in his book on the Bhagavad Gita, everyone has faith in something, including those who don't believe in scriptures or don't acknowledge the existence of God. Atheists may have faith in logical thinking or scientific theories. This is also a type of faith. The idea that 'religion is faith' and 'science is knowledge', is debatable because science is a form of faith. Charles Towne, Nobel Prize winner in physics, said, "We scientists believe in the existence of the external world and the validity of our logic. Nevertheless, these are acts of faith because we cannot prove them." Scientists discovered the connection between the energy and matter, but cannot explain the source of the abundant energy in the universe. They explained the structure of a molecule but do not know who designed the molecular structure for each element. And, where does the energy residing in an atom come from?

TOPIC 34 - Manifestation of Three Gunas

🌼 *Krishna now explains why the faith of people varies.*

17.3 सत्वानुरूपा सर्वस्य श्रद्धा भवति भारत श्रद्धामयोऽयं पुरुषो यो यच्छ्रद्ध: स एव स:
The faith of everyone conforms to their nature, which is made of faith. People are what their faith is.

The quality and the target of our faith are based on the nature of our minds.

17.4 यजन्ते सात्विका देवान्यक्षरक्षांसि राजसा: प्रेतान्भूतगणांश्चान्ये यजन्ते तामसा जना:
Those in the mode of goodness (sattvic) worship celestial gods; those in the mode of passion (rajasic) worship the yakshas and rakshasas; those in the mode of ignorance (tamasic) worship ghosts and spirits.

Whom you worship is determined by the predominant mode of your nature. Tamas (mode of ignorance) attracts you to ghosts and spirits; Rajas (mode of passion) to the yakṣhas (semi-celestial beings who have power and wealth) and rākṣhasas (powerful beings inclined to sensual enjoyment, revenge, and wrath); sattva (mode of goodness) to celestial gods.

17.7 आहारस्त्वपि सर्वस्य त्रिविधो भवति प्रिय: यज्ञस्तपस्तथा दानं तेषां भेदमिमं शृणु   The food people like is according to their dispositions. The same is true for the sacrifice, austerity, and charity they prefer. Now hear of the distinctions from Me.

A person's taste for a type of food is determined according to the three Gunas prevalent in them. The mind and body have a relationship in that one affects the other. The Upanishad says, "āhāra shuddhau sattva shuddhiḥ," which means, "By eating pure food, the mind becomes pure."

17.8 आयु:सत्वबलारोग्यसुखप्रीतिविवर्धना: रस्या: स्निग्धा: स्थिरा हृद्या आहारा: सात्विकप्रिया:
Sattvic people like foods that increase life, virtue, strength, health, happiness, and satisfaction. Such foods are juicy, succulent, nourishing, and naturally tasteful.

The qualities of the food described in this verse lead some to conclude that Krishna is referring to vegetarian food. However, nowhere in Gita, Krishna directly promotes vegetarian food or prohibits non-vegetarian food. Sages believe a vegetarian diet is healthy and beneficial for cultivating the qualities of the mode of goodness that are conducive for spiritual life. Some argue based on the logic that the anatomical structure of the humans indicate that vegetarian food is more suitable for them than the non-vegetarian food.

17.9 कट्वम्ललवणात्युष्णतीक्ष्णरूक्षविदाहिन: आहारा राजसस्येष्टा दु:खशोकामयप्रदा:
Rajasic people (in the mode of passion) prefer foods that are too—bitter, sour, salty, hot, pungent, dry, and spicy. Such foods produce pain, grief, and disease.

Rajasic people go for hot and spicy food. The spices and ingredients used in the cooking of such food carry a sharper flavor that dominates the natural taste of the food.

17.10 यातयामं गतरसं पूति पर्युषितं च यत् उच्छिष्टमपि चामेध्यं भोजनं तामसप्रियम्
Tamasic people (in the mode of ignorance) prefer foods that are overcooked, stale, putrid, polluted, and impure.

Some believe that the description of food in this verse fits non-vegetarian food. Again, that is their interpretation, but not a consensus because vegetarian food also can be "stale, overcooked, impure, and rotten". In summary, people have argued if Gita approves non-vegetarian food or not. Once again, it is the author's conclusion that Gita does not seem to support or oppose non-vegetarian food in explicit terms. The benefits of a vegetarian diet are many as proven by science, and therefore more and more people worldwide are choosing it as a healthier option to non-vegetarian food.

17.11 अफलाकाङ्क्षिभिर्यज्ञो विधिदृष्टो य इज्यते यष्टव्यमेवेति मन: समाधाय स सात्विक:
Sacrifice done per the scriptures (Vidhi drishtah) unselfishly (Aphala-ākāṅkṣhibhiḥ), as a duty, is Sattvic (in the mode of goodness).

Sacrifice done 1. as a duty to God, 2. per the scriptures, and 3. without anticipation of rewards for personal pleasure is Sattvic. In other words, do the Yajna (sacrifice) or whatever else you are doing according to the principles of Karma Yoga.

7.12 अभिसन्धाय तु फलं दम्भार्थमपि चैव यत् इज्यते भरतश्रेष्ठ तं यज्ञं विद्धि राजसम्   The sacrifice performed for material benefit or with the deceitful aim is the mode of passion (rajasic).

Krishna says that sacrifice may be made with a grand ceremony, but if it is for the sake of desire-prone rewards, prestige, and show, it is rajasic in nature.

17.13 विधिहीनमसृष्टान्नंमन्त्रहीनमदक्षिणम्श्रद्धाविरहितंयज्ञंतामसंपरिचक्षते   Sacrifice done without faith, contrary to the injunctions of the scriptures, and in which no food is offered and no mantras chanted and no donation made is to be considered Tamasic, in the mode of ignorance.

Sacrifice done according to one's whim disregarding scriptures out of laziness and belligerence is tamasic.

17.14 देवद्विजगुरुप्राज्ञपूजनं शौचमार्जवम् ब्रह्मचर्यमहिंसा च शारीरं तप उच्यते   Worship of the gods, the Brahmins, the spiritual master, the wise, and the elders—when this is done with cleanliness, simplicity, celibacy, and non-violence is the austerity of the body.

Rig Veda says: "sacrifice done by purifying the body, with austerity, with pure intent one can reach the final state of yoga."

17.15 अनुद्वेगकरं वाक्यं सत्यं प्रियहितं च यत् स्वाध्यायाभ्यसनं चैव वाङ्मयं तप उच्यते
Truthful Speech that is pleasant, agreeable, and beneficial and the recitation of Vedas is "verbal austerity".

Manu Smriti says: "Speak the Truth in such a way that it is pleasing to others. Do not speak the Truth in a manner injurious to others. Never speak untruth, though it may be pleasant. This is the eternal path of morality and dharma."

17.16 मन:प्रसाद:सौम्यत्वंमौनमात्मविनिग्रह:भावसंशुद्धिरित्येतत्तपोमानसमुच्यते   The calmness of mind, compassion, silence, discipline, and purity of heart are "mental austerity."

The austerity of the mind is superior to the austerity of body and speech. You can exercise control of the body and speech with a controlled mind. Keep the mind away from negative thoughts as these are harmful. Focusing the mind on positive sentiments is called the austerity of the mind. Thoughts determine your destiny, illustrated by the arrow chart:

Thoughts become >>words >>actions >>habits >>character >>destiny

17.17 श्रद्धया परया तसं तपस्तत्त्रिविधं नरैः फलाकाङ्क्षिभिर्युक्तैः सात्विकं परिचक्षते

When sincere people with keen faith practice these three-fold austerities without attachment to material rewards, such austerities are Sattvic (in the mode of goodness).

17.18 सत्कारमानपूजार्थं तपो दम्भेन चैव यत् क्रियते तदिह प्रोक्तं राजसं चलमध्रुवम्

Austerity performed for ostentation in anticipation of honor, respect, and adoration is Rajasic (in the mode of passion). Its benefits are questionable and temporary.

Guests soon forget the "show" and often criticize the flashiness of parties held by the host for the apparent reason to display wealth and showmanship.

17.19 मूढग्राहेणात्मनो यत्पीडया क्रियते तप: परस्योत्सादनार्थं वा तत्तामसमुदाहृतम्

Austerity performed with idiotic notions, and that involves tormenting the self and hurting others is tamasic (in the mode of ignorance).

Refer to verses 17.5 and 17.6 in Topic 33 on Scriptural Injunctions for examples of the type of tortures the tamasic people do in the name of austerity. However, these are not austerities but extreme acts of torture and against the preaching of Krishna. The performers of tamasic austerities may be heading towards the entry to hell.

17.20 दातव्यमिति यद्दानं दीयतेऽनुपकारिणे देशे काले च पात्रे च तद्दानं सात्विकं स्मृतम्

Charity given to a deserving individual because it is the right thing to do, without expecting rewards in return, and at the proper time and place is sattvic (in the mode of goodness).

According to scriptures, the selfless donation given to deserving people during the age of Kali purifies the mind.

17.21 यत्तु प्रत्युपकारार्थं फलमुद्दिश्य वा पुन: दीयते च परिक्लिष्टं तद्दानं राजसं स्मृतम्

Charity offered with reluctance, in expectation of returns and rewards is Rajasic (in the mode of passion). Its benefits are temporary.

17.22 अदेशकाले यद्दानमपात्रेभ्यश्च दीयते असत्कृतमवज्ञातं तत्तामसमुदाहृतम्   Charity given in the wrong place at the wrong time to an undeserving person without respect, and in contempt is tamasic (in the mode of ignorance).

An example of tamasic donation is a donation to a drug-addict who buys drugs with it and then robs a bank under the influence of the drug.

TOPIC 34 - Manifestation of Three Gunas

TOPIC 35

Significance of Om Tata Sat

Krishna brings up the mantra 'Om Tat Sat' in context with characteristics of Brahm. Om is the original symbol or a mantra, "an invisible vibratory power, the direct creator and activator of all creation" (a quote from Yogananda Paramhansa), a sacred syllable that designates Brahm. It is the cosmic sound some say they hear in an advanced state of meditation. The Sanskrit word Tat stands for "that", Brahm, the ultimate reality beyond any description and human thought. And another Sanskrit word "Sat" stands for "that which is" and "that which is good". Sat is God, beyond creation. Collectively these words give the mantra 'Om Tat Sat' a deep meaning that only the good and eternal really exists. The opposite of sat is asat, which says the evil is not real and it is not eternal but transient. Om tat sat symbolizes a transcendental aspect of the absolute truth beyond the name, form, space, and time. It is a part of the prayers of the worshippers of the formless.

❦ *Krishna says:*

17.23 ॐ तत्सदिति निर्देशो ब्रह्मणस्त्रिविधः स्मृतः ब्राह्मणास्तेन वेदाश्च यज्ञाश्च विहिताः पुरा
Syllables 'Om Tat Sat' symbolically represent Brahm. The priests (Brahmanas), scriptures, and Yajna (sacrifice) originated from Om Tat Sat.

Rise above the Gunas to reach the highest level known as Om Tat Sat.

17.24 तस्माद् ॐ इत्युदाहृत्य यज्ञदानतपःक्रियाः प्रवर्तन्ते विधानोक्ताः सततं ब्रह्मवादिनाम्
Therefore, the followers of the Vedas always begin mantras by uttering Om first when performing Yajna or offering charities or undergoing penance.

The syllable Om is a symbolic representation of the impersonal aspect of God called Brahm. Om is the ancient sound that pervades creation. Om is included at the beginning of mantras as a beej (seed) mantra to invoke auspiciousness.

17.25 तदित्यनभिसन्धाय फलं यज्ञतप:क्रिया: दानक्रियाश्च विविधा: क्रियन्ते मोक्षकाङ्क्षिभि:
Those who want liberation and not personal rewards add the word "tat" when doing activities involving austerity, sacrifice, and charity.

Chanting Tat, along with austerity, sacrifice, and charity indicates that one is performing these activities not for material rewards, but for attaining the level of Brahm.

17.26 and 17.27 सद्भावे साधुभावे च सदित्येतत्प्रयुज्यते प्रशस्ते कर्मणि तथा सच्छब्द: पार्थ युज्यते यज्ञे तपसि दाने च स्थिति: सदिति चोच्यते कर्म चैव तदर्थीयं सदित्येवाभिधीयते   The term Sat means existence and goodness. Sat also signifies an auspicious action, therefore, activities such as donation, penance, and austerity are called Sat.

Sat signifies goodness and virtue. Meritorious acts such as charity and penance are described as Sat, which also means eternal and always authentic.

17.28 अश्रद्धया हुतं दत्तं तपस्तसं कृतं च यत् असदित्युच्यते पार्थ न च तत्प्रेत्य नो इह   Any good activities such as sacrifice, penance, and charity done without faith are called Asat (the opposite of Sat); they are useless in this world and the next.

Krishna emphasizes the importance of faith by stating the sacrifices, austerities, and charities done without faith are useless in this life and the next. The Bible says the authentic faith is more valuable than gold that perishes. Faith is whatever you believe in with certainty. Trust, confidence, belief, assumptions, and expectations are other names for faith only.

Devotion and faith (bhakti and shraddha) are the foundations for spiritual practice. Faith in God, the scriptures, the teacher, the spiritual path, dharma, the theory of liberation, and the laws of God are a few examples of faith, deemed as the highest virtues. The human senses (Indriyas) cannot see or know God, yet faith drives the devotees to follow rigorous routines of their chosen path to attain God's grace.

TOPIC 36

Spreading the Divine Message of Gita

This section on Spreading the Divine Message of Gita is combined with Topic 38 on Sharing the Message of Gita.

TOPIC 37

Effect of Three Gunas

This topic explains the theory of Karma Yoga in view of the three Gunas. It is not the action that binds the soul but the attachment to the action. One must not abandon the obligatory duties, no matter whether those are considered high or low. Distinct types of renunciation motivated by attachment or the lack of it, according to the three Gunas, are defined here. Also covered here is the theory of action relative to the five elements necessary to accomplish the actions – the body, the senses, ego, efforts to do the action, and divine will. Then, Krishna explains the three factors that propel actions: Jnana (knowledge), Jneya (the object of knowledge), and Jnata (the knower), and also, three kinds of Knowledge, Action, and Doer according to the three modes.

Intellect and determination which propel, control, and direct action are explained in view of the three Gunas. The topic at the end summarizes the theory of action in the commentary under verse 18.39.

The three Gunas affect everyone in Maya's domain from hell to heavens, without exception. People possess unique natures depending on the proportions of the three Gunas inherent in them because of the past karmas and impressions.

18.4 निश्चयं शृणु मे तत्र त्यागे भरतसत्तम त्यागो हि पुरुषव्याघ्र त्रिविध: सम्प्रकीर्तित: Hear My conclusion on the subject of renunciation; "it has been declared to be of three kinds".

Saint Kabir said: "One is not brave just because he can fight with arrows and swords; the one who renounces Maya and pursues bhakti is courageous." Renunciation is for the brave-hearted, hence Krishna addresses Arjun as purush-vyaghr (the lion among men) in this verse.

18.5 यज्ञदानतप:कर्म न त्याज्यं कार्यमेव तत् यज्ञो दानं तपश्चैव पावनानि मनीषिणाम्   One should not abandon activities relating to sacrifice, charity, and penance; in fact, one must perform these activities.

Krishna says one must never renounce sacrifice, charity, and penance as these actions elevate the soul and are beneficial for people. Such measures help spiritual growth and liberation.

18.6 एतान्यपि तु कर्माणि सङ्गं त्यक्त्वा फलानि च कर्तव्यानीति मे पार्थ निश्चितं मतमुत्तमम्
These activities must be done without attachment and expectation for rewards; this is My absolute and best judgment.

Acts of sacrifice, charity, and penance should be done selflessly in devotion to God. This verse summarizes the theory of Karma Yoga discussed in Topic 3 earlier. The reason the karmas bind the soul is not the action itself, but the attachment and expectation of rewards to satisfy desires.

18.8 दु:खमित्येव यत्कर्म कायक्लेशभयात्यजेत् स कृत्वा राजसं त्यागं नैव त्यागफलं लभेत्
Giving up prescribed duties because they may be difficult or uncomfortable amounts to working in the mode of passion (rajasic). Such renunciation of actions is never elevating for the soul.

One must not relinquish obligatory duties. For example, Arjun must fight the righteous battle being a warrior.

18.9 कार्यमित्येव यत्कर्म नियतं क्रियतेऽर्जुन सङ्गं त्यक्त्वा फलं चैव स त्याग: सात्विको मत:
The obligatory action done because it is one's duty, without attachment and the desire for reward, is sattvic renunciation (like goodness).

The highest kind of renunciation is not to stop but continue to perform our obligatory duties, giving up attachment to the results. So, you abandon attachment and selfishness, not the actions. Such renunciation is Sattvic (in the mode of goodness); it raises the spiritual level. Renouncing family in pursuit of bliss, but with the mind attached to the sense objects is not a spiritually elevating action.

18.13 पञ्चैतानि महाबाहो कारणानि निबोध मे साङ्ख्ये कृतान्ते प्रोक्तानि सिद्धये सर्वकर्मणाम्
Now learn from Me these five elements necessary for accomplishing all actions, as taught by the Sankhya system.

Sankhya philosophy develops knowledge of the self by analysis of the elements within the body and in the world. Sankhya was initiated by Maharshi Kapil believed to be an avatar (incarnation of God). The following describes what drives actions and how they are performed.

18.14 अधिष्ठानं तथा कर्ता करणं च पृथग्विधम् विविधाश्च पृथक्चेष्टा दैवं चैवात्र पञ्चमम्
The five factors of action are: 1. The body, 2. the means (the senses), 3. The ego, 4. The effort for the performance of the act, and 5. The divine will.

TOPIC 37 - Effect of Three Gunas

The doer of karmas is the soul; although the soul itself does not act, the body-mind-intellect mechanism powered by Jeev Shakti (life force) perform the actions under the jurisdiction of the soul. Hence, the soul is the knower and the doer, and a factor in completing actions. The senses perform the actions. Without the working senses (tongue, skin, eyes, nose, and ears), the soul cannot feel the sensations of taste, touch, sight, smell, or sound. Thus, the senses are listed as factors in doing actions.

However, if one puts no effort, nothing gets done. Therefore, cheshthā (effort) is another ingredient of action. God bestows skills to perform actions, according to past karmas. Hence, God is listed as one of the factors responsible for the action.

The Praśhna Upaniṣhad says: "It is the soul that sees, touches, hears, feels, tastes, thinks, and comprehends. Thus, the soul is both the knower and the doer of actions."

18.15 and 18.16 शरीरवाङ्मनोभिर्यत्कर्म प्रारभते नरः न्याय्यं वा विपरीतं वा पञ्चैते तस्य हेतवः तत्रैवं सति कर्तारमात्मानं केवलं तु यः पश्यत्यकृतबुद्धित्वान्न स पश्यति दुर्मतिः   These are the five factors in all actions, right or wrong, done by thought, word, or deed. The lack of understanding misleads people to think of themselves as separate agents. The impure intellect impairs the ability to see the truth.

The soul does govern the body, mind, and intellect, but without the body given by God, the soul cannot do anything at all. If the body were not energized by God's Jeev Shakti, it can do nothing. The message that can be derived from this verse is: 1. Be free from the pride of doership; 2. Give credit for our efforts to God for the tools and skills He gave us; 3. Realize we are not the enjoyers of our actions; 4. The ultimate enjoyer of our activities is God.

Enjoying the benefits of everything we do without thanking God and offering results to Him is selfish and further binds the soul. Refer to verses 9.26/9.27 in Topic 7 regarding the spirit of offering to God.

18.18 ज्ञानं ज्ञेयं परिज्ञाता त्रिविधा कर्मचोदना करणं कर्म कर्तेति त्रिविधः कर्मसंग्रहः Knowledge, the object of knowledge, and the knower are the three factors that induce action. The organ (instrument of work), the act itself, and the doer—these are three constituents of action.

Krishna presents the three-fold factors that propel actions. These are jnana (knowledge), jneya (the object of knowledge), and jnata (the knower). "Knowledge" provides understanding to the "knower" about the "object of knowledge." This triad jointly induces action. The second set named in this verse is the karm tripuṭī (the triad of action). It includes the karta (doer), karaṇ (the instrument of action), and karm (the act itself). This triad of work jointly constitutes the content of the action. The "doer" utilizes the "instruments of action" to perform "the action". Next, Krishna relates them to the three modes to explain why people differ in their motives and actions.

18.19 ज्ञानं कर्म च कर्ता च त्रिधैव गुणभेदतः प्रोच्यते गुणसङ् ख्याने यथावच्छृणु तान्यपि There are three kinds of Knowledge, Action, and Doer (in Sankhya philosophy) according to the three modes; I will now explain these distinctions to you.

Topics 28 and 34 explained how the three Gunas bind the soul, how they influence the faith and the choice of foods, and the three categories of sacrifice, charity, and penance. This verse 18.19 introduces the three types of knowledge, action, and doers, according to the three modes (Gunas). The Sankhya philosophy is recognized as the authority in the analysis of material nature. Sankhya states the cause for misery is the desire of the Purusha (the soul) to enjoy Prakriti (nature and everything made from it).

18.20 सर्वभूतेषु येनैकं भावमव्ययमीक्षते अविभक्तं विभक्तेषु तज्ज्ञानं विद्धि सात्विकम्
Sattvic Knowledge (in the mode of goodness) is when a person sees a single undivided indestructible reality (God) in all beings, not a separate reality in separate beings.

Shrimad Bhagavatam states: "there is only one entity in existence, without a second." That entity is God; formless Brahm in the nirguna sense and the one with a form like Krishna, Ram, and Shiv. He supports everything and everyone, without needing the support of anyone. He is complete all by Himself, and everything is His. When we see the entire creation in its unity with God, it is considered sattvic knowledge. It is the knowledge of oneness with the Almighty, the One and only One. Guru Nanakdevji envisioned one God (Brahm) known as Ek Onkar in Sikhism.

18.21 पृथक्त्वेन तु यज्ज्ञानं नानाभावान्पृथग्विधान् वेत्ति सर्वेषु भूतेषु तज्ज्ञानं विद्धि राजसम्   Rajasic knowledge (in the mode of passion) is when a person sees many individuals and unconnected beings in separate bodies.

When the world is not seen in its connection with God, and thus the living beings are perceived with distinctions of race, class, creed, sect, and nationality, that is rajasic knowledge. Sattvic knowledge unites and resolves disputes, and rajasic knowledge divides and causes disputes.

18.22 यत्तु कृत्स्नवदेकस्मिन्कार्ये सक्तमहैतुकम् अतत्त्वार्थवदल्पं च तत्तामसमुदाहृतम्
Tamasic knowledge (in the mode of ignorance) is that which clings to a single effect as if it were a whole. It is irrational, not founded on truth, and trivial.

The tamasic people believe their perception, whatever it may be, to be the Absolute Truth. They come up with weird concepts, previously unheard of. Their understanding is entirely irrational; it is neither based on scriptures nor reality, but they zealously impose their beliefs on others. In the name of God and religion, they create disruption and disorder in society. They violently guard their idiotic ideas.

18.23 नियतं सङ्गरहितमरागद्वेषतः कृतम् अफलप्रेप्सुना कर्म यत्तत्सात्विकमुच्यते   Sattvic action follows scriptures; it is free from attachment and aversion and done without a desire for rewards.

Having described three types of Knowledge, Krishna now describes three kinds of Action. The action in the mode of goodness is doing one's duty under the scriptures, provided it is free of attachment, aversion, and desire to enjoy the results.

18.24 यत्तुकामेप्सुना कर्म साहङ्कारेण वा पुन: क्रियते बहुलायासं तद्राजसमुदाहृतम्   The rajasic action is driven by selfish desire and pride, and is stressful.

Rajasik action is characterized by desire, sense gratification, ambition, stressfulness.

18.25 अनुबन्धं क्षयं हिंसामनपेक्ष्य च पौरुषम् मोहादारभ्यते कर्म यत्तामसमुच्यते   Tamasic action is prompted by delusion and beyond one's ability; it disregards the consequences, loss, and injury to others.

Tamasic action (in the mode of ignorance) does not consider what is right and what is wrong; it is driven solely by self-interest and ignores hardships and injury to others. Such action is a waste of effort, time, and resources, and only results in serious physical, social, and legal problems. Examples- gambling, cheating, stealing, corruption, drinking.

18.26 मुक्तसङ्गोऽनहंवादी धृत्युत्साहसमन्वित: सिद्ध्यसिद्ध्योर्निर्विकार: कर्ता सात्विक उच्यते   When without ego and attachment, and when enthusiastic, determined, and equipoised in success and failure, the performer is said to be Sattavik (in the mode of goodness).

The primary motivation of Sattvic performers is spiritual growth.

18.27 रागी कर्मफलप्रेप्सुर्लुब्धो हिंसात्मकोऽशुचि: हर्षशोकान्वित: कर्ता राजस: परिकीर्तित:
The Rajasic performer craves to enjoy results, is greedy, angry-natured, impure, and reacts to joy and sorrow.

Rajasic performers are driven by worldly progress, wealth, and power. Their life is mixed with delights and sorrows.

18.28 अयुक्त: प्राकृत: स्तब्ध: शठो नैष्कृतिकोऽलस: विषादी दीर्घसूत्री च कर्ता तामस उच्यते
A Tamasic performer is undisciplined, vulgar, stubborn, deceitful, lazy, hopeless, and procrastinating. Tamasic doers are negative, unhappy, and morose, and have no goal.

A summary of the three types of doers: The Sattvic doers are detached, Rajasic doers are attached to selfish action, Tamasic doers are devoid of discrimination. However, the one who is not concerned about the results and surrendered to God rises above the three modes.

18.29 बुद्धेर्भेदं धृतेश्चैव गुणतस्त्रिविधं शृणु प्रोच्यमानमशेषेण पृथक्त्वेन धनञ्जय   Now I describe in detail the distinctions in intellect and firmness, according to the three modes of material nature.

The last nine verses discussed knowledge, action, and the doer in the three modes. This verse explains two additional factors - intellect and determination, which propel, control, and direct action.

18.30 प्रवृत्तिं च निवृत्तिं च कार्याकार्ये भयाभये बन्धं मोक्षं च या वेत्तिबुद्धि: सा पार्थ सात्विकी
The one with sattvic intellect understands the proper and improper action, the duty and non-duty, what is to be and not to be feared, and what is binding and what is liberating.

Sattvic intellect is shining with the light of knowledge; it helps in making the proper decision. Verse 18.63 says, "I have explained to you the knowledge that is more secret than all secrets. Ponder over it deeply, and then do as you wish."

18.31 यया धर्ममधर्मं च कार्यं चाकार्यमेव च अयथावत्प्रजानाति बुद्धि: सा पार्थ राजसी
The one with rajasic intellect cannot distinguish between righteousness and unrighteousness, and right and wrong.

The one with rajasic intellect has attachments and aversions, likes and dislikes, and can't differentiate valuable and worthless.

18.32 अधर्मं धर्ममिति या मन्यते तमसावृता सर्वार्थान्विपरीतांश्च बुद्धि: सा पार्थ तामसी
The one with tamasic intellect is covered in darkness, believing irreligion to be religion, and perceives untruth to be the truth.

Tamasic intellect lacks knowledge, proper judgment, and logic, often leading to prohibited actions and violation of the law.

18.33 धृत्या यया धारयते मन:प्राणेन्द्रियक्रिया: योगेनाव्यभिचारिण्या धृति: सा पार्थ सात्विकी
The sattvic firmness or will is developed through Yoga; it restrains the activities of the mind, the life-forces, and the senses.

Sattvic determination (Dhṛiti) is characterized by mental strength, which removes obstacles and keeps focus on the goal. Yoga disciplines the mind and renders the ability to control the senses.

18.34 यया तु धर्मकामार्थान्धृत्या धारयतेऽर्जुन प्रसङ्गेन फलाकाङ्क्षी धृति: सा पार्थ राजसी
But that firmness by which one holds to Dharma, pleasures, and wealth, inspired primarily by attachment and desire for reward is rajasic.

Rajasic firmness is centered on enjoying results of actions with the entire focus on sensual pleasures and wealth acquisition.

18.35 यया स्वप्नं भयं शोकं विषादं मदमेव च न विमुञ्चति दुर्मेधा धृति: सा पार्थ तामसी
Adhering to the stupid decisions driven by dreams, fear, grief, despair, and conceit are tamasic determination.

Tamasic determination is due to the influence of unproductive thoughts.

18.36 सुखं त्विदानीं त्रिविधं शृणु मे भरतर्षभ अभ्यासाद्रमते यत्र दु:खान्तं च निगच्छति
Now learn about the three kinds of happiness in which the soul dwells, and can end all suffering.

Having discussed the constituents of action and the factors that motivate and control the action, the next topic is the goal of action – happiness and how it varies under the influence of the three Gunas.

18.37 यत्तदग्रे विषमिव परिणामेऽमृतोपमम् त्सुखं सात्विकं प्रोक्तमात्मबुद्धिप्रसादजम्   The sattvic happiness is like poison at first, but sweet in the end. It rises from the pure mind and intellect based on knowledge of the Self (Atmjnan).

TOPIC 37 - Effect of Three Gunas

Two types of happiness are Shreya (beneficial) and Preya (pleasant). Shreya is bitter in the beginning, enjoyable in the end.

Preya is pleasant in the beginning, but bitter in the end.

18.38 विषयेन्द्रियसंयोगाद्यत्तदग्रेऽमृतोपमम् परिणामे विषमिव तत्सुखं राजसं स्मृतम्

Rajasic happiness is derived from the contact of senses with objects; it is like nectar at first but poison at end.

Divine bliss comes from renunciation, not indulgence.

18.39 यदग्रे चानुबन्धे च सुखं मोहनमात्मनः निद्रालस्यप्रमादोत्थं तत्तामसमुदाहृतम्

Tamasic happiness is elusive. It arises from sleep, laziness, and negligence.

Tamasic happiness is foolish from the beginning to the end. Examples: joy felt from harmful habits like alcohol, cigarettes, gambling, etc. It is very difficult to break these habits.

SUMMARY of verses 18.13 through 18.39:

1. *The five causes of action are the body (adhishthanam, the place of residence or the body), the owner of the body (karta), various senses (Karanam or instruments), different functions performed by the body (chestah), and the super soul (daivam). All actions by body, mind, and speech, whether good or bad, are caused by these five factors.*
2. *Three factors that induce or propel action are knowledge (Jnanam), the object of knowledge (Jneyam), and the knower (parijnata).*
3. *Three factors involved in accomplishing any work are the senses (Karanam), the actual work, and the performer of the work.*
4. *Two factors that control and direct are intellect and determination.*
5. *Three kinds of happiness are Shreya (unpleasant in the beginning but ultimately beneficial), Preya (pleasant in the beginning but ultimately harmful), and the illusionary happiness from wrong habits like smoking, drinking, drugs.*

18.40 न तदस्ति पृथिव्यां वा दिवि देवेषु वा पुनः सत्वं प्रकृतिजैर्मुक्तं यदेभिः स्यात्त्रिभिर्गुणैः

No one on earth or in the heavens among the gods (Devatas) is free from the influence of these three modes of nature (Triguna). The three modes influence everyone without exception.

Maya's domain covers the abodes of all gods and Lord Brahma. Everyone without exception is affected by the Gunas. Sattva is dominant in the heavens. People possess different natures depending on the proportions of the three Gunas inherent in them as a result of the past karmas and impressions.

TOPIC 38

Sharing the Message of Gita

Krishna tells Arjun that those who teach the knowledge of Gita to sincere devotees will go to him without a doubt. He says no one does loving service more than the ones who spread his message to dedicated people. Krishna holds the study of Gita as worship. He says merely hearing Gita's discourse will free one of sin and qualify him for higher abodes. However, Krishna cautions, not to discuss Gita with those not interested in listening and abuse God with a mean disposition. Such doubtful people without faith will not listen, no matter how hard you try to teach them. So, respectfully, leave them to their ways.

18.67 इदं ते नातपस्काय नाभक्ताय कदाचन न चाशुश्रूषवे वाच्यं न च मां योऽभ्यसूयति   You should not give this knowledge to those who are not austere, not devoted, not interested in listening (to spiritual topics), and envious of Me.

The knowledge of Gita should not be given to unqualified and atheist people. Why provide the divine instructions to those who lack faith in God?

18.68 य इदं परमं गुह्यं मद्भक्तेष्वभिधास्यति भक्तिं मयि परां कृत्वा मामेवैष्यत्यसंशय: Those who teach (spread) this most sacred knowledge amongst My devotees perform the greatest act of love. They will come to Me "without a doubt".

God's promise – teaching Gita to the qualified opens doors to his abode. Sharing Gita's message with those who are eligible attracts God's grace. Being devoted pleases God, but enlightening others draw the special grace of God.

Kabir says, "dāna diye dhana nā ghaṭe, nadī ghaṭe na nīra; apane hātha dekha lo, yoṅ kyā kahe kabīra." Meaning - "Wealth does not decrease by giving in charity; a river does not become narrow, though people take water from it. I am not saying this without basis; see it yourself in the world." Thus, spiritual knowledge does not decline by sharing it with others; in fact, whoever spreads Gita's message to the believers receives the highest blessing of Krishna.

18.69 न च तस्मान्मनुष्येषु कश्चिन्मे प्रियकृत्तम: भविता न च मे तस्मादन्य: प्रियतरो भुवि   No human being does more loving service to me than those who share the knowledge of Gita with others, nor there shall ever be anyone on this earth dearer to me.

Teaching Gita to the qualified, Krishna says, is the highest gift. The gift of spiritual knowledge is considered the highest of all types of gifts as it can transform the recipient permanently and point him to the spiritual path. The teacher should be humble and think of himself as God's instrument. Sages rank four types of charities according to this stated order: 1. Jnan Daan - the gift of knowledge; 2. Aushadh Daan gift of medicines and medical treatments; 3. Anna Daan - the gift of food; 4. Dhan Daan - the gift of money.

18.70 अध्येष्यते च य इमं धर्म्यं संवादमावयो: ज्ञानयज्ञेन तेनाहमिष्ट: स्यामिति मे मति:
And I proclaim that those who study this sacred dialogue of ours will worship Me (with their intellect) through the Jnana Yajna or sacred offering of spiritual knowledge; such is My view.

Studying Gita is held as worship. The Sanskrit word Yajna is translated as "sacrifice" by many authors; however, its broader meaning is "devotion, worship, offering," and refers to any ritual done in front of a sacred fire, often with mantras. Yajna has been a centuries-old Vedic tradition. The tradition has evolved from offering oblations and libations into the sacred fire as symbolic offerings in the presence of sacred fire (Agni).

18.71 श्रद्धावाननसूयश्च शृणुयादपि यो नर: सोऽपि मुक्त: शुभाँल्लोकान्प्राप्नुयात्पुण्यकर्मणाम्
Even those who only listen to this knowledge with faith and without envy, will be liberated from sins and attain the auspicious abodes where the pious dwell.

Krishna declares that merely hearing Gita with faith will free you of sins and qualify you for the higher-level abodes.

An actual story is related now to illustrate the power of listening. A disciple of Shankaracharya, called Sananda, demonstrates the power of listening to the Holy Scriptures. He would listen to Sankara's discourses with great faith, although he was illiterate and could not comprehend the Guru's teaching. One day, he was washing his Guru's clothes near a river, and when it was time for the class, the other disciples requested Guru to begin. Shankaracharya asked everyone to wait till Sananda returned, saying it is true Sananda could not understand the discourses, but he did listen to them regularly and faithfully. To show the power of faith, Shankaracharya called Sananda to return. On hearing his Guru's words, Sananda hurried and ran on the river, by the power he acquired (a Siddhi) by merely listening to the discourses with faith. Krishna guarantees Arjun that just by listening to the sacred dialogue with faith will gradually purify the listener.

TOPIC 39

End of Gita - Conclusions and Impressions

After hearing all discourses, Arjun declares that his illusion is dispelled and he will follow Krishna's instructions without exception.

Sanjay, the assistant of Kaurava King Dhritrashtra, who heard all Krishna's discourses remotely, is ecstatic. He declares and cheers again and again at the astounding and magnificent dialogue between Krishna and Arjun. He says he is drowning in a profound joy after hearing Krishna. The brilliant cosmic form of God stunned him. Sanjay concludes with great respect to Krishna and Arjun, "Wherever there is Yogeshvar Krishna, and the supreme archer Arjun, there will be eternal splendor, triumph, wealth, and virtues." He says he is certain of his conclusion. Krishna's teaching has been enormously valuable to generations of people, still is, in guiding spiritual seekers on their journey from ignorance to enlightenment. Krishna reiterates to Arjun not to pass on the knowledge of Gita to those who are not austere, not devoted, do not want to listen, and are envious of him.

❧ Krishna says:

18.72 कच्चिदेतच्छ्रुतं पार्थ त्वयैकाग्रेण चेतसा कच्चिदज्ञानसम्मोह: प्रनष्टस्ते धनञ्जय   Have you heard me with a concentrated mind? Have your ignorance and delusion been destroyed?

Krishna inquires if Arjun's delusion is vanished after hearing the entire discourse of Gita.

❧ Arjun replies:

18.73 अर्जुन उवाच नष्टो मोह: स्मृतिर्लब्धा त्वत्प्रसादान्मयाच्युत स्थितोऽस्मि गतसन्देह: करिष्ये वचनं तव   You have eradicated my douhts and delusions. I understand by your grace. I have no doubt now and will act according to your will.

Arjun was confused and overwhelmed with sorrow, looking at the Kaurava's army, and he gave up his weapons. He could not overcome the grief. After listening to Krishna's discourse, he is no longer perplexed. He submitted to the will of God and agreed to follow Krishna's instructions. He says, "tvat prasādān mayāchyuta," meaning, "By your grace," not merely by your discourse, that my ignorance was destroyed.

❧ Sanjay says to Dhritrashtra:

18.74 सञ्जय उवाच इत्यहं वासुदेवस्य पार्थस्य च महात्मन: संवादमिममश्रौषमद्भुतं रोमहर्षणम्   Thus, I have heard this pleasant conversation between Krishna and Arjun. So thrilling is the message that my hair is standing on end.

Sanjay is elated and speechless, hearing the dialogue. He is so stunned that his hair rose, standing on end, which is symptom of sincere devotion.

As a related note, devotional ecstasy is exhibited by eight symptoms: 1. becoming motionless, 2. sweating, 3. hair standing on end, 4. choking of the voice, 5. trembling, 6. color of the face becoming ashen, 7. shedding tears, and 8. fainting.

18.75 व्यासप्रसादाच्छ्रुतवानेतद्गुह्यमहं परम् योगं योगेश्वरात्कृष्णात्साक्षात्कथयत: स्वयम् By the grace of Veda Vyas, I have heard this supreme and most secret Yoga directly from the Lord of Yoga, Krishna himself.

Sanjay heard Gita as spoken, remotely. His Guru Ved Vyas blessed him with this power to view and hear what happened on the battleground, as he sat in the palace with the blind king Dhritarashtra. Ved Vyas possessed all the clairvoyant powers himself. He was the author of the Brahma Sutras, the Puranas, and the Mahabharat, and considered an avatara of God.

18.76 राजन्संस्मृत्य संस्मृत्य संवादमिममद्भुतम् केशवार्जुनयो: पुण्यं हृष्यामि च मुहुर्मुहु: As I repeatedly recall this astounding dialogue between Krishna and Arjun, O King, I cheer again and again.

Sanjay is overwhelmed with divine Bliss and sharing his experience with Dhritarashtra. Divine bliss (Ananda) cannot be described, as one has to experience it. It is a calming and thrilling experience one feels when encountering God. The divine Bliss is eternal. In comparison, the worldly joy felt by the senses is temporary (Anitya) and dwindles rapidly.

18.77 तच्च संस्मृत्य संस्मृत्य रूपमत्यद्भुतं हरे: विस्मयो मे महानराजन्हृष्यामि च पुन: पुन: And remembering that brilliant cosmic form of Lord Krishna, I am amazed, and my joy overflows.

Sanjay remembers the marvelous universal form of God and feels ecstatic. As a narrator and a messenger, he becomes an unexpected recipient of bliss. He benefited from Vyasa's grace. It is pathetic that Dhritrashtra, the greedy father of the evil Kauravas, silently receives the greatest of the teachings but does not express gratefulness to Krishna.

18.78 यत्र योगेश्वर: कृष्णो यत्र पार्थो धनुर्धर: तत्र श्रीर्विजयो भूतिध्रुवा नीतिर्मतिर्मम

Wherever there is Yogeshvar Krishna, and the supreme archer Arjun, there will be eternal splendor, victory, prosperity, and virtues. Of this, I am certain.

Quite appropriately, Sanjay offers his prayer at the end. Gita concludes with a sincere pronouncement. Regardless of the strengths of the two armies, the only judgment in this war is that triumph will always accompany God and his pure devotee, and so will supremacy, and prosperity. Wherever the Yogeshwar Krishna and his devotees are present, the light of truth will decidedly defeat the darkness of lies and deceit. Fortunate are the listeners of the song of Gita full of nectar.

TOPIC 40

God's Glories – Vibhutis

Krishna reveals his inconceivable divine nature and announces himself as the source of everyone and everything visible and invisible in the universe. He is Brahm and beyond dualities; he is happiness and suffering; he is birth and death. A glimpse of him can be experienced in the highest state of Yoga. Arjun had briefly heard about Krishna's glory but wants to hear more. Krishna obliges Arjun by revealing a few more examples of his divine opulence (vibhutis). He mentions a few eminent names and objects from ancient scriptures in his examples of vibhutis; the commentaries explain these names whenever possible. Krishna says that anything and anyone excellent, impressive, and most beautiful in every category of vibhutis is nothing but himself. The best in any class should remind us of Krishna. He is the river Ganges, he is the sun, he is Indra, and he is the syllable Aum. He says he is the inner Self in all beings, the object of worship and meditation. Even the Devatas and highly evolved sages cannot name all his vibhutis.

Krishna emphasizes that only divine grace can destroy ignorance and impart the right knowledge. God bestows his grace on devotees who have single-pointed focus and who surrender to him. The infinite God who is beyond the bounds of time and space is the source who creates, sustains, and destroys everything.

❧ Krishna says:

7.8 रसोऽहमप्सु कौन्तेय प्रभास्मि शशिसूर्ययो: प्रणव: सर्ववेदेषु शब्द: खे पौरुषं नृषु   I am the taste in water, the radiance in the sun and moon, the sacred syllable Om in the Vedic mantras, the sound in ether, and ability in human beings.

We easily remember when we see something excellent in any category. "The best in the class" of everything should remind us of God's presence everywhere.

7.9 पुण्यो गन्ध: पृथिव्यां च तेजश्चास्मि विभावसौ जीवनं सर्वभूतेषु तपश्चास्मि तपस्विषु
I am the pure fragrance of the earth, the brilliance in the fire, the life-force in all beings, and the austerities in the austere.

7.10 बीजं मां सर्वभूतानां विद्धि पार्थ सनातनम् बुद्धिर्बुद्धिमतामस्मि तेजस्तेजस्विनामहम्
I am the eternal seed of all beings, the intellect of the intelligent, and the splendor of the glorious.

7.11 बलं बलवतां चाहं कामरागविवर्जितम् धर्माविरुद्धो भूतेषु कामोऽस्मि भरतर्षभ
I am the strength in strong persons free of desire and passion, and I am the sexual activity that is not adverse to dharma.

Desire is hankering for what we do not have, and attachment is the tendency to holding and guarding our possessions. Selfishness creates attachment. Acting, when attached to someone or something, weakens you. Here is an example. The Pandavas knew that Drona was too powerful and could not be killed quickly, so, instead of Drona, they went after his son Ashwatthaamaa. Drona was deeply attached to his son. So, Drona became too weak to fight and defend as he was overcome by worries for the safety of his son Ashwatthaamaa. Consequently, Drona got killed in his moment of extreme weakness.

By turning to God, our attachment to people and worldly objects declines. Therefore, Krishna says that he is the strength that is free from selfish desire and attachment.

7.12 ये चैव सात्विका भावा राजसास्तामसाश्च ये मत्त एवेति तान्विद्धि न त्वहं तेषु ते मयि   The three Gunas (Satva, Rajas, and Tamas) originate from Me. They abide by Me, but I am not in them.

The three modes are born from Maya Shakti, one of God's powers. Refer to verse 7.25 under Topic 15 for the description of all God's powers. Krishna is the excellence in all objects, entities, and beings.

9.16 and 9.17 अहं क्रतुरहं यज्ञ: स्वधाहमहमौषधम् मन्त्रोऽहमहमेवाज्यमहमग्निरहं हुतम् पिताहमस्य जगतो माता धाता पितामह: वेद्यं पवित्रमोङ्कार ऋक्साम यजुरेव च   I am the Vedic ritual, the sacrifice (Yajna), the oblation offered to ancestors, the medicinal herb, the Vedic Mantra, the clarified butter (ghee), the fire, and the act of offering (all elements involved in the performance of Yajna). Of this universe, I am the father, the mother, the sustainer, the grandsire, the purifier, the goal of knowledge, the sacred syllable Om, the Rigveda, Samveda, and Yajurveda.

God is the source for everything needed in performing Yajna and the original creator of the Vedas, the books containing ancient knowledge.

9.18 गतिर्भर्ता प्रभु: साक्षी निवास: शरणं सुहृत् प्रभव: प्रलय: स्थानं निधानं बीजमव्ययम्
I am the goal, the support, the Lord, the witness, the abode, the shelter, the friend, the origin, the dissolution, the foundation, the treasure-house, and the imperishable seed.

189

Our relationships with worldly relatives are temporary and based on selfish motives. God alone is our perfect relative, who is both eternal and selfless.

9.19 तपाम्यहमहं वर्षं निगृह्ळम्युत्सृजामि च अमृतं चैव मृत्युश्च सदसच्चाहमर्जुन I am heat, I withhold and send forth the rain, I am immortality and also death, I am what there is and there is not.

Before the universe came into existence, only God existed. After the universe is dissolved, only God will remain. God is the source of all resources and there is nothing apart from God.

🦋 *Arjun says:*

10.16 and 10.17 वक्तुमर्हस्यशेषेण दिव्या ह्यात्मविभूतय: याभिर्विभूतिभिर्लोकानिमांस्त्वं व्याप्य तिष्ठसि कथं विद्यामहं योगिंस्त्वां सदा परिचिन्तयन् केषु केषु च भावेषु चिन्त्योऽसि भगवन्मया Tell me about your divine opulence by which you occupy all the worlds and reside there. How may I know you, and what forms can I think of you when meditating?

Arjun is requesting to Krishna to reveal his majestic opulence. Arjun realizes that God is not detached from us, but he is everywhere with his manifestations. So, he is asking Krishna to explain the details of his expressions.

10.18 विस्तरेणात्मनो योगं विभूर्तिं च जनार्दन भूय: कथय तृसिर्हि शृण्वतो नास्ति मेऽमृतम् Describe again in detail your divine glories and manifestations. I never get tired of hearing your words like nectar.

Krishna's glories are infinite. Arjun is not satisfied and wants to hear more. Similarly, the sages who gathered to listen to Sukhdev's discourse on Srimad Bhagavat said, "The devotees of Krishna are never tired of hearing about his glories. The more you hear it, the more you want to hear."

🦋 *Krishna says:*

10.19 श्रीभगवानुवाच हन्त ते कथयिष्यामि दिव्या ह्यात्मविभूतय: प्रधान्यत: कुरुश्रेष्ठ नास्त्यन्तो विस्तरस्य मे I shall now briefly describe my glories (Vibhuti) to you. There is no end to their details.

Upanishad says, "God is infinite and has innumerable forms in the universe. Although he runs the universe, he is yet the non-doer." This is why Krishna says he will "briefly" describe his glories.

10.20 अहमात्मा गुडाकेश सर्वभूताशयस्थित:अहमादिश्च मध्यं च भूतानामन्त एव च I am seated in the heart of all living entities (Paramatma). I am the beginning, middle, and end of all beings.

God resides within our soul (Atma) as Paramatma (super soul). The soul's power comes from the super soul. Both the soul and the super soul are eternal. Taittriya Upanishad says,

TOPIC 40 - God's Glories – Vibhutis

"God is the one from whom all living beings have emanated; God is the one within whom all living beings are situated; God is the one into whom all living beings shall unite."

10.21 आदित्यानामहं विष्णुर्ज्योतिषां रविरंशुमान् मरीचिर्मरुतामस्मि नक्षत्राणामहं शशी

I am Vishnu among the 12 sons of Aditi; the sun among the luminous objects; Marichi among the Maruts; and the moon amongst the stars in the night sky.

The most prominent among each category is singled out as God's glory. Kashyap Rishi had two wives - Aditi and Diti. Aditi had 12 sons; all were celestial avatar: Dhata, Mitra, Aryama, Shakra, Varun, Amsha, Bhaga, Vivasvan, Pusha, Savita, Twashta, and Vaman (Vishnu); Vishnu being the most prominent of the 12 sons. Diti had 49 forms of Maruts (winds) - Avaha, Pravaha, Nivaha, Purvaha, Udvaha, Samvaha, Parivaha, and others, not named here. Of all the Maruts, Marichi was the most distinguished.

10.22 वेदानां सामवेदोऽस्मि देवानामस्मि वासवः इन्द्रियाणां मनश्चास्मि भूतानामस्मि चेतना

I am the Sama Veda amongst the Vedas, Indra amongst the celestial gods, the mind amongst the senses, and the consciousness amongst the living beings.

Indra tops the celestial gods in fame, power, and rank; he possesses the dazzling glories of God. The mind is the king among the senses as none of the senses can function without the mind. Consciousness differentiates the soul from unconscious matter. Without consciousness, the body is dead. Hence, the Vedas state: "God is the sentience in the sentient." Samveda among the four Vedas is most musical and sung in praise of God; it evokes devotion among listeners. The Sama Veda contains musical rules like regulated order of words, phonological rules for the combination of sounds (sandhi), and recitation of letters. Sung correctly, the Sama Veda hymns evoke devotion among the singers and listeners.

10.23 रुद्राणां शङ्करश्चास्मि वित्तेशो यक्षरक्षसाम् वसूनां पावकश्चास्मि मेरुः शिखरिणामहम्

I am Shanker among the Rudras, Kuber among the yakshas, Agni among the Vasus, and Meru among the mountains.

Eleven Rudras are Har, Bahurup, Tryambak, Aparajit, Vrisakapi, Shankar, Kapardi, Raivat, Mrigavyadh, Sarv, and Kapali, of which Shankar is eminent. Eight Vasus make the structure of the universe, and they are —land, water, fire (Agni), air, space, sun, moon, and stars. Agni gives warmth and energy to the rest of the elements. The semi-demons are known as Yaksha, who are very fond of obtaining and collecting wealth. Kuber is their leader; he the God of wealth and the treasurer of the celestial gods.

Meru Mountain is located in the celestial region, according to the scriptures; it is rich in natural resources, and it forms the axis around which heavenly bodies rotate.

10.24 पुरोधसां च मुख्यं मां विद्धि पार्थ बृहस्पतिम् सेनानीनामहं स्कन्दः सरसामस्मि सागरः

I am Brihaspati among priests, Kartikeya among warrior chiefs, and the ocean among the reservoirs of water.

Again, the best in every category reflects the opulence of God. Brihaspati is the chief priest in heaven, who performs ritualistic worship and ceremonies. Kartikeya, the son of

TOPIC 40 - God's Glories – Vibhutis

191

Lord Shiva, is the commander-in-chief of the celestial gods, thus the chief of all military commanders. Krishna further says that amongst stagnant bodies of water, he is the massive ocean.

10.25 महर्षीणां भृगुरहं गिरामस्म्येकमक्षरम् यज्ञानां जपयज्ञोऽस्मि स्थावराणां हिमालयः
I am Bhrigu among the great seers and Om among the sounds. I am the Holy Name among the chants (Jap Yagna) and the Himalayas among the immovable things.

Bhrigu is the greatest among the seers in wisdom, fame, and devotion. Aum/Om is a sacred sound and a Vibhuti of God, (refer to verses 7.8 and 8.13). It is the divine sound that pervades creation and often shows up as the first letter in Vedic mantras to invoke auspiciousness. Anhad Naad means "primordial sound" which exists as the sound of the universe, and is not produced by striking two objects. Aum is also considered as the sound of the cosmos and human consciousness, an ultimate sound that goes beyond space and time, a sound that has no beginning or end.

Scriptures say the original vibration from which all other vibrations originate is the sound AUM. Chanting Aum unites us with God. The Aum sound is always within us, but we don't hear it as the mind is preoccupied with thoughts. With progress in meditation, the mind becomes still and connects with the inner soul where the Aum sound resides and reverberates constantly. It is said that as one advances in meditation, different sounds are heard such as birds chirping, bell, lute, flute, ocean waves, and ultimately Aum, before the absolute bliss is experienced.

Japa Yajna can be done anywhere, anytime; it is purifying and is highly recommended for spiritual progress in Kali Yuga.

10.26 अश्वत्थः सर्ववृक्षाणां देवर्षीणां च नारदः गन्धर्वाणां चित्ररथः सिद्धानां कपिलो मुनिः
I am the banyan tree among trees, Narada among heavenly sages, Chitrarath among the Gandharvas, and Kapil among the Siddhas.

The banyan tree is vast and provides cooling shade in a large area. Narad was a Guru of great personalities, such as Ved Vyas, Valmiki, Dhruv, and Prahlad. Highly talented singers and musicians inhabit Gandharva planet; Chitrarath is the best of the Gandharvas. Siddhas are yogis who reach spiritual perfection and acquire various siddhis (powers). See the commentary under verse 7.3 in Topic 15 for more details on acquired siddhis. Kapil was an avatar of Vishnu; he revealed the Sankhya philosophy and taught Bhakti Yoga.

10.27 उच्चैःश्रवसमश्वानां विद्धि माममृतोद्भवम् ऐरावतं गजेन्द्राणां नराणां च नराधिपम्
I am Ucchaihshrava among the horses, Airavat among the royal elephants, and a monarch among humans.

Ucchaihshrava is a celestial winged-horse of Indra, the king of heaven. It is white and is the fastest horse in the universe, according to scriptures. It emerged during the churning of the ocean by the Devas (celestial gods) and Asuras (demons). Airavata is a white elephant that serves as the vehicle of Indra. It is also called "the elephant of the clouds".

Airavata elephant and Kamdhenu cow (verse 10.28) also came out of the ocean after its churning.

10.28 आयुधानामहं वज्रं धेनूनामस्मि कामधुक् प्रजनश्चास्मि कन्दर्प: सर्पाणामस्मि वासुकि:

I am Vajra (thunderbolt) among weapons, Kamadhenu among the cows. I am Kamdev, God of love, among all causes of procreation, and Vasuki among serpents.

The thunderbolt was made from bones of sage Dadhichi, and Lord Indra used it to defeat the demon Vritrasura. Kamdhenu is the sacred cow that emerged during the churning of the ocean by the Devas and Asuras. Kamdhenu grants desires and prosperity. Kamdev is the God of love. He is a force of attraction between the opposite sexes for procreation.

10.29 अनन्तश्चास्मि नागानां वरुणो यादसामहम् पितृणामर्यमा चास्मि यम: संयमतामहम्

I am Anant among the snakes, Varun among the aquatics, Aryama among the departed ancestors, and Yamraja (the Lord of death) among the dispensers of law.

Anant is the divine serpent, Lord Vishnu rests on; it has a thousand hoods (mouths). It has been singing God's glories with each mouth since the creation but is still not done singing the infinite grandeur of God.

Varun is the celestial God of the ocean. Aryama (the third son of Aditi and Kashyap) is the head of departed souls. Yamraja is the heavenly God of death; he carries the soul from the body and dispenses justice on behalf of God.

10.30 प्रह्लादश्चास्मि दैत्यानां काल: कलयतामहम् मृगाणां च मृगेन्द्रोऽहं वैनतेयश्च पक्षिणाम्

I am Prahlad among the demons, time among all that controls, the lion amongst animals, and Garuda (an eagle-like sunbird) among the birds.

Prahlad was a great devotee of God and the son of a powerful demon Hiranyakashipu. God destroyed Hiranyakashipu to protect Prahlad. Time is called Kaal, the transforming principle, a subduer that wears out all entities of the universe. Refer to verse 11.32 in Topic 7 on Punchline Verses. Garuda is the perfect vehicle of Lord Vishnu. Garuda is the most powerful among all birds. The lion is the most potent wild animal and represents the best of God's might.

10.31 पवन: पवतामस्मि राम: शस्त्रभृतामहम् झषाणां मकरश्चास्मि स्रोतसामस्मि जाह्नवी

I am the wind among the purifiers, Lord Ram among the wielders of weapons, the crocodile among the water creatures, and the Ganges among the flowing rivers.

The wind is a great purifier; it converts impure water into vapor, carries away the dirty smells, and it makes the fire burn by fueling it with oxygen. Rama is the most powerful warrior, and his bow was the deadliest weapon on the earth. The Ganges is a holy river that started from the divine feet of the Lord. Its water does not decompose, which was a proven fact before the river got polluted. Among aquatic animals, the crocodile is the biggest and most powerful.

10.32 सर्गाणामादिरन्तश्च मध्यं चैवाहमर्जुन अध्यात्मविद्या विद्यानां वाद: प्रवदतामहम्

I am the beginning, middle, and end of all creation. I am the science of spirituality among sciences and the logical conclusion among debates.

God is the beginning (adi), middle (Madhya), and end (anta) of all beings and the panch mahabhuta (space, air, fire, water, and earth). The universal principles of logic are a manifestation of the power of God.

Logic enables communication and helps cultivate knowledge. The science of spirituality frees one from bondage and unites the intellect with God. Vedas, vedangas, and many other scriptures are the primary source of spiritual knowledge. Vedangs consists of 1. Śhikśhā, 2. Kalp, 3. Vyākaraṇ, 4. Nirukti, 5. Jyotiṣh, 6. Chhanda. Vedas are 1. Ṛig, 2. Yajur, 3. Sāma, 4. Atharva. Other scriptures are 1. Mīmānsā, 2. Nyāya, 3. Dharma Śhāstra, and 4. The eighteen Puranas. This is a partial list as it is not easy to make a complete list of all Santara Dharma scriptures that exist and those that were destroyed by the barbarian invaders.

10.33 अक्षराणामकारोऽस्मि द्वन्द्वः सामासिकस्य च अहमेवाक्षयः कालो धाताहं विश्वतोमुखः

I am the letter "A" among all letters, and the dual word in grammatical compounds. I am an endless time (Kaal) and Brahma among the creators.

The letter "a" is the first vowel of the alphabet. It is essential as Sanskrit letters are formed by combining a half-letter of a consonant with "a." Hence, the letter "a" is the most critical alphabet. It is also the first vowel of the alphabet. Kaal is the imperishable time that controls all beings. Krishna says he is Brahma himself with faces all around, who creates this cosmos.

10.34 मृत्युः सर्वहरश्चाहमुद्भवश्च भविष्यताम् कीर्तिः श्रीर्वाक्च नारीणां स्मृतिर्मेधा धृतिः क्षमा

I am the all-devouring death. I am the original and things that are yet to be. I am fame, prosperity, beautiful speech, memory, intelligence, courage, and forgiveness, among feminine qualities.

God devours everything in the form of death. He is also the generating principle for all future beings. Presiding deities or the goddesses of the feminine attributes mentioned in this verse are in the parenthesis: Fame (Kirti), Prosperity (Shree), Fine speech (Vak), Memory (Smriti), Intelligence (Medha), Courage (Dhriti), and Forgiveness (Kshama).

10.35 बृहत्साम तथा साम्नां गायत्री छन्दसामहम् मासानां मार्गशीर्षोऽहमृतूनां कुसुमाकरः

I am Brihatsama among the Sam Veda hymns, and Gayatri amongst poetic meters. I am Margashirsh among the twelve months in the Hindu calendar, and spring among the seasons.

Among Samaveda mantras, there is a particular mantra called Brihat Sama, sung at midnight. It is a highly spiritually charged invocation of God; therefore, it is called Brihat Sama (large Sama), the most powerful of the mantras. It is chanted with music.

The Gayatri mantra, as follows, is the very root and essence of all Rigveda mantras. It bestows wisdom and enlightenment by the grace of the Sun (Savita) that represents the source and inspiration of the universe. Gayatri Mantra invites light into the mind to dissipate darkness, meaning the negative energy. The Mantra fosters peace and confidence, sharpens knowledge-yielding faculty, and releases hidden power. It is believed to be the most potent of all mantras, when sung with proper emphasis on the syllables and vowels.

Oṃ bhūr bhuvaḥ suvaḥ tatsaviturvareṇyaṃ bhargo devasyadhīmahi dhiyo yo naḥ prachodayā (Rigveda 3.62).

Gayatri's meaning, according to Shri Satya Saibaba, "The Mantra is addressed to the Immanent and Transcendent Divine, 'Savita,' meaning 'that from which all this is born.' The Gayatri has three parts - (i) Adoration (ii) Meditation (iii) Prayer. First, the Divine is praised, then It is meditated upon in reverence and finally, an appeal is made to the Divine to awaken and strengthen the intellect, the discriminating faculty of man."

Margshirsh month has the best climate of all months when it is not too hot nor cold. Similarly, the spring season is the most pleasant of all seasons.

10.36 द्यूतं छलयतामस्मि तेजस्तेजस्विनामहम् जयोऽस्मि व्यवसायोऽस्मि सत्वं सत्ववतामहम्
I am the gambling of the cheats and the splendor of the splendid. Of the many games of deceiving others, I am gambling, such as dice-play. I am the victory of the victorious, the resolve of the resolute, and the virtue of the virtuous.

God is present even in an expert trickster, a gambler. "All activity that leads to success and victory is Me only," says Krishna.

10.37 वृष्णीनां वासुदेवोऽस्मि पाण्डवानां धनञ्जय: मुनीनामप्यहं व्यास: कवीनामुशना कवि:
I am Krishna among the descendants of the Vrishnis, and Arjun among the Pandavas. I am Ved Vyas among the sages and Shukracharya among the great thinkers.

Krishna is the leader and the best among the Yadavas (the Vrishnis). He considers Arjun as the best among the Pandavas. Vyas was a great master, who wrote the Mahabharata, the Brahma Sutras, and the Puranas and classified the Vedas. Sukracharya was outstanding among the leaders of moral principles in political science.

10.38 दण्डो दमयतामस्मि नीतिरस्मि जिगीषताम् मौनं चैवास्मि गुह्यानां ज्ञानं ज्ञानवतामहम्
I am the rod of the punishers and the right conduct among those desirous of victory. I am the silence of secrets and the knowledge of the enlightened.

1. Punishment is most severe among restraining forces. 2. The right conduct and diplomacy are the desired traits in a winner. 3. All secrets accompany silence.

10.39 यच्चापि सर्वभूतानां बीजं तदहमर्जुन न तदस्ति विना यत्स्यान्मया भूतं चराचरम्
I am the generating seed of all beings. No moving being or stationary entity can exist without Me.

Verses 7.10 and 9.18, in the current topic 40, mention "the eternal seed"; verse 10.39 here says "the generating seed"; all these phrases in these verses mean the same. Life is born from eggs or the womb or the sweat or earth, not including other beings like the ghost, evil spirits, and mane, whose origin is also God.

TOPIC 40 - God's Glories – Vibhutis

10.40 नान्तोऽस्ति मम दिव्यानां विभूतीनां परन्तप एष तूद्देशत: प्रोक्तो विभूतेर्विस्तरो मया
My divine opulence and manifestations are endless. What I have mentioned here are
only examples of My infinite glories.

God's glories are infinite. Scriptures say that Lord Anant (divine serpent, which is Lord
Vishnu's resting place) has been singing Lord's glories since the beginning of the creation
and is still not done singing the infinite glories.

10.41 यद्यद्विभूतिमत्सत्वं श्रीमदूर्जितमेव वा तत्देवावगच्छ त्वं मम तेजोंऽशसम्भवम्   All
that is glorious and excellent, know for sure that that is born of a tiny portion (Ansh)
of my splendor

All verses 10.20 through 10.39 list more than eighty of the God's infinite opulence. Some
people ask if everything is God's opulence, why mention? This is because Arjun asked
how to think of him. Answer - "Wherever you see a manifestation of glory, think of Me."

10.42 अथवा बहुनैतेन किं ज्ञातेन तवार्जुन विष्टभ्याहमिदं कृत्स्नमेकांशेन स्थितो जगत्   But
what is the use of knowing these details? I exist pervading this entire universe by a
fraction of myself.

The entire creation of countless universes is held merely within a miniscule fraction of
God. Counting and naming His unlimited extraordinary manifestations is impossible.
Krishna is the ancient seed, the origin of all creation that comes into existence. Nothing
can exist without him, the soul of everything. Anytime anywhere you see magnificence
in anyone or anything he created, know that to be Him.

TOPIC 41

Meaning of few Esoteric Terms

Explained here are a few esoteric terms such as Jnana, Vijnana, Brahm, Adhyatma, Karma, Adhibhuta, Adhidaiva, and Adhiyagna. Note that some of these terms carry multiple meanings and interpretations; due to varying background of individual commentators on Gita.

❧ Krishna says:

7.2 ज्ञानं तेऽहं सविज्ञानमिदं वक्ष्याम्यशेषतः यज्ज्ञात्वा नेह भूयोऽन्यज्ज्ञातव्यमवशिष्यते
I will disclose to you fully the knowledge (Jnana) combined with the direct realization and experience (vignana). After knowing this, nothing else remains to be known in this world.

What are the Gnana (knowledge) and Vignana (realization)? The knowledge learned from the scriptures by the senses, mind, and intellect is jñāna. The knowledge resulting from sadhana (effort) and purification (Atma shuddhi) is Vijnan; it is wisdom based on direct realization and experience. Ramakrishna Paramhansa says, "One who has merely heard of fire has Ajnana. One who has seen fire has jnana. However, the one who has actually built a fire and cooked on it has vijnana."

❧ Arjun asks:

8.1 and 8.2 अर्जुन उवाच किं तद्ब्रह्म किमध्यात्मं किं कर्म पुरुषोत्तम अधिभूतं च किं प्रोक्तमधिदैवं किमुच्यते अधियज्ञः कथं कोऽत्र देहेऽस्मिन्मधुसूदन प्रयाणकाले च कथं ज्ञेयोऽसि नियतात्मभिः   What are Brahm, Adhyatma, Karma, and Adhibhuta? Who is Adhidaiva? Who is Adhiyagna in the body? How is he the Adhiyagna? How are You to be known at the time of death by those of steadfast mind?

197

The questions from Arjun in verse 8.1 and 8.2 were introduced in verse 7.30 included in Topic 19. Krishna's answers are below in verse 8.3 and 8.4. Brahm is the Imperishable, the Supreme; His essential nature is called Self-knowledge; the offering (to the gods) which causes existence and manifestation of beings and which also sustains them is called action.

✱ *Krishna replies:*

8.3 श्रीभगवानुवाच अक्षरं ब्रह्म परमं स्वभावोऽध्यात्ममुच्यते भूतभावोद्भवकरो विसर्ग: कर्मसञ्ज्ञित: My highest nature is the imperishable Brahman, it gives every creature its existence and lives in every creature as the adhyatma. My action is the creation and the bringing forth of creatures.

This verse is defined differently by each commentator, some using esoteric language. Above is a direct translation by Eknath Eswaran from his book entitled "The Bhagawad Gita", offered in simple and easy to understand language. Some define 'action' (karma) as the work done to fulfill needs for sustaining life.

8.4 अधिभूतं क्षरो भाव: पुरुषश्चाधिदैवतम् अधियज्ञोऽहमेवात्र देहे देहभृतां वर The adhibhuta is the perishable body; the adhidaiva is Purusha, eternal spirit. The adhiyajna, the supreme sacrifice, is made to me as the Lord within you.

The above translation is from Eknath Eswaran's book "The Bhagawad Gita".

Verses 8.3 and 8.4 answer six of the seven questions from Arjun. Remembering God at the time of death takes a lifetime of surrender and a single-pointed focus on God; refer to Verse 8.9 and 8.10 below.

8.9 and 8.10 कविं पुराणमनुशासितार मणोरणीयांसमनुस्मरेद्य: सर्वस्य धातारमचिन्त्यरूपमादित्यवर्णं तमस: परस्तात् प्रयाणकाले मनसाचलेन भक्त्या युक्तो योगबलेन चैव भ्रुवोर्मध्ये प्राणमावेश्य सम्यक् स तं परं पुरुषमुपैति दिव्यम् God is omniscient and most ancient. He is the controller, subtler than the tiniest particle, the support of all, inconceivable, bright as the sun, beyond the darkness. Whoever keeps the mind steady as learned from the practice of Yoga at the time of death, fixes the concentration between the eyebrows, and continuously remembers the Lord with devotion, will attain Him.

In pure devotion, the mind is focused on God's forms. The one well versed in Yoga practice can hold concentration between the eyebrows (the spot known as the spiritual eye).

In Aṣṭāṅg Yoga done under expert guidance, the life force is conserved and channeled to the brain via the spine to activate more significant parts of the brain to develop a broader view of the power of God. The brains are like million-watt amplifiers, requiring immense input power for them to function at their maximum capacity. Ashtang yoga and bhakti generate very high levels of "input power". Those not practicing Yoga utilize most of their god-given power (Jeev Shakti) in regular tasks to sustain the body and satisfy the senses. Very little of their Jeev Shakti reaches the brain and activates only a small portion of it. That is like trying to run the million-watt amplifier with a nine-volt battery. Therefore, their brain transmitters work at low efficiency and can only sustain essential body functions like breathing, digesting, recreation, circulation, reproduction, and excretion. Human brains, when fully activated, produce incredible power and impart many siddhis (extra-ordinary spiritual powers) discussed elsewhere in Gita, for example, see verses 7.3 (topic 15) and 18.46 (topic 21). These siddhis are acquired from extended yoga practice and are different than the powers the avatars or ansh of God have; the latter are born with those powers due to the Yoga Maya Shakti. For example, enlightened saints like Ramkrishna, Saibaba, and Guru Nanakdevji were born with the spiritual powers. Swami Yogananda Paramhansa says the subject of spiritual science and extra-ordinary powers has a scientific base, something one must discover via one's own spiritual journey.

TOPIC 42

History of Ancient Knowledge of Yoga Taught in Gita

The knowledge of Gita is ancient and Krishna says he taught it to celestial deities thousands of years before Arjun's birth. Arjun is confused about Krishna's existence that long ago because he considered Krishna a contemporary and a human just like him. Krishna explains that Arjun does not know all his previous lives and only Krishna knows all past births of Arjun. Krishna discloses that He is eternal without beginning and end, and there was never a time when He was not there. Krishna says the precious ancient knowledge of yoga over time was lost and that He is reviving the divine knowledge via the discourses given to Arjun.

❧ Krishna says:

4.1 श्रीभगवानुवाच इमं विवस्वते योगं प्रोक्तवानहमव्ययम् विवस्वान्मनवे प्राह मनुरिक्ष्वाकवेऽब्रवीत्   I taught this eternal science of Yoga to the Sun-god, Vivasvan, who passed it on to Manu, and Manu, in turn, instructed it to Ikshvaku.

The eternal science of Yoga is ancient, passed down through the guru-disciple hierarchy. Manu is considered the progenitor of humanity. For more details on Manu avataras (divine incarnations), refer to verse 10.6 under Topic 16 on Creation.

4.2 एवं परम्पराप्राप्तमिमं राजर्षयो विदुः स कालेनेह महता योगो नष्टः परन्तप   The Brahm Jnani or saintly kings thus benefited from this science of Yoga in a continuous tradition. But, in the rather long intervening period, the knowledge about the original science of Yoga was lost to the world.

Divine knowledge originated from God. It was passed down by hearing and memorizing. With time, the tradition discontinued and the knowledge was lost. Also, pleasure-oriented disciples contaminated the knowledge by flawed interpretation. When ancient spiritual knowledge is corrupted or lost, God reestablishes the divine treasure and the tradition Himself, or sometimes through a qualified saint. See Verse 4.7 in Topic 7 where Krishna says that one of the reasons He descends in the human form is to reestablish spiritual science.

4.3 स एवायं मया तेऽद्य योग: प्रोक्त: पुरातन: भक्तोऽसि मे सखा चेति रहस्यं ह्येतदुत्तमम् The same ancient wisdom of Yoga, which is the supreme secret, I am today revealing to you because you are my friend as well as My devotee, who can understand this.

Krishna renewed and passed the ancient knowledge of Yoga to qualified disciples. The qualifications to receive the knowledge are 1. Closeness based on faith, trust, and respect, 2. Devotion, and 3. Ability to understand. This verse also means the knowledge can be grasped by those having these qualifications.

❧ Arjun voices his doubt to Krishna:

4.4 अर्जुन उवाच अपरं भवतो जन्म परं जन्म विवस्वत: कथमेतद्विजानीयां त्वमादौ प्रोक्तवानिति You were born much after Vivasvan. How am I to understand that in the beginning, you instructed this science to him?

Arjun views Krishna as a human, like him. He is confused about Krishna's age, thinking that Krishna has a human body made from Maya Shakti. The answer to Arjun's question in the next verses reveals the mystery of God's human birth and his human body.

❧ Krishna explains to Arjun:

4.5 श्रीभगवानुवाच बहूनि मे व्यतीतानि जन्मानि तव चार्जुन |तान्यहं वेद सर्वाणि न त्वं वेत्थ परन्तप Both you and I have been born many times; you have forgotten the past births, while I remember them all.

Paramatma vs. Atma. God and the soul have similarities: both are eternal, conscious, and blissful. Differences between God and the soul are:

1. *God is all-pervading; the soul only permeates the body.*
2. *God is all-powerful, while the soul is not - the soul cannot liberate itself from the clutches of Maya without God's grace.*
3. *God creates the laws of nature, while the soul must abide by these laws.*
4. *God carries the entire universe, while the soul is carried by God.*
5. *God is all-knowing, while the soul does not have complete knowledge even in one subject, particularly in its bonded state.*
6. *God remembers the past and knows the future of everyone, whereas the soul does not.*

TOPIC 42 - History of Ancient Knowledge of Yoga Taught in Gita

TOPIC 43

◆━━●━●━━◆

Guru's Role According to Gita

Krishna settles a controversy about whether a Guru is necessary for the spiritual development of an aspirant, and why one can not receive knowledge by individual efforts by listening to sages and reading scriptures. Krishna says, an enlightened saint who has experienced the truth himself can instruct the faithful aspirant and impart wisdom in him. An enlightened Guru can remove ignorance and teach the actual substance of Krishna's teaching, leading him to higher levels.

❧ *Krishna says:*

4.34 तद्विद्धि प्रणिपातेन परिप्रश्नेन सेवया उपदेक्ष्यन्ति ते ज्ञानं ज्ञानिनस्तत्त्वदर्शिन: An enlightened Saint has seen the truth and can instruct you in wisdom. Inquire from him with reverence, and render service unto him.

Sankaracharya says, "Until you surrender to a Guru, you cannot be liberated from Maya." How do you meet a Guru? The grace of God, past karma, and intensity of desire to meet a guru bring you in contact with a "tatvadarshinah" (a self-realized) and Jnani (imparts knowledge), a Sadguru; either a living human or his preaching. Ask questions to Guru with reverence, not to trap him. Render service to Guru, but do so sincerely, not unwillingly.

4.35 यज्ज्ञात्वा न पुनर्मोहमेवं यास्यसि पाण्डव येन भूतान्यशेषेण द्रक्ष्यस्यात्मन्यथो मयि
After realizing knowledge and attaining enlightenment from a Guru, you will not be deluded. By that knowledge, you will see all living beings in yourself and within Me.

Like darkness cannot envelop the sun, 'illusion' cannot touch the enlightened soul. Spiritually elevated sages realize that the world is nothing but the energy of God, and all people are His parts. Therefore, one should show a divine attitude toward everyone.

TOPIC 44

Power of Knowledge

Krishna says that with 'knowledge' you can cross the limitation imposed by Maya and remove the effect of sins. With humble prayer and God's grace, one should receive authentic knowledge from a realized Guru. Accurate knowledge received with devotion to God and prolonged spiritual practice eliminate the reactions of accrued Karma, freeing the soul of its bonded state, leading to liberation. However, those who lack faith and knowledge and have a doubting nature, suffer a downfall. Krishna says the skeptical souls will find no happiness in this world or the next and will continue to suffer in the cycle of rebirths.

❧ Krishna says:

4.36 अपि चेदसि पापेभ्य: सर्वेभ्य: पापकृत्तम: सर्वं ज्ञानप्लवेनैव वृजिनं सन्तरिष्यसि   Even if you are the most sinful of all sinners, yet you will for sure cross all sins by the raft of knowledge.

Performing the Yajna with God as a goal would liberate the jnani - knowledgeable. With knowledge, you can transcend the Maya to sever the soul's bondage.

4.37 यथैधांसि समिद्धोऽग्रिर्भस्मसात्कुरुतेऽर्जुन ज्ञानाग्नि: सर्वकर्माणि भस्मसात्कुरुते तथा As the blazing fire reduces fuel to ashes, so does the light of knowledge reduce all actions to ashes.

Knowledge eliminates the karmic reactions and the soul's bondage.

4.38 न हि ज्ञानेन सदृशं पवित्रमिह विद्यते तत्स्वयं योगसंसिद्ध: कालेनात्मनि विन्दति   There is nothing as purifying as divine knowledge. One who has attained purity of mind

203

through the prolonged practice of Yoga, receives such knowledge within the heart, in due course of time.

The realized knowledge is acquired by practice and blessing of God. God's grace purify, elevate, liberate, and unite a dedicated follower.

4.39 श्रद्धावान् लभते ज्ञानं तत्पर: संयतेन्द्रिय: ज्ञानं लब्ध्वा परां शान्तिमचिरेणाधिगच्छति

Those with deep faith and striving to achieve mind control attain knowledge. By knowledge, they quickly achieve permanent peace.

Upanishads say, "The Vedic knowledge is revealed to faithful devotees." Faith means firm confidence in the words of the Guru and the scriptures.

4.40 अज्ञश्चाश्रद्दधानश्च संशयात्मा विनश्यति नायं लोकोऽस्ति न परो न सुखं संशयात्मन:

But those who lack faith and knowledge and have doubting nature, they suffer a downfall. The skeptical souls have no happiness in this world or the next.

Even, the devoted person who has a desire for knowledge will make progress, but the one who is satisfied with the senses and refuses to know will steadily decline in spiritual path.

Bibliography

1. Bhagavad Gita, The Song of God, by Swami Mukundananda
2. Bhagavad Gita, The Divine Life Society, Swami Sivananda
3. The Bhagavad Gita, Royal Science of God-Realization, Yogananda Pamahansa, Self-Realization Fellowship
4. The Bhagavad Gita, Introduced and Translated by Eknath Easwaran
5. Devi Gita, Translated by Swami Satyananada Sarasvati
6. The Gospel of Selfless Action: The Gita According to Gandhi, by M. K. Gandhi
7. Dnyaneshwari, Gita by Sant Gyaneswar
8. The Bhagavad Gita with Commentary of Sri Aurobindo
9. The Bhagavad Gita, The Song of God Retold in Simplified English, Edward Wiljoen
10. The Bhagavad Gita As It Is Original by Swami Prabhupada, ISKCON
11. Srimad Bhagavat by Gita Press, Gorakhpur
12. Isopanishad, Translated and Interpreted by Swami Prabhupada, ISKCON
13. The Uddhav Gita, the Final Teaching of Krishna, Source: Srimad Bhagavat
14. Ashtavakra Mahageeta, Discourses on the Great Mystic Ashtavakra, by Osho (Acharya Rajaneesh)
15. Gita Vahini by Satya Saibaba
16. Sai Satcharitra, Life and Teaching of Saibaba of Shirdi, by Dabholkar
17. The Bhagavat Gita, a Walkthrough for Westerners, Jack Hawley Author

Endorsement

"*This excellent volume, with its novel approach of organization by topic, offers a new way to engage the perennial wisdom of the Bhagavad Gita. The reader can strategically consult the text for cross-referenced access to its insights, all traditionally explicated. Modern readers will discover how the ancient text supports their personal and contemporary search for spiritual guidance. No one with a serious interest in the Gita should be without this work.*"

Prof. Dr. Charles G. Elerick, Professor of Languages and
Linguistics, The University of Texas at El Paso

"*Vino Mody is a devoted disciple of Sri Sri Saidas Babaji. His insight and creativity are reflected in how he organizes the book by major topics instead of by chapters, making the contents easier to grasp. Arjun raises monumental questions to Lord Krishna in the Srimad Bhagavad Gita, the ultimate Upanishad. When Krishna says, "Come to me and be detached from all relations," He essentially proves that He was a Sagun form of Brahm. Vino Mody provides unbiased analytical evidence to show that Krishna declared Himself as the Lord.*"

Dr. Rabinder Singh Masroor, Retired Associate Professor of Punjabi
at the Kurukshetra University, Renowned lyricist of many
spiritual poems, Onkar Dham, Kurukshetra, Haryana

"*I was very happy to go through Sri Vino Mody's commentary on the Srimad Bhagavad Gita. It appears to be a very well thought out and erudite dissertation on the Song Celestial. I'm sure it will be of immense benefit to sincere and in-depth students of the Bhagavad Gita. All the best to the author.*"

Maataji Vanamali Devi, Author of Several Books on Spiritual Science,
Vanamali Gita Yogashram Tapovan, Rishikesh, India

206

Other Publications of The Author

1. Quality in Design, Manufacturing and Deployment of High Volume Electronics, Year, ISBN: 978-9386210753
2. Metrics for Winning Customers in Electronics, 2017, ISBN: 978-9386210746
3. Invented and Made in the USA, year, ISBN: 978-1-4575-5398-1

- https://store.whitefalconpublishing.com/products/metrics-for-winning-customers-in-electronics
- https://store.whitefalconpublishing.com/products/quality-in-high-volume-electronics-design-manufacturing-and-deployment